UNBRIDLED DEMOCRACY

and Other Philosophical Reflections

by George Lowell Tollefson

Palo Flechado Press

Unbridled Democracy and Other Philosophical Reflections

ISBN-13: 978-0-9983498-1-7

Library of Congress Control Number: 2017917422

Palo Flechado Press, Eagle Nest, NM

Contents

Prefatory Remarks

What is being presented in this book is a preliminary introduction for a work which is to come: a multivolume study of human awareness which is grounded in philosophy of mind and extends to a systematic explanation of consciousness, thought, and emotion. However, that remains a work in progress, more than six years in the making at this point.

The present volume exhibits a more relaxed and random selection of topics, brief in treatment and considering such subjects as the subjective character of politics and political economy, the influence of institutional practices on spiritual life, the spiritual origin and character of mind, the relationship of science and mathematics to the limits of mind, and a philosophy of art. Most of the entries in this book were extracted from notes which were recorded when I was teaching philosophy. They were subsequently revised for this work, while additional entries included in it were inspired by the same notes.

October 10, 2017

Unbridled Democracy

UNTIL a way is found to create peace within individual people, the peace which is achieved between them will be next to worthless.

THE Achilles heel of democracy lies in a tyranny of the majority. This consists of a complacency of that majority, which makes possible a domination of the political environment by financial interests and social pressure groups.

WHAT is most important is the life of the spirit: a life of the emotions well regulated by the mind. But where emotion is given priority and the mind is made unclear, the emotions can be manipulated. Until this problem is solved, democracy will always fail.

A FREE and successful republic is a political order in which social placement depends upon talent and self-improvement. It is not a radical democracy in which everyone is treated socially and morally as the same. Rather, it implies an aristocracy of the mind, a society in which merit is respected and rewarded.

Equality under the law, the legal basis of a successful republic, is a political concept which guarantees fairness, or justice, to each member of society. But in social and ethical matters, there can never be an equality. For the former depends upon talent and self-improvement. And the latter depends upon individual moral development. These differ with every person.

WESTERN style democracy, as described by John Locke and Jean Jacques Rousseau, is based on a high regard for the rights of the individual. In a certain sense, it places the individual's interests above those of the state. For the state is thought to be founded upon the intelligence and will of its citizens. In Locke, they are thought to be rational beings. In Rousseau, they are assumed to be fundamentally good.

These ideas are unlike those of the classical form of a democracy or republic, as in Greece and Rome or the thought of Plato and Aristotle. These ancient societies and thinkers put a person's duty to the state above his personal interest. The interests of the individual were clearly subsumed within the community.

This difference between the ancients and the moderns seems to be due to the influence of Christianity with its emphasis on the importance of the individual person. But the fact should not be overlooked that the interests of the individual can only be realized through the community. Conversely, if the individual is not recognized, his creative capacity will be greatly reduced. So finding a balance is of the greatest importance.

THE first and most compelling half of Thomas Jefferson's Declaration of Independence is derived point by point from John Locke's Second Essay Concerning Civil Government. But Jefferson brings to these ideas a conviction and elevation of sensibility which transforms them into an inspiring monument to human dignity and self-determination.

THE founding of the American republic in the Age of Reason was based on the idea that free people would use reason to discover moral, social, and political truth. But the French Revolution released irrational forces into Western Civilization. Though it claimed to be based upon principles of reason, it began the Romantic era, where emotion was seen to be the principal organ of insight and truth. People, it was thought, could reflect on and decide political and ethical issues based on how they "felt" about them and how they subjectively "saw" the circumstances.

This was the point at which radical democracy made its entrance into modern affairs. It represented a subversion of reason. But since each person became individually worthy of attention and investigation, it also prepared the way for a deeper understanding of matters concerning the human soul, which is composed of both reason and emotion. If people can get a sober minded grip on this fact, they will see that they have much more to reason about now than they did before the French revolution. But reason they must.

THE American experiment is based upon a false premise. It is the idea that man is a rational animal, which was carried over from the European Enlightenment. Man is not a rational animal. No one reasons all the time. And most human beings almost never reason. These latter individuals practice opinion, prejudice, wishful thinking, superstition, egoism, and a process of rapid association followed by rationalization. But they do not truly reason.

Nevertheless, the great success of the American republic over the last two hundred and twenty-eight years has been possible because the American people have *believed* that they are a reasoning people. But as personal discipline and civic-mindedness break down and the people turn inward toward their individual interests, which are largely emotional and sensual, this common belief becomes less important. As a result, national cohesion weakens and breaks down. And the nation's fortunes begin to sink to that irrational base upon which all nations are truly founded.

THE American public has an enormous appetite for sweets: endless desserts that make so many of them slow and rotund, sugary ideas that are easy to swallow while providing little constructive energy, and sentimental emotions that falsify life by rendering it artificially and deceptively comfortable.

THE strength of the democratic spirit is to allow no person's overlordship over another. Its great failing is to confuse the character of a person of low character with that of a person who is not of a low character.

ALL governments get their power from the consent of the people. But they do not as a general rule get it from the *overt* consent of the people. For people are often complacent, self-involved, indolent of mind. When they are such, much can be impressed upon them without their assent or resistance. Hence tyrannies, usurpations, and the dominance of special interest groups. There is also the shifting of personal identity to that of the social group, accompanied by a willingness to submit to strong leadership which will fulfill the interests of the group.

UNLESS a safeguard is maintained, such as a continued intellectual vigilance, democracy can become extremely self-destructive. For, without such watchful care, it inevitably degrades itself over time. This is because there can be no other guarantee that the people as a whole have the wisdom to conduct their own affairs. The reason for this is that a majority of the people incorporates a more than equal share of the least qualified in judgment: those who are incapable of rational thought and sustained reflection concerning their relationship to the common experience of their lives.

DEMOCRACY begins by releasing enormous human potential, as in the case of ancient Athens or the modern Western world. But eventually it seeks to suppress that same potential. Freedom becomes more and more an idea subsumed under the notion of equality. And an emphasis on equality arouses jealousy towards exception. No person of genuinely exceptional merit or ability is tolerated to rise above the common potential. This applies, in particular, to intellectual merit.

This can now be seen to be expressed in many forms. Science applauds the small discovery but looks with suspicion upon the large. Group research takes precedence over individual insight. Graduate levels of education become a cloning process, whereby the candidate for advancement is taught what communal box he is permitted to think within. Sports are celebrated because they represent an exclusive emphasis on external bodily awareness.

Preventive medicine develops more and more invasive procedures, which emphasize the fact that one's innermost parts are not private. Political and other leaders are hounded for any personal failings which might be discovered, regardless of their executive or legislative accomplishments. Skill, insight, and a penetratingly meaningful understanding of life are gradually removed from the arts and philosophy. These fields grow increasingly superficial, losing themselves in intricate designs and forms of argumentation containing little life-illuminating substance.

These are all institutional and social assaults on personal consciousness. To their number should be added a growing emphasis on volunteer work and other forms of public participation that take the individual outside of the depths of his mind, outside of his private mental life, and into a realm where trivial physical and social acts are performed. Less and less time is left for quiet thinking. Yet this is where creativity takes place, the fruits of which would catapult the exceptional person above his presumed and envious peers.

If a person is trying to think inside his car, a boom box will appear beside him in another vehicle, blasting all thoughts from his mind. Or this thought-shattering disturbance may come from a neighboring house. Yet the police grow more and more unwilling to deal with such situations because they seem increasingly common, expected, accepted, and normal. Dogs bark day and night, two or three of them to a subdivision lot. And the owners feel little or no embarrassment at the intrusion.

This is no anomaly. It is an inevitable sickness of democracy, resulting from a transference of emphasis over time from individual freedom and uniqueness to individual equality, or sameness. Such a state of affairs erodes away everything which had originally given birth to the fledgling democracy and sustained it.

DEMOCRACY is predicated on the myth of consensus. But in fact it is majority rule. Majority rule carries with it an inevitable tendency toward tyranny of the many over the few. The few are the less vigorous, the less blindly passionate, those who are not united in an avoidance of reflection. Thus, as the mythical character of consensus is laid bare, social divisions deepen until a rift necessitates authoritative control.

Tyranny of the majority does not always follow from the limited self-interest of a majority party. It can result from a universally felt need to establish order. But what is universal is the need, not a consensus as to how or who should impose such order, or what kind of order should be imposed.

Order is an expression of control. Control is an application of force. Even in the American Civil War, Abraham Lincoln, who might be considered in some sense a patron of popular rule—even this man used undemocratic means to bring about a national consensus and reestablish order concerning the issues of slavery and union. No doubt Mr. Lincoln hoped the myth of popular consensus could be restored after the war. It has been for a time. But with ever-present strains.

THE principal gift of Western civilization to the world is not democracy. It is the rule of law. This is law based on reason and not emotion, prejudice, bias, or wishful thinking. Republics which are not fully democratic are the political entities most likely to establish the rule of reason through law. They are usually composed of distinct social groups, such as a property holding class and a non-property holding class. Laws are made by them to clearly delineate distinctions, obligations, and general rights.

On the other hand, an unbridled democracy prefers to imagine there are no distinctions. As it progresses from an idea of fairness to one of sameness, it thrives increasingly on ego and emotionalism rather than reason. Egoism and emotionalism differ from person to person. Thus no uniform standard exists. Or insofar as it does, it will be continually eroded.

When the early American republic, for which the U.S. Constitution was written, established reason as the basis for its legal relations, that emphasis on reason produced an idea of equality of treatment, particularly under criminal law. But as the republic has become more openly democratic, popular emotionalism has arisen and with it an unwillingness to recognize any standard of superiority among persons, either in talent, station, or character. Money is the only standard. Thus the idea of equality under the law is converted into a notion of sameness everywhere. And the idea of sameness attaches directly to people themselves. It is felt that all people should be regarded as similar in all things.

Consequently, since people are not really similar in talent, station, or character—particularly in matters of personal conduct and rational development—the reasonable basis of society is undermined. In this way, the descent of a moderately democratic republic into an unbridled democracy destroys the very reason-centeredness from which that republic claims its origin.

RETRIBUTIVE justice cannot be said to be moral in character. Yet the conditions which occasion it are rules assented to in a relationship of trust. These rules possess the character of obligations either tacitly or deliberately agreed upon by all the members of a society. They are therefore moral in character.

THE power of the people is a myth and only works so long as the people believe in the myth. The American Constitution is a peace of paper, a beautiful document suggesting an extraordinary trust in the reasonableness of people. But if those people lose faith in it, if they feel they must repeatedly take to the streets in displays of ungoverned emotion, thus expressing no respect for the role of reason in public affairs, the Constitution has no power of its own. That power ultimately resides in the military.

IT has been said that God always sends a prophet to warn a great nation of its impending downfall. It has also been observed that such figures are inevitably abused and scorned. However one wishes to view it, Alexander Solzhenitsyn came to the United States, as well as to other venues in the Western world. He was jeered off the public stage and ignored. Perhaps the saddest fact is that he was addressing the entire Western world, not just a single nation. No one listened. The possible sinking of the star of Western civilization is a far greater tragedy than the fate of any one nation.

REASON produces law because it sees conceptually what the heart anticipates in emotional feeling. This feeling cannot be put into place without reason. So, once it is in place, law relieves the burden of old irritations and constraints while imposing new ones. For the emotions continue to develop in subtlety, outpacing the conceptual bonds of reason. Thus it is out of this that an additional conceptual response must come. There must be a continual modification of the laws. For it is by such leaps and bounds as these that civilizations are made, mature, and molder away.

Political forms are extensions of law into the social structure. They regulate the relations of groups as well as individuals: groups of governance, institutions, and commerce. So the process of conceiving, perfecting, modifying, or dissolving governments is not unlike that for any system of laws. There must be continual conceptual growth to keep pace with the emotional life of the community.

In other words, what is politically conceived in the intellect will initially support then subsequently conflict with the spirit of a people, first giving it room for growth, then stifling its development. This is a dialectic somewhat different from the Hegelian and Marxist forms. It is the dialectic taught by Jesus of Nazareth. For spirit is greater than intellect. Spirit is a living form. Intellect is the garment it wears for a particular occasion.

THERE is a continual counterbalancing of power against reason and law in the Western tradition. Too much power, and reason is trodden down. Too much reason and, well, there has never been too much employment or recognition of the moral influence of practical reason. John Stuart Mill, in his essay *On Liberty*, eloquently expresses the importance of keeping power at bay, so that reason might have room to develop.

Karl Marx, on the other hand, subordinates everything to power. The true dictatorship of the proletariat—that is, the forced rule of an overwhelming majority—is a naked expression of power. Out of it somehow, in the newfound environs of a classless state, is supposed to develop a reasonableness and tolerance. It is assumed that after the revolution, the demands of reason, as they apply to human relations, morals, etc., can be worked out. This will presumably allow a free play of individually creative expression in accordance with the dictates of reason and human nature.

But is this possible? Human nature, it should not be forgotten, loves power. Where power cannot be attained, it even loves a submission to power. For the ego wants to stand out, one against another, either independently or by association. And the ego is often more persuasive than the mind. So force usually ends in force. Once naked power becomes independent of reason, putting it back under such a governance is problematic at best. It most cases, it is not possible.

A MINORITY does not have the right to impose its norm on a majority. But a majority does have a right, under reasonable circumstances, to impose its norm on a minority. If this were not the case, social harmony would be impossible. Norms are a form of decorum. And the functional purpose of decorum is to promote social harmony.

Thus, if a society imposes a dress code, a small portion of that social body may not, in turn, impose a different code on the majority. This is not an argument as to the relative value of dress codes. It is a recognition that social harmony must be respected. A collapse of that overbalances the importance of individual expression.

Nevertheless, as John Stuart Mill pointed out, the greater the level of tolerance that can be endured without a complete disruption of social harmony, the greater the freedom for creative innovation and subsequent advance of the human condition. But the fact remains that the key consideration is social harmony and the maintenance of norms.

This is why legal recognition and protection for gay people has been established. But it does not authorize an imposition of their lifestyle on the heterosexual majority. For a minority cannot insist upon norm replacement, except where that norm individually targets that minority and does so in a pointed and exclusive way.

CAPITALISM is not the equivalent of a free-market system. Without careful regulation, it is a parasite which devours its host. And its host is the free-market system.

THE reason poverty has been so difficult to eliminate is that a privileged class wants other members of its society to be poor. This is because the relative poverty of the many provides for the proud distinction of the few. Thus a privileged class will exert it influence toward an active suppression of the underprivileged.

In this light, it can be understood that having money is not about the possession of material goods. For these are merely ostentatious toys. Rather, the principal motivation toward an accumulation of wealth is a concern with the social exclusion of the have-nots. So the point here is that the rich do not merely wish to put on a show. They want to maintain a platform upon which to do it.

For them the issue is as much about the depth of the underclass as it is about the elevation of themselves. Looking down upon someone is their fundamental need. For these reasons, economic justice cannot be achieved in the present context. So, if the progress of civilization is to continue, a way must be found to get beyond this state of affairs. It will certainly involve a change in states of mind.

THE capitalist system does not support a free market. The only members of the capitalist marketplace who may be considered free agents are those who shape and control it. They are the entrepreneurs. If the definition of a free market is restricted only to its entrepreneurs, then it may be considered free so long as they are in competition with one another.

Entrepreneurs build and maintain infrastructure. Infrastructure is a combination of two things: the means of production and the means of distribution. A new or industrious entrepreneur will seek to change or improve one of these two elements, perhaps both in some cases. An established entrepreneur, with no inclination toward further innovation, will seek to maintain the status quo.

But infrastructure is no more than a box the gift of modernity comes in. In the sphere of commodities and services produced, there is the creator of new ideas, inventions, and insights. In the capitalist system, this individual is in the employ of the entrepreneur or her representative. For this reason the marketplace cannot be said to be a free marketplace for the creator. Her destiny lies in the hands of another: a financier to support the development of her innovations, an existing means of producing them, a chain of established outlets for them.

A note apart: The financier or investor is of course an abettor of entrepreneurship. Thus she is an entrepreneur herself, controlling the money side of infrastructure. It is also a circumstance worthy of note to observe that services are more often components of infrastructure than not. A society of nearly pure services would thus be like a nervous system waiting to be installed in a body.

The entrepreneur may be called a developer of means, a facilitator. Therefore, let the creator of ideas, inventions, and insights be labeled a creator of things: intellectual and physical commodities. Since the final and purposeful outcome of any market process is the volume and quality of commodities produced, one cannot help but see that these are in the control of those who do not produce them. When one thing is contingent upon another, it cannot be said to be free, but merely conditioned by that which is free. For this reason, a capitalist system cannot be said to be a free market system.

THERE are two fundamental types of intelligence: instrumental and reflective. A democratic capitalist society generally favors the instrumental form of intelligence, which conduces to an attitude of cunning. Though not necessarily. A good will and honest demeanor among the people may prevent it. But not often. As a rule, and in varying degrees, instrumental intelligences fall into the cunning cycle of a ruthless, competitive, market-driven society.

THERE are two fundamental types of people: reflective and cunning. Human beings almost always choose one of these modes of life and abandon the other. The great majority of human beings are of the cunning persuasion. It is a shortcut to a seeming peace found in material security—a security that can never be genuinely achieved.

The entire history of the world has been a history of cunning people controlling both those less gifted in cunning than themselves and those more gifted in reflection. So it is in the present world. In economies, the cunning gain control of financial means. In politics, they obtain mastery of the instruments of power. Thus the less gifted among the cunning, as well as the reflective minority, are made to serve their interests. Yet the creative gifts which have been bequeathed to the human race have come from the minds of the reflective and the labor of the less gifted among the cunning.

In the present world, monetary power has assumed a broad identity. It embraces more than factories and other types of manufacturing. It now includes infrastructure. But in truth, it always has. For it is the middleman, with all his connections with other middlemen, who controls infrastructure. And middlemen are always in the middle of things. Thus they control access to markets. They run governments day to day. They dole out subsidies to the reflective creator.

Because of this control, largely by men of little imagination and inferior intellect, both the creative and the less strong must seek the favor of the strongly cunning and their middlemen. So, in return for their vital efforts, they are rewarded with a small portion of credit for what is theirs. Consequently, as has always been the case, mediocrities not only rule the world. They get the greater share of the credit for having made it.

IT seems that most laws are based on property relations with human needs built around them. The situation should be reversed. Laws should be based on human needs. Property should follow. But how is this to be achieved? Communism created an alternative legal structure which was also built around property. Human beings were fit into the new social order with little regard for their needs, which were spiritual as well as physical. To put the spirit first—without the slavery of superstition and external control—that is the challenge.

ALL of civilization has been an effort in providing comfort and joy. The question is how to do this. A balancing of its quest is like considering the difference between a flower and the perfume taken from it. A wildflower provides simple pleasure and delight precisely because it is not possessed. It belongs to everyone.

The perfume extracted from that flower is possessed because it is made by human labor. It cannot change hands without permission. For that reason, it is never enjoyed for its own sake but for other purposes. That should reveal something about the role of property. Because property is rarely possessed for its own sake alone, it often limits freedom and produces misery.

WITNESS the evils of a worship of production as an end, rather than as a means! This problem has placed humanity in opposition to itself and the planet it inhabits for more than two centuries. Yet people persist in refusing to see how it lies behind so many of the horrors of the modern world. Communism, Fascism, and terrorism have been and remain a reaction to it. An overreaction, perhaps. Which is why it expresses the hidden magnitude of the horror.

MODERN materialism does not originate with capitalism. Adam Smith's argument that commodities are the source of wealth rather than currency helped to release the forces of the Industrial Revolution. But the pernicious belief that a pervasive and unending increase in material wealth could be the means alone for achieving human happiness—that belief, which extends back in history at least as far as the sixteenth or seventeenth centuries—is the evil that plagues the modern world.

CAPITALISM, as an idea that productivity should be an end rather than a means to an end, is one of the worst ideas ever to inhabit the mind of man. This is not to condemn a free market. It is simply an attempt to denounce a fixation on material productivity as an end, as a final purpose for human activity, for both individuals and for society as a whole.

This ethically ridiculous idea has given a part of the world enormous material wealth. But it has also been the cause of most of the abuses of the last two hundred years. In fact, its negative effect goes back further than that—to a time before it had been rendered into a fixed and articulate idea by Adam Smith.

To say that it created Fascism, Nazism, Marxism, Communism, and radical Islamic terrorism as a reaction to its inherent coldness, cruelty, and immorality is not an exaggeration. It is even now destroying the planet—its biology, its topography (its lands and waters), and its climate. It has fueled and will continue to fuel the ferocious rapacity of industrial wars.

While fattening some people, it has brought unspeakable unhappiness to the suppressed lives of many others. Is there no one who cares? Is it enough to say that prosperity will eventually spread over the whole earth, when it will do so at such a cost? Shall people bury their hollow souls in gold embossed caskets, purchased in vanity and then lowered into a meaningless oblivion?

It is amazing that anyone could ever mix such a mindless and heartless worship of mammon with the compassionate vision found in the teachings of Jesus of Nazareth. And this is not to cite his direct statements to the contrary. The entire panorama of systematic greed and selfishness, predicated upon a Christianized culture and ethics it cannot own, as it slides down the corridors of history—reaching back even to slavery!—is surely a miracle to behold.

IN capitalism there is inevitably a speculative aspect to the profit margin. To understand how this occurs, let us suppose that someone produces a widget of superior quality, something never before seen and from which the human race is about to receive immense benefit. This person would like to have her genius appreciated. And she does not want to wait until she is so old she cannot enjoy a monetary benefit from her extraordinary innovation. Moreover, the marvelous widget cannot be obtained anywhere else because she is the first to produce it.

So she rushes it into production and puts it on the market for two dollars. Now, since simple clarity is the goal, let us say that two dollars is the average total disposable income per month of most prospective customers for this product. But the actual production cost of the widget is one dollar. For extreme clarity, let us observe that the entire productive value (labor, investment, personal maintenance of the producer, etc.) of the widget is tucked into its production cost. That leaves a purely speculative profit margin of one dollar.

The widget producer is going to make a one hundred percent profit on her product. She has an exclusive patent. So she is not worried about immediate competition. However, she is not foolish enough to think that she can get by with such a thing for very long, unless there is some mechanism to take up the slack. That mechanism is increased general production in the future. This is increased production of all goods and services across the marketplace. It is the reason why an economy *must* grow.

So imagine that this increase in general productivity in the marketplace is so great that, within a short time, the widget's prospective buyers each obtain a disposable income of four dollars per month. That is four dollars purchasing power per month, as opposed to two dollars purchasing power per month when the widget was first placed on the market.

Now what they are paying for the widget is, in fact, what it was originally worth in terms of production costs: one half of their disposable income per month. That was its hidden value which lay concealed beneath the large profit margin, when people desperate to get it were expected to expend their whole monthly income on it. It was the original true value of the widget. So the disruptive ripple in the market appears to have smoothed out over time.

The problem is, in ordinary circumstances the widget producer is not the only one doing this. The increasingly crowded rush for good times is what accounts for a general rise not only in productivity, but in expected return on that productivity. The growing market becomes intensely speculative. In fact, there are so many people behaving the same way, the economy begins to overheat. That is, it begins to outpace itself.

So the market approaches crisis as a result of so much speculative greed, so much general expansion of expectation tied to an enlarging profit margin throughout the marketplace. In the fevered atmosphere, real productive value is almost forgotten. And eventually, productivity simply cannot keep up. Finally, the strain is so great that the market collapses into recession.

IN their 1848 *Communist Manifesto,* Karl Marx and Friedrich Engels declared that capitalism would convert every nation on earth into its own image. Why is this? It is because selfishness and the quest for power are the ruling passions of capitalism. These motives have been the way of the world, the mark of a materialist outlook on life, since time immemorial.

What nation can stand against the tools of material progress placed in the hands of self-interest and the quest for dominance? It must acquiesce, conform, and join the general struggle. Not until all the world is consumed in this way can a higher spiritual vision rise from this abatement of moral values.

TO understand the wide diversity of the world's moral systems, it is useful to consider two things. First, moral systems are generally composed of laws enforcing a condition of mutual trust. To live in cooperative social relations, human beings need to know they can expect their neighbors not to do them harm, be it theft, slander, murder, or whatever. This part of morality is universal because it is based on human nature.

But the second consideration is different. Underlying the institutions and practices of any social body are the economic arrangements of that society. If they are pastoral or agricultural, and if historical associations with other societies have inclined the economic structure toward a patriarchal form, this will be reflected in the moral law. The ancient Hebrews were such a people.

On the other hand, there are people living in Nepal who have developed a polyandrous, matriarchal society due in part to a limited supply of arable land. Again, the modern Western, democratic, capitalist world needs the free movement of the largest possible body of available labor, male and female. So women's rights have been enabled to gradually emerge from previous prejudice.

Any of these systems might have developed differently based on general prehistory, geographical location in reference to resources and climate, fortunes of war, and association with other societies. But in general, their social and moral structure will be compatible with the dominant economic structure. Aside from a universal enforcement of a condition of mutual trust, the institutions and laws of each society will strongly reflect this economic influence.

ON the whole, the American people are strong in quantitative analysis but lack subtlety in qualitative judgment. Like Americans, the Romans had little patience for ideals or abstractions, unless these could be shown to have a practical foundation. But qualitative thinking was also freely expressed by them in a way which is alien to the American temperament.

Under the Greek influence, the Romans came to see the humanities (philosophy, literature, and history) as preeminently useful. Americans, on the whole, do not. Perhaps this is due to the all-consuming presence of science and technology, which are often uncritically viewed by Americans in quasi-religious terms.

BALANCING the objective and the subjective is always difficult. If a person concentrates upon building a perfect society, she must override some individual desires. If she wishes to maximize individual freedom, she must sacrifice some degree of social harmony. How then does she balance these two opposing interests?

This question does not only apply to the individual and the state. It arises in any institutional situation. The problem is as broad as the philosophical gap between mind and body. And just as the mind / body conflict in philosophy cannot be fully resolved, so the subjectivity / objectivity impasse continually arises. It is in religion as well as in politics and philosophy. It is in education: the divide between an emphasis on the humanities and the arts on one side, technology and science on the other.

THOMAS Hobbes, understanding the universal role of fear in human relations, chose the recognition of self-defense as a foundation for the development of civil society. Yet self-defense is an expedient consideration. It may induce some men to cultivate a relationship of trust with others. But it is this trust alone, not the motive of self-defense, which is the foundation for all moral and civil relations.

THE "state of nature" is a powerful conceptual tool. But it is unnecessary as a forerunner of social relations. Relations of trust, originally arising from the social impulse, are natural. They do not need an atmosphere of savagery at their back. Their development is largely unconscious and incremental.

They are socially evolutionary. And being so, they are malleable, demonstrating a capacity for forming complex and varied social structures. But here a caveat should be introduced: beware that these complex social structures do not create a condition of social anonymity, where scoundrels, thieves, and demagogues may conceal themselves under a covering of rote custom and impersonal law.

THE idea of justice differs, depending on the social-economic evolution of a society. That is why the ethical ground of a society is not justice but trust. Different peoples have different ideas of justice. But everyone has the same need for security of person and reputation. If people are to live together in harmony, they must be able to trust one another not to do harm.

For example, a man must know his neighbor will not physically harm, steal from, or malign him. If he knows this, he can go about his business in peace. He will not need to be always on his guard. That is trust. But justice in an aristocratic society, or a patriarchal one, or a matriarchal one, would be different from justice in a democratic society because the hierarchy of interrelationships would differ. Nevertheless, the need for trust and its resultant harmonious interchange in personal relationships would remain the same.

THE true nature of a social contract is not that of a social order deliberately formed, as in the apparent case of the U.S. Constitution. A social contract is an arrangement of relations among a relatively homogenous group of people which occurs unconsciously over time. It may then, as in the case of the framing of the U.S. Constitution, be given an acknowledged formal status. But this always follows a long and hidden ferment.

THE human heart is adjustable and can easily become inured to pain, including the suffering of some other person or creature. Therefore, it is best not to trust to simple pieties and self-deceiving ideals when setting out in pursuit of universal peace. See things as they are. Know the human heart for what it is with all its limitations. Then see what can be made of it in the interest of a better world. But under no circumstances entertain the notion that peacemaking is a simple task.

WAR is more than diplomacy by other means. It is often prosecuted out of a desire to eliminate another viewpoint, or at least to prove a viewpoint to be superior.

IT may be that the organized and institutionalized violence which is called war is not only a product of the state, but the very mortar which holds it together. Once people settled into agricultural communities, got together in cities, and developed a division of labor, they became numerous and anonymous to each other.

This meant that the general trust could not be founded on familiarity. It was simply a set of ideas and rules that all men and women should follow for the mutual good, so that they might have community. It required an enforcer. And this is how institutionalized violence was introduced. Once introduced, the concept could be extended to relations between states, where no trust existed. Hence the formation of a militia, a trained and martially disciplined body of troops.

THE terrible beauty of war! It is a strange thing that something so horrible can have such a favorable aesthetic impact on memory. What is it that causes this? That is, beyond the camaraderie, group identification, and testing of one's limits, or having come through. Only one thing: there is an infinitesimal gradation in difference between the satisfaction of creation and that of destruction. They are, in some sense, one and the same. Their nexus is change. And change effected is the material expression of will.

WAR presents paradoxes. It is said that, because of the killing and destruction, war is ugly, a terrible thing. Who would deny that? War unleashes savage and selfish instincts. Yet it is also beautiful, as only pure destructive power can be beautiful. An absolute destructive power alone demonstrates the close relationship between coming-into-being and going-out-of-being. For it is no more miraculous to create than it is to destroy. Hence the beauty in both.

But there is another paradox. War also kindles within a disciplined body of soldiers a communion of fundamental emotions rarely seen in a peaceful atmosphere. These emotions often occasion selfless acts, such as one soldier giving his life for others. Such acts are much more broadly spaced in the course of peaceful lives. In addition, many peaceful acts, if not destructive, are frequently selfish.

The principal difference between war and peace is not the presence or absence of good and bad qualities. It is the level of grandeur upon which they are played out. War, by raising life to a continuing level of crisis, burnishes every human act found within it, whether it be good or bad. However, none of this suggests that war should be celebrated.

It merely indicates that, if the best part of humanity is not to be lost, a heightened authenticity or honesty of emotion and selflessness of motive, readily found on the battlefield, must be diligently sought out in the more mundane pursuits of peaceful life. When they are found, they should be clung to.

UNDERSTANDING the nature of war helps in understanding history. Understanding history contributes to an understanding of human nature. Understanding human nature provides a means for changing history. Changing history may someday bring an end to war. Or at least, it may bring an end to international war. Homegrown insurrections are another matter. It will take a much deeper understanding of human nature to solve the internal problem of social injustice.

THE greatest single danger of supreme political and military power is that it produces myopic vision. History is strewn with the wreckage of empires that could not see the world in any terms but their own. The desire to create order out of chaos is good. The Romans understood this. But they also understood that when a nation begins to think it is the superior life form on the planet, it is soon proven to be mistaken.

WHY do people always want to look at the international arena through rose-colored glasses, when it clearly functions according to the ethics of a street brawl?

HITLER was not solely responsible for the Holocaust. Neither was Germany. All of Western civilization was. Germany, and finally Hitler, were simply the vortex into which certain historical forces gathered and from which they were finally released in expression. Perhaps the most important stream that fed the great cataract was early Christianity with its growing bigotry towards Judaism.

THE present terrorist problem, referred to from the Western perspective as the "war on terror," is not religious in nature. It is a war of modernism against medievalism and vice versa.

THE present state of international anarchism in the form of terrorism and internecine war is a result of the increasing development and threat of a single world community. Increased communications, enhanced means of transportation, and the globalization of big business have brought it about. Capitalism, which sought far-flung markets and resources in the past, is also now questioning its own values because its influence is already everywhere and can be spread no further. So it has turned inward upon itself.

In the wake of this confusion comes a variety of world views. One of them is Western Civilization. Another is Medieval Islam. And yet another is the hybrid East—half Eastern, half Western. There are also the different religions. Not all these views can prevail at once. That is why social unrest, terrorism, and local wars are world-wide.

But what about the international conscience? Is there such a thing? There is not. There is only an appearance of consensus. Nations are in a state of anarchy in relation to one another. They obey no universal ethical code because none exists. However similar the individual national codes may be, they are always separated by an immense gulf of mistrust and self-interest. They are not binding outside their borders.

An individual nation's institutions—its points of view, prejudices, mores, and laws—are bound together by the glue of mutual trust within that community. They are established and maintained for the maintenance of mutual trust, regardless of the means by which they came into existence. But this environment of mutual trust does not float in an atmosphere of simple good will. If it did, there would not be any police forces.

Violence, or at least a threat of violence, underlies the whole. In some cases it is a stabilized violence, which only rarely need be called forth. This relative stability is usually due to the fact that past demonstrations of violence within national communities have been convincing and remain in the collective memory. The American Civil War is an example. It brought about a union in a way that the Declaration of Independence and the Constitution did not.

Applying this national model to the international arena, as some have thought to do, it can easily be understood why the United Nations is so ineffective. There can be no international community of trust if there is no underlying threat of force to weld it together. But how many nations are willing to be the first to lay down arms in the interest of all?

In other words, what nation would be willing, in effect, to turn over its national sovereignty to a world body backed by military strength? Would it be the most powerful nation, which already has the greatest means of imposing its will? Certainly not, if its world view is likely to be overridden by the hordes of other perspectives at large in the world. And this is not to mention an economic reduction in the quality of life, which would prove necessary to wealthy nations if the world's resources were to be more equally shared out.

But this is going to happen anyway. As multinational business has become less and less attached to any particular homeland, great economies are already beginning to suffer. The world is moving in the direction of a single economy. Political and ethical uniformity will follow as a necessary effort to shape that world. But the question is: whose world view will prevail?

The primary effect of a world view is an ethical arrangement. How people see themselves on a universal scale determines how they think they should relate to one another. Since in any one community there can be only one dominant view, providing one way for people to relate to one another, other world views must be relegated to an ever-diminishing status within that community.

Thus there must be consistency in laws, mores, etc. Such a uniformity provides mutual agreement and understanding, which augments trust. Where there is understanding and trust in the community, it will allocate resources, both human and material, in a way which is universally conceived as fair and appropriate.

This is an ethical system which must be undergirded by the placement of force—force which should rarely be used, but which, nevertheless, must be present. The single community, undergirded by such force, thus becomes an ethically bound social structure. But the problem is: whose structure will it be? This is what worries the terrorists, insurrectionists, anarchists, etc. It is also what worries their opponents.

A MORAL idea is only enabled to effect results when it is embedded in prescribed practice. So, though an adherent of natural law ethics might proclaim that ethical rules can be deduced from nature, this does not mean that they can of themselves have any appreciable effect upon the behavior of humankind. Just because it can be determined that they exist in the minds of people does not mean they will be acknowledged or followed. Nor is there any guarantee they will be adhered to if they are universally agreed upon in principle.

Only when they are embedded in positive law and social prejudice—that is, only when they are concretely expressed in a social community, their observance and nonobservance rewarded and punished by central authority or social censure, only then are ideas able to effect certain results. In the former case, they must be backed by physical force, while in the latter by some form of communal ostracism. For it is when an ethical community is given means to regulate and enforce that it can be said to exist.

Thus people should not base their hopes for world peace on ideas and sentiments. For these are no more than momentary affectations of the imagination and the emotions. For this reason, it does not matter if international law is codified in a world body, if reasonable provisions have not been made for giving that body teeth. Peace is possible. But it is a possibility only when sovereign states are willing to transfer sufficient power and rights to a communal association of nations for their mutual benefit.

So world peace should not be striven for with wishful thinking. Good, for all the verification of it that can be found, is no more than an idea. It cannot be wished into existence. For it is among many conflicting ideas which are to be found in the mind, any one of which may hold sway in a moment, soon to be replaced by another.

To think that uncooperative forms of behavior are not implanted in the human heart is to step unarmed onto the battlefield of life. For life, as it is daily lived, is not a cooperative venture. At least, it is not so beneath a surface of pretensions and often feigned good will. Cooperation at best is isolated and limited. Material existence is a struggle of one entity against another, each one seeking advantage where it can be found. Upon the least amount of reflection, this is a condition which is easily recognized. For its evidence is openly revealed in the individual actions of people.

Nevertheless, to hold that good is only an idea is not to deny a possibility of goodness. It is not to deny that it can be embedded in institutions. For here, with properly thought out guarantees of their enforcement, the products of reason can hold sway. Thus practical reason alone is the means for an establishment of good, inasmuch as such a thing is possible under the grasping circumstances of physical existence.

A MAJOR difficulty in bringing into being a world organization based on law lies in the fact that any system of laws reflects the particular world view of a specific society. On this planet, there are some sharply divergent world views. So it does not matter that some things are alike in the laws of different societies. For they can mean something different to each of them.

THERE is a superior, spiritually transformed human race yet to come. When that happens, the three principal political forms—monarchy, aristocracy, and democracy—will be one and the same.

SO what is it that makes human beings into artists, philosophers, mathematicians, scientists, etc., when, insofar as is known, other creatures on earth have overlooked these disciplines? It is nothing more than a habit of forming conventions, which are themselves products of infrastructure. In general, that infrastructure is culture.

Culture is a collection of conventions handed down through deliberate learning. The conventions codify practices and procedures in the use of reason. Thus even art is a form of reasoning in this broadened sense. For a work of art must convey an attitude, which is a set of emotions governed by a concept. And the formation and use of that concept is an exercise of reason.

The concept might involve nothing more than an idea of love, pleasure, pure emotion, or the enjoyment of a pleasant scene. Nevertheless, it is a concept and therefore a product of reason. People learn to understand such concepts by learning how to "read" them, say in paintings. This is to say that a person learns how to reason about emotions as they are presented to them under the control of reason. Such a reading is accomplished according to a convention. The convention determines that a painting must be looked at in a certain way. Music must be heard in a certain way. A novel must be read in a certain way.

A political constitution is another such convention. It does not matter if it is literally true that the social contract arose out of a state of nature, as imagined by Thomas Hobbes, John Locke, and Jean Jacques Rousseau. What matters is that people are becoming more aware that a political structure may be understood according to principles of reason and that laws may be held to the dictates of reason. Thus politics and law have become part of the rational infrastructure of civilization.

So this infrastructure, or culture, is civilization. And the level of any particular civilization may be measured by the rise and accumulation of such conventions in every sphere of human activity. The more this has occurred, and the more a rational integration is developed between such conventions, the higher the civilization.

However, this truism only holds if reason remains operative throughout. For this to occur, a culture's spheres of formalized infrastructure must be kept open to question and should be continually subject to modification by new, well thought out insights. If this fails to be the case, if unquestioned authority, prejudice, and emotion become the rule rather than reason, then the civilization either stagnates or falls into disarray.

THE negative is the backbone of the positive in matters of the spirit as well as in the physical, in ideas as well as in action. This is the dialectical process as developed in different ways by both Georg Wilhelm Friedrich Hegel and Karl Marx. Both men were concerned with the firm resolution which arises from an opposition.

A positive idea always rests upon its opposite. The person who formulates an idea or theory has been required to consider contradictions to his way of thinking. Thus the strength of his final position gains its vigor from that opposition. Taken to the level of human intellectual and moral development, the result is the same. Humanity's understanding of itself grows more comprehensive through the failure of its ideas. New and better ideas replace them.

In the realm of action, it is the same. According to Karl Marx and his collaborator, Friedrich Engels, class oppositions have brought about the advance of civilizations. This advance cannot be realized without such oppositions because any new world order is realized by means of a contradiction between two older orders in which elements of both orders enter into the synthesis of the new order.

Now, at a more mundane level of events, consider this. General Robert E. Lee was as important as President Abraham Lincoln in abolishing slavery and cementing a firmer union between the States. If upon the Confederacy's first firing on Fort Sumter, the North had been able to rush massive military forces into the south to overwhelm and subdue the rebellion at its outbreak, the result would have been inconclusive. For the South would not have been convinced of defeat.

But General Lee's aggressive and spirited employment of the Army of Northern Virginia, causing the North numerous lost battles, stalemates, and a general anxiety over a period of several years, attested to the strength and vigor of the Confederacy's military argument. For from this, it would appear that its people were of a firm resolve.

Consequently, when that argument was finally overturned by the advantage of superior force, there could not be any doubt as to the conclusiveness of the blow. Lincoln's final perseverance and decisive victory were built in this way from the raw materials of General Lee's stubborn resistance and of the Army of Northern Virginia's determination to give all it had for what it believed in a struggle against impossible odds.

JUSTICE is not a strictly moral concept. For it combines the expedient (punishment and reward) with the moral (a community of trust). Punishments and rewards are meted out according to rules governing the established relationships of a community of trust. But it is only the rules, not punishments and rewards, which reflect the community.

Punishment itself is predicated on a type of collective revenge. And to a greater or lesser extent, it is fulfilled through some sort of social restraint, or outright removal, of the offender. This is expedience. In other words, it is a form of individual and social self-defense meted out by authority. Trust has been breached. And the offender must be dealt with as an enemy of the community of trust.

The same is true of rewards, since they imply incentives. They are given to individuals, businesses, and groups to enhance social conformity. But when an incentive is required to assist a relationship of trust, that relationship is imperfect. It is flawed to some degree by self-interest. For it is a denial of an appeal to the general good, which should function as the only motive for appropriate behavior.

This brings up the problem of a "just war." Is it moral? In itself, it is not, because it is the expedient side of justice that is exercised when a nation goes to war. Of course, in an imperfect world this does not mean that there are not times when a nation should go to war. It simply means that the prosecution of a war is an expedient action. This is true even though the considerations for taking such an action concern a supposed "breach of trust." For, like a punishment, it is an action carried outside any bond of trust.

In the first place, there can be no real community of trust between sovereign nations for which there is no overriding authority. In the second, once war is enjoined, it is carried out in a moral vacuum of expedience. It is either aggression or self-defense, even if a high principle is what brings it about.

Aggression is clearly a breach of trust. But though self-defense may be necessary, from a strictly moral perspective it is little better. For self-defense is always an expedient action—operating outside any environment of trust and at best only referring back to it as an origin of the act.

So how can it be determined if a war should be prosecuted or not? Internal national standards of right and wrong are its only reference. There can be no universal set of standards. For there must be a community of trust to set them. So a nation must—and in a practical sense, always will—answer to its own principles for taking an expedient action.

It must look into itself because it is only within the nation that there is an established and enforced community of trust. That community is the one taking the action, and one which will be affected by its consequences. Outside of such a community, there is no authorized foundation for such a decision.

If the opinions of other peoples, or nations, are considered, the acting community's state of war is clearly understood by these others to be a matter of expedience, just as it should be understood by the acting community itself. To these others, it cannot be concealed under the cover of a moral act because it is not their act. Thus there is no incentive to justify it by self-deception. For, unless by some chance these other nations have standards identical with those of the acting community and are in agreement with it, it is not in their interest.

Institutional Religion

FAITH in the spirit is nothing. Life in the spirit is everything.

IT has been said that God does not have a religion. What a wonderfully freeing revelation this is to one strangled in the fetters of tradition!

HUMAN beings are told to ponder in their hearts the great truths concerning their souls. Yet most often, all they are inclined do is either analyze them or accept them from authority.

NO written or spoken scripture can be considered absolutely sacrosanct. For a scripture is a document produced by human beings, however inspired. There is but one infallible scripture, which lies at the core of human nature. It is the spiritual ground of human experience, which is generally concealed beneath the sensory confusion of life. The function of external writings and oral revelations is to bring this inner awareness to light, where it can represent spiritual relations to the mind.

THE miracle of consciousness is greater than the miracle of a resurrection.

TRUTH is sincerity of heart.

THE world's great religions are immersed in a struggle for power over men's behavior. This is particularly true of the Semitic religions. The problem is that this attempt to control behavior becomes a preoccupation with moral codes. The particular moral code in question is made equivalent to the will of God.

But morality cannot be made equivalent to spirit, lest spirit be placed in a position of self-contradiction. How can spirit lead men to commit no murder and yet send them into war (as occurs in the Hebrew scriptures)? Again, many Christians once viewed slavery as acceptable. Now they do not.

A conception of spirit must lie beyond the moral codes people live by, which codes are ever-changing and evolving. A transcendent deity is moral precisely in the sense that it is beyond, that it transcends the divisive and conflicting relations of humanity. Spirit is approached, not for the particular, momentary view, but for the larger, inclusive, eternal relation of things about which human understanding is ever growing in experience.

NIETZSCHE was right: in certain respects, Christianity died on the cross. But that is not the fault of the carpenter—a man of genius. It is the work of those who came after him and could not see with his breadth of vision. Nietzsche recognized this fact. For even the New Testament apostles share this limitation.

They were good men. They were sincere men. What they have to say in their epistles is true. But it is only one side of the truth. Preoccupied with the needs of their time or blinded by a one-sided perspective, they would seem not to have shared, and certainly did not express, the full measure of their master's vision. If Plato missed anything in Socrates, he did not miss half so much as these men did in Jesus of Nazareth.

THE poet Shelley and Jesus of Nazareth were both visionaries who have yet to be properly understood. Their insights extend beyond the earthbound thoughts of most people. For even the best educated bear too much of the weight of the material in their thinking. This is why they have not been able to understand them.

IN modern times, religion has failed because it has become encrusted with low ideas. It is not the life of spirit which has failed, but the mind.

IN accordance with the gospel representation of Jesus of Nazareth, he was one of the most original figures in human history. He shocked his society by totally shifting its values inward. He taught his disciples that they could go out and do what he did: cast out spirits and heal the sick. Through faith, they had the power of the universal spirit in them.

He also separated individual from institutional religious practice: the Sabbath was made for man, not man for the Sabbath. In other words, laws were made for people, not people for laws. He taught people to pray in privacy because what is in a person's soul cannot be approached in a group setting.

He instructed his disciples to swear by nothing in heaven or on earth, since a person should affirm or deny on the basis of his own integrity. Otherwise his avowal or disavowal is meaningless. It cannot be helped by superstition or external authority. In addition, all people are expressions of the universal spirit. So the individual heart is more important than things sworn by.

But what has institutional religion done? It has shifted values outward again, away from the individual into an emphasis on doctrine and communal conformity and practice. Individuals rely on a group environment to relate to spirit as much or more than they do on a private one. In Christian institutional practice, Jesus has been turned upside down. He has been left standing on his head.

SUPERSTITION is difficult to define. Religion, or spirituality at any rate, is a search for transcendence. It is an attempt to find that which is greater and more unified than the things of daily experience. This is true even of animistic religions. All, at bottom, are a search for spiritual transcendence and unity.

But superstition takes a different tack. It is a kind of shunt between the desire for transcendent meaning and the material need for a sense of security. By reaching out to grab hold of something concrete, rather than risking the airy hopefulness of a full transcendence, a person falls into superstition. If transcendent meaning is lost sight of, even for a moment, the result is superstition.

UNIVERSAL spirit can only be loved in an admiration for the beautiful. This is a synthesis of thought and emotion which defies any analysis.

THE idea, according to institutional religion, that human beings should do good for the sake of the carrot (heaven) or the stick (hell) is disgusting. It is totally unethical. A person should do good because of her love of the good. Only then can she be virtuous. The above motives are composed of self-interest and fear. There is no virtue in them.

THE intellectual love of spirit is the love of an intellectual approach to spirit. What there is to love is the character human beings possess when they extend their minds toward spirit.

A FUNDAMENTAL religious assumption in modern times ought to be that there is mystery in nature. But there is no magic.

IT has been said that human beings are made in the image of God. But in truth, for most people, spirit is made in a human image. As a person grows in spiritual understanding, in breadth and tolerance of outlook, his conception of spirit changes accordingly. Spirit is like an idealized portrait, a mirror image of man. Human beings cannot truly see spirit because they are limited by what they can see of themselves in spirit.

WHAT is religion? Religion should be a recognition of the preeminence of spiritual being. Though the material may be regarded in various ways, religion always posits the prior importance of spirit. This emphasis on spirit, when applied to individual human beings, provides an opening in an apparently causal world for a recognition of free will. For this reason, religion is inherently prescriptive. It is moral, placing an emphasis upon a person's responsibility for her acts.

PERSONHOOD cannot be attributed to the spirit. How could this possibly be known? But the human capacity to have a personal relationship with the spirit can be affirmed. Many people of faith would adamantly insist on the efficacy of their personal interaction with the spirit. There is no reason to doubt their assertion. Leave it at that and go no further.

THE three great Semitic religions share this one flaw: they encourage an anthropomorphic conception of spirit. This god of theirs seems inevitably to be a jealous and possessive god who demands loyalty. Loyalty to such a god being paramount in the believer, the believer finds it impossible to be consistently honest with himself.

HUMANISM and Christianity are not incompatible. Much of the spirit of Renaissance Humanism grew out of Christianity. Some of the influence was Greek, or Classical. But much of it was Hebraic and especially Christian. An example would be the modern respect for women and the individual person. So much of the social consciousness that would today do away with religious constraints is, in fact, Christianity without a name.

INSTITUTIONAL religion often adapts truth to social expedience. It generally conceives of itself as the guardian of morals. For this reason it is apt to substitute moral rules for moral insight. But the problem is that moral perceptions change over time. For this reason, social expedience involves an element of drift. It changes a little—but not entirely—as circumstances change.

Nevertheless, the amount of accumulated drift over time, however slight in its increments, may become sufficient to falsify the spiritual insight which supports the moral rules. When this happens, moral values become confused. Thus the core of spiritual truth which was enclosed within those values may finally be lost.

For this reason, a hard won truth should never be sacrificed for the sake of the conveniences of the moment. It is better to endure present social difficulties than it is to destroy long term hope. It is thus preferable that a social system should collapse altogether, rather than lose the possibility of building a better society in the future. Truth is humanity's greatest asset. Truth in spiritual insight and moral values all the more so.

THERE is no substitute for sincerity of heart. Sincerity of heart makes the mind strong, the will supple, and the feelings gentle. Where there is sincerity, there will be the clearest thinking possible. There will be the molding of desires and actions to the nuances of situation. And there will be an emotional sensitivity conditioned by sympathy.

SINCERITY would seem to be the cardinal virtue. Do everything with a sincere heart. Shake hands firmly. Hug people as though it were meant, in accordance with the person and the occasion. Be tolerant and accepting because tolerance expresses a general regard for the other person, their whole person. Disapproval should be expressed with an expectation and hope of improvement. It should be directed toward an action and not the person. The person is a son of the universal spirit.

THE most difficult task in understanding the character of spirit lies in considering how human beings are invested with it. Each person does not have a part of universal spirit in her. She has all of spirit in her. So it might be said that spirit is indivisible. But if so, how is spirit's presence in each separate human being to be accounted for? This would imply division, much as the human race is divided into individuals.

A person must go East to find an answer. There someone might observe that physical reality with its appearance of division is an illusion. For the true character of being is oneness. But this is not acceptable to a Western sensibility with its emphasis on individuality and on the reality of the material realm.

So this person must return from the East, but without abandoning it. Not wanting to let go of either the Eastern or Western perspective, she may proclaim the dual and complete reality of both the material and the spiritual. It is as though they are flipsides of one another. And to entertain one is to momentarily forgo the other. For both together are one reality, a reality which can only be experienced in halves.

Together these two realities are like a mirror with its glass surface and its black paper backing. The black paper backing can be equated to the material realm. For it is opaque. It stops the penetration of human vision and returns it to the viewer, just as material experience will not grant a view of spirit.

But all the while, the viewer's vision has passed through the glass, reached beyond it, and come back to her through it. That hidden transcendence is spirit. The fact that she sees only a reflection of the familiar material realm is an illusion. She has seen a great deal more, though she does not know it.

There is one glass and one backing, just as there is spirit and matter. But though they can only be understood separately by the mind, they are experienced together. So together they are one. And when a person gazes into them combined, what she sees may differ according to the character of her cultural orientation. If she is accustomed to the material, she sees the material. If she is accustomed to spirit, she finds spirit.

There are individual personal sightings as well. Each of these is also an expression of the combined character of the mirror. For it is limited human perspective that creates both the cultural and individual sightings which are found in the mirror. But limitation in perspective is not fragmentation. For in each sighting, the whole expression of the mirror is received, an expression of its glass and black paper backing.

Another, and perhaps simpler, way of considering the issue would be to think of looking through the different facets of a prism. If the prism is universal spirit, and individual people are what are seen through particular facets of the prism, then each person is wholly spirit but a different expression of the same.

TO fear the spirit as an angry being is false. Spirit is universal. And universal spirit does not need to take revenge upon human beings for their disloyalty, because it does not need their loyalty. In a deep sense, a human being is this spirit. Thus, to be fully herself, she has a need to express it. To live a meaningful life, her mind must be fully transformed into spirit. For spirit and consciousness are one. And consciousness gains its most profound depth of knowledge and assurance from that which it purports not to know: itself.

Think of this universal spirit as a gardener. The gardener plants a seed and waters it. The seed grows and becomes a tree, providing shade, beauty, and a home for birds. The gardener loves the tree and cares for it tenderly, watering, fertilizing, and pruning it. But he does not demand its loyalty. The tree pleases the gardener by simply being a good healthy tree.

So what should the tree do in its relationship to the gardener? It should be a good, healthy tree. That is what pleases the gardener. It should bear fruit appropriate to its kind. That is, good fruit. It should be as naturally a tree as it possibly can be. It should not be grass or a vine or a fungus. It should be what it is.

So what should people do? They should behave like the tree. They should be as naturally human as they can be. But what is it to be human? To be human is not to allow oneself to be twisted or destroyed by evil, as when a fungus rots or a vine chokes a tree. A person should be clean and naturally functioning according to her kind both inwardly and outwardly.

What is her kind? She is a rational being. She can understand consequences. She can feel the pain in others and recognize how her actions might cause it. She should therefore strive to do no harm. She can also take a position of respect and wonder concerning the overall nature of things, which will always be far beyond her full comprehension. Because she can imagine a universe with laws, she can expect a lawgiver. If she is in awe of the universe, she should have a profound respect for its source. That is her nature as a rational being.

Anything else is a distortion. It makes a person spiritually unhealthy. If a person is unhealthy, she will produce unhealthy fruit, just as, if an apple tree gives unhealthy fruit, it is understood that the tree itself is under some kind of stress. It is not growing and producing naturally. It is an unhealthy tree.

The human relationship to spirit is no different. Spirit is the ground of all being and the source of all truth. A human being does not revere spirit because it needs for her to do so. She reveres it because *she* needs to do so. Human beings were not made for religion. Religion was made for human beings. It was given to make them happy and should be as natural as happiness is.

If it makes people unnatural—that is, not themselves—they should discard it. The one universal spirit did not bifurcate its creation. It did not put religion on one side and humanity on another as two estranged entities, the former subordinating the latter. There would be no religion if it were not natural to have one. People are as fitted to it as a bee to its hive. Or at least they should be.

THROUGHOUT history monotheistic religion has often shown itself to be cruel. How is this so? It happens when people become dogmatic in defense of their perspective on ethical questions. Sometimes, out of what they see as loyalty to an anthropomorphic god, they will suspend natural feeling and judgment and proceed to persecute those who do not agree with them. This generally happens because institutionalized religion, being an instrument of the state, turns spiritual feeling into an inflexible moral law upholding the harmony and order of the community. It must then be defended at all costs.

THE unspeakably horrible ethics of laissez-faire capitalism—materialism, greed, competition, let the buyer beware, etc.—is fundamentally incompatible with the teachings of Jesus of Nazareth. It is a discipleship of physical bodies alone, which can in no way be brought into harmony with a spiritual state of mind.

But what can be done? Can the material demands of the body be ignored? Is it not true that any ethical system based on human reason, imagination, and experience must reflect material reality, the joys and pains of physical existence? The material realm is divisive by nature and must take into consideration events and conditions which do not accord with the ideal of an undivided, unified character, which is a product of a spiritual state of mind.

When Jesus of Nazareth spoke of turning the other cheek, going the extra mile, giving up one's coat and cloak, persevering in faith, he spoke from a point of view that assumed total immersion in the spiritual. When one with the universal spirit, the human mental condition is one of peace, fearlessness, and union with spirit. It is totally non-divisive, totally immaterial. What can reason, imagination, and experience contribute to this, since they are inevitably products of the material realm?

It is true they cannot directly pursue the spiritual state of mind set forth by Jesus. But what they can do is create a platform of awareness and behavior that is a good place to regain one's bearings when falling out of the spiritual state, as people regularly do. In other words, an ethical awareness should be empathetic and fair.

But empathy and fairness are categories that apply to material experience. They reflect human instincts. As such they are imperfect, subject to repeated error, especially where a sense of personal insecurity is concerned. Nevertheless, they can reflect the spiritual in the way a pool reflects the sky, where all the heavens are contained in a finite body of water. For this reason, an ugly or deceitful demeanor towards one's neighbor is never to be sanctioned. That is because it is not beneficial to anyone, even in a finite sense.

Let the infinite sense of good be ever so far above the material sense of good. Yet they are close enough to reflect and influence one another. How can this be said of a competitive, mutually destructive mentality?

That is why spiritual values and a discipleship of physical bodies alone are incompatible.

THE apostle Paul said that there are evil principalities and powers at work in the world. Is this not akin to the negative effect of bad habits spoken of by Socrates, Plato, and Aristotle? What is a habit but a state of mind reinforced by practice? What are these principalities and powers but limited spirits in the sense that they are states of spirit?

Is not a state of mind a spiritual state? Then habits, good or bad, are states of mind, or states of spirit. A mind in the grip of a bad habit, an addiction, an obsession, or a state which occludes its approach to the common sense of reality, is a mind under the control of an evil spiritual state or condition. In varying degrees, it is a mind possessed.

Spirit as Universal Consciousness

THE universe is alive. Spirit permeates all of it and resides wholly in every part of it. For spirit is the ground of being. It is both unlimited and indivisible. This is what it means for it to be *in*finite, or *not* finite. That is why it must be both omnipresent and wholly present. Consciousness—not its content—is spirit.

HUMAN beings find it impossible to comprehend the death of a person (the extinguishment of a living spirit). But every experience of sentient life confirms it. This is the opposition between the unity of consciousness and the disunity of the senses.

CONSCIOUSNESS is self-limiting universal spirit. That is what human beings are, each and every one.

ALL people are sons of spirit. For all are self-limiting universal spirit. Spirit is one: one consciousness self-limited to many individual centers of consciousness, one infinite awareness limited to many material centers of finite awareness. Yet universal spirit, being one, remains unlimited in itself.

IF human awareness were to acknowledge itself as an expression of spirit, it would be subject to a different set of laws than those which appear to govern matter. But this cannot be known so long as a stubborn reason insists that a quantitative analysis of the content of consciousness reveals a greater miracle than consciousness.

SO much of what human beings do and know is spontaneous and beyond words. Yet a veil of reason is placed over everything. And the veil becomes reality.

SØREN Kierkegaard's "leap of faith" demands an infinitely great leap over an infinitesimally small chasm, a chasm which lies between matter and spirit. The greatness of this leap is an overcoming of will in its dependence on rational understanding.

THERE is an ongoing intellectual tension which forms a nexus between the dynamic of spirit and human awareness. Science and philosophy must work within it. But they should always strive toward spirit.

NATURE in its fullness is a dynamic process which has no identifiable coordinates. As such, it is spirit. But the materially oriented human mind cannot grasp nature as spirit. For it must find a way to identify itself within it. In doing so, it converts an inherent dynamism, both of itself and of experience, into a static template, which is thrown over both. From this vantage point, it fills the world with coordinates relative to a material perspective. Thus the universe exists only as a construct of the mind. Nevertheless, this is not to say such a construct is false. Rather, it is a limitation placed on spirit for the sake of analysis.

EVERY person has a choice between contentment and happiness. The way of civilization is the way of contentment, safety, rules. The other way is full or risk but the reward, though difficult to achieve, is fulfillment.

THE joy a person expresses is linked to all things because her joy is the expression of spirit. And spirit is one.

A PERSON is not immortal because his life extends throughout the history of time. He is immortal in simply being. Therefore, the joy he expresses today is for all time and extends beyond time. For it is rooted in simple being.

FROM a material perspective, where all is division and opposition, compromise is necessary. But truth never need be compromised because it rests upon an indivisible unity of spirit. Material fact is no exception. For spirit is the ground of being. For this reason, not all goals can be achieved by compromise. Moreover, the most enduring ones are often furthered by defeat. A search for truth must seek for the unity that lies beneath things. And defeat in such a pursuit is a victory.

IT may be that at the time of death a human spirit is simply diffused within the universal being within which it is grounded. This would seem to imply a loss of personal identity. But why should this be so? In the first place, why should personhood be denied to that from which all things emanate? If the universal spirit carries personhood as a potential, as it carries within itself all other things actual or potential, why should that same universal spirit not express personhood within itself and in its relationship to a human response?

And in the second place, if this is so, why should universal spirit, which is after all universal, not also encompass the many persons? Insofar as they emanate from the universal ground of all being, all persons who have ever lived or will live may persist within it beyond the present finitude. In such a case, personal identity could not perish.

THERE is a spirit of life. Everything emanates from it. Each individual human life is a full expression of this spirit, which is in all things at once and entirely within each thing. It is therefore necessary that a person should be joyful and full of the spirit of living. That includes a respect for everything which emanates from spirit. For, as spirit is the ground of one being, it is also the ground of another. Each being is the spirit.

Every individual emanates from one spirit. Moreover, each person is a full expression of that spirit. Each thing, animate or inanimate, is a full expression of one spirit shared by all and possessed exclusively by each. A leaf is a full expression of spirit. There is no part of spirit which is left over from the leaf. But every other leaf is also spirit. And there is only one spirit. A leaf can be said to be put forth by a plant. The plant is spirit. Or the leaf puts forth itself. It is spirit. It is thus joyful in living.

ONE must examine the character of genuine spiritual life to understand it. That way of life is a progress, both for the general body of men and women and for each individual person. An individual grows in spiritual character, in spirit-mindedness. For this to occur, there must be fermentation.

There must be spiritual progress through a continual examination of oneself and the character of spirit. As spiritual development occurs, the individual grows to see himself differently. And as he sees himself differently, he comes to understand the character of spirit and spiritual life in new ways. No one person can do this for another. It is a matter between the individual and the spirit.

NATURE, when looked at in isolated segments, can be seen as both fascinating and cruel. But when considered as a whole, it can be understood as an expression of the inscrutable dynamic of spirit. It is then experienced as filled with a mysterious harmony. If the fragmentary material view of nature excites, wounds, and intrigues the human mind, the universal spiritual outlook elevates the mind into a state of peace and joy.

Both Jesus of Nazareth and the Buddha understood the natural world in this way. That is to say, they understood reality, material and spiritual, as a unity. They recognized it both materially as divisive and transcendently as healing. Thus they sought to present a vision which was a bridge between the two.

As a result, both the faith of Jesus and the nirvana of the Buddha demand a letting go of a material mentality. For wholeness and freedom can only be found within an individual person when she relinquishes the divisive and oppositional states of mind which proceed from such a view.

Nevertheless, the Christian emphasis on an enduring self and the early Buddhist vision of extinguishment, or dissipation of the self into the all, do appear to be incompatible. But perhaps a ground of reconciliation lies in the question of the meaning of self? Christian and Muslim mystics have held that it means immersion in the oneness of universal spirit. But they do not hold that this necessitates a loss of self. For the self cannot be lost. It is simply restored to its original condition of oneness with spirit as one of the multiple selfhoods of spirit.

It can be seen then that Jesus and the Buddha were both concerned with a unified state of being, which is universal spirit. It is a state in which human beings already exist, inasmuch as they are dynamic, self-regarding organisms. For as such, they may in their understanding extend their own dynamism to a spiritual state. It is the extension of a free will to its ground of liberation in spirit. Thus they can understand themselves as expressions of the inclusive dynamic of spirit. Though this would be accomplished without the possibility of a full intellectual comprehension of its meaning.

Jesus did not define the universal spirit and the Buddha did not speak of it because such expressions invite a complex and limited analysis. For analysis fosters a material state of mind. Or, which is the same thing, it encourages the interpretation of spirit in material terms. That interpretation is inherently a denial of spirit.

A TRANSCENDENT faith in spirit, once acknowledged as faith, allows for the imposition of spiritual values upon nature. Then having thus established a framework of standards for a hierarchy of "goods" which may be chosen in life, people are able to legitimately *see* these goods in nature.

THE material world is an expression of spirit. Every species of sentient life expresses the same type of general awareness that human beings do. Each kind of animal life differs only in the apparatus with which it processes the information it receives from its environment. All are conscious. And all may even have a sense of self.

PLATO'S strength lies in his recognition that there is something in human awareness which is not material. Aristotle's strength lies in the recognition that reality is only grasped in terms of the material. But this latter position does not mean that human awareness is limited to the material. It simply means that human reason is a correlative of the material, that it must use material instruments to construct an understanding of the spiritual.

This dichotomy, which is a dichotomy of approach, remains with humanity to this day. It is a problem of knowledge which forces the human mind to one side or the other of the issue. The mind must, it would seem, choose either the idealist or the empirical approach to knowledge. Even Kant ended up more on the side of the ideal and was not able to fully reconcile the two. Such a titanic failure must give anyone pause. But the effort must go on. A thinker must now begin by picking up the broken shards of Immanuel Kant, or by going back to David Hume and George Berkeley. For this is how philosophy works.

WHEN the terms "real" or "realism" are being used, what is being referred to is an attitude toward the physical and emotional experiences of life. For purposes of faithful observance and depiction in art and literature, these physical and emotional experiences are assumed to have a combined objective existence. That is, they are real to a person, though, as a compound, they occur inside him, beyond sensory observation.

Thus the use of the word "real" in this sense is not a statement concerning what is possessed of physical being or what is not. Such speculation proves itself to be meaningless when the urgent business of living is under consideration. For this reason, spiritual states, such as mystical states and matters of faith, can be considered real if they have a basis in personal experience. For they are an integral part of this or that person's reality.

Without having recourse to external evidence to support it, an individual person is acquainted with the indivisibility and unity of his own state of consciousness. It is part of his reality and may lead to further understanding, such as the belief that others have the experience as well or that all things, living and inanimate, share a foundation in conscious being. There is no reason not to accept such an insight derived from inner experience. It may have as much of a foundation in the mind—where all things are experienced and understood—as anything regarding what is external to the senses. It is therefore real, or at least potentially so.

IS there really much difference between an idea and an act? An idea is an act foreshadowed or reflected upon. This is true even when one idea merely leads to another idea. For ideas change minds, however slightly, altering their balance toward some future action in this direction or that, thus producing a different inclination.

Conversely, an act is an argument by means of a hammer, language, paintbrush, sword, or other physical means. This indicates the close association between human thoughts and material events. They are born of the same source: the spiritual / material structure of the world, of which human beings are an integral part.

The only possible fallacy which could arise from this way of thinking would be to assume that the material limits the spiritual. While it is true that a close relationship exists between the data of the senses and that of thought, it cannot be demonstrated that the physical itself is not of a spiritual origin. Neither has anyone succeeded in demonstrating, other than by suggestion and temporal association, that the mind is of a physical origin.

THE material world is like a work of art. It is so complexly integrated that an inexhaustible fund of relations arise from it. In fact, it can be assumed that just to keep the material world in existence requires an unimaginable fund of interest and commitment on the part of its progenitor. So, just as an exact interpretation of Rembrandt's viewpoint in any of his paintings will never be known, neither will anyone ever fully conceive the spiritual ground of the universe.

The human mind may come to understand the material whole in its parts, and in a composite of those parts, but never in its ground of origin. For a human mind to peer beyond the superficial crust of material reality, even when assisted with its most subtle reasonings, is at best an uncertain endeavor. To know this ought to be a human being's first act of reverence. But it should not keep him from trying to understand what he can. Modesty, not ignorance, is what is required.

ACCEPTANCE of a belief in a personal god is the acceptance of a responsibility which comes with varying levels of commitment. The more intense the relationship, the more personal it is, the greater will be a person's felt sense of responsibility for her actions. For, if her actions are measured in terms of what she believes to be the god's will, they must be of great importance to her. Thus her responsibility is immense.

But if the person-to-god relationship should be less centered in the life of that person, many projects may be carried out by her without reference to the relationship. And those acts which are in fact referenced to it will carry less weight. But the cost of this is a loss of sincerity of commitment. And this can reflect a lack of serious involvement in life.

A believing person's loyalty to her god is her loyalty to herself, a commitment to what she perceives to be the proper course to pursue in a life which belongs exclusively to her, but which is indexed to her belief in a personal god. Thus it can be seen that a greater commitment to the person-to-god relationship is simply a more ambitious program for life. For, if it should turn out that there is no god, what would be found lacking is an enlarged moral purpose. In her view, her life would become disoriented and less meaningful.

It is true that personal focus can be achieved in a morally purposeless universe. But she has not chosen it. She has not conceived its possibility. For she believes that in such a universe, any largeness of design in the project of living would be all but unattainable. There would be for her a numbing sense that her actions would thus be designed for only a moment of existence, a moment passed on a speck of dust, where she is spun about in an immeasurably vast and meaningless mechanism. So, by lending a sense of benevolence and purpose to the universe, the idea of a personal god provides her with a possibility for unlimited development in her thoughts and emotions. Her acts follow from these.

WHEN a person relates herself to nature, say to a bird singing in a tree amidst green leaves and against a blue sky on a sunny day, she may want to praise universal spirit. But it is not spirit she is thinking of. It is a bird in a tree. So what is her emotion? Is it gratitude to an anthropomorphic artisan who made these things?

If she tries to probe into the matter, what she will see is that she empathizes with the bird. She senses its exuberance and shares in it. She feels the bright sunlight and the summer breeze. And she is grateful that appreciative life is not confined to her or her kind. She is enlarged by the connection.

It is in this kinship with other life that she feels a connection with universal spirit. But she would not limit spirit to it, to a simple life form, or to nature at large. She would not assume that universal spirit is to be understood as simply a connection between living things. Nor would she say that spirit is the dynamic interaction of all things.

What she would say is that the point at which such a dynamic between her and nature becomes a detached, self-actuated self-awareness is the point at which it is spirit. Furthermore, she sees that the detachment works from both directions. For the natural world can be seen as having been spun out of a dynamic of spirit, which precipitates into nature its constituent elements and their relations. Thus she would acknowledge that what comes from the dynamic interchange between herself and nature is more than a sum of so many parts.

So in turning away momentarily from the isolated perspective of her own physical being, that person is partaking of an enlarged self-awareness. When she empathizes with the bird, she does more than connect with it in imagination. She acknowledges her own spiritual being, because she recognizes the spiritual unity between things. She sees universal spirit.

THE quality of life on earth is in jeopardy due to a gap between material and spiritual concerns. As the danger of human beings deteriorating the resources and variety of life on the planet they inhabit continues to increase, an alternative way for human beings to think about themselves must be found. For neither a predominately materialist nor a predominately spiritualist view has worked.

In fact, a deliberate focus on one side of the issue, either material or spiritual, has led to unsatisfactory results which are clearly manifested in human history. A strictly material perspective liberates tendencies toward selfish exploitation. And a strictly spiritual point of view stagnates the human mind.

So whether humanity sees nature as its material opponent to be overcome and subdued for its uses, or whether it sees itself as spiritually exempt from nature and therefore as a "steward" of something which will be left behind or remade in eternity, the result in either case is reckless and imbalanced.

People must see reality as simultaneously material and spiritual. They must acknowledge both realms, the material and the spiritual, as coextensive views of a single reality. This is not a plea for pantheism. It is not an assertion that nature and spirit should be inextricable from one another in terms of human understanding.

It is an insistence that explanations of material and spiritual views are ultimately concerned with the same topic. The subject matter is different. But the ground is the same. Yet a problem does continue to present itself. It is that to speak in terms of one is to exclude the other, at least for the duration of an inevitably one-sided discussion concerning either perspective. This remains the case in spite of the fact that together they constitute the fullness of reality.

THE gift of spirit to humanity is a gift of spiritual synthesis. This is the capacity in every human being to create a synthetic whole of herself, a spiritual unity and oneness of thought within herself. It is an individualized world view. Few people achieve it. And the reason they do not is that they depend on others to do their thinking for them.

This is why there can be no unreflective adherence to doctrine or dogma in genuine spiritual life. To do so is to obstruct spiritual synthesis, to impede the attainment of an individualized world view. An individualized world view is the only instrument which can create a whole and integrated vision whose principles can be an expression of harmonious inner strength, rather than a crippling mass of contradictory ideas.

Of course, there is danger in this. There is always an element of danger in freedom. But that is the nature of spiritual life. Spirit is understood to be self-actuated being. That is its independence and separation from the material. So, if people are to realize their character as grounded in spirit, they must resemble spirit in this. They must achieve an inward and independent separation from the material.

Let it be put another way. An animal, a sentient creature other than man, is naturally spiritually unified. But this wholeness comes from the physical integration of its being, which is superbly designed to blend with its physical environment. Only disease or extreme cruelty, distorting the animal's nature, can shatter this harmony.

Human beings are different. They internalize so much of their environment, any blending of themselves with that internalized environment must be achieved by a deliberate effort. This is a process and adjustment of mind. Liberated mind is spirit. Reason, though a weak instrument, can free humanity from an unreflective existence. Thus harmony can be achieved with the physical facts of existence without a yielding to what is not spirit. It is in this sense that human beings are said to be living spirits.

Spirit is always an expression of unity rather than a division of parts. Spirit is unlimited and indivisible. So must human beings be. This means a person cannot allow any alien formula, though it were materially correct, to fragment her inner being. For this is what happens when a person blindly follows principles she is not allowed to question or disagree with.

HUMAN beings are born into the world in a state of innocence. But they soon learn of the material limitations of physical life. They develop a limited sense of themselves. Yet at the same time, they are conscious beings. Consciousness is immaterial. It is not limited. And this is where the deepest sense of self is centered.

However, the world presses on, making its limited material demands. So, instead of the spiritual perspective (the consciousness centered view) having a liberating effect, it combines with the material perspective. Thus the desire to persist in being is combined with a desire to protect that being. The immaterial quality of being is forgotten. And the mind and will join in a mad rush to prevail over every perceived limitation and opposition, over every imagined threat and injury. This is the worldly material view, reinforced by a perverted spiritual perspective.

TO grow in wisdom is to grow in spiritual mindedness. It is to grow in a general understanding of the relationship between a human being and human experience. This understanding is wisdom, or largeness of mind. Such largeness of mind provides a more comprehensive vision of life—something which reaches beyond the material to a fuller, more integrated range of human experience. As consciousness lies at the basis of human experience, and as simple, pure consciousness is immaterial in character, so should consciousness lie at the center of any explanation of the real.

WHAT is it in nature that makes people love it? Is it the detail—the myriad paraphernalia of life studied by biologists, geologists, meteorologists, and the like? Certainly there is interest in these details. But it is the whole, often when it is least focused upon it, that connects a human being with the whole within herself. If this pleasure is augmented by an attention to detail, then, from that person's spiritual and emotional perspective, this is good. But more often than not, the details overwhelm and cause her to lose sight of the whole.

IN its initial character, human awareness is the full dynamic of a human person. Though mental and physical experience appear to be only centered in a person's consciousness—the former directly so, the latter indirectly—a person's full awareness is in fact the whole of that person. It is that person and her circumstances. It is mind in the broadest sense: consciousness and its sensory content together. That is, it is the unveiling of a person through time—a life.

A person and her world are one. But they do not appear to be. For, though consciousness as such is one and indivisible, the content of consciousness is an unveiling through time which causes a person to see herself in terms of that content. In this way, she experiences herself incrementally in such a manner that the future appears to be hidden from the present moment. Moreover, the past presents itself as an accumulation, which is dead in activity.

But time, which appears to be incremental in its development of this view, is not incremental as an expression of spirit. As an expression of spirit, it is like the purity of simple consciousness in that it does not begin or end or have a middle. Time and spirit are one: unlimited, indivisible, a unity.

But in the immediate character of its presentation of finite experience to human awareness, time, or spirit, exhibits the whole of that experience in an order. It is an order which is not a sequence. For it is presented as a unity. Yet it is this order which is "read off" incrementally by human awareness in the form of sequential time, thus generating a past, present, and future.

So it is that a material world undergoing change is brought to bear upon a human sensibility. Consequently, it is in this way that a person's fundamental unity of awareness is made to submit to a fragmented experience. Thus a person is induced to understand herself incrementally, under an illusion of incremental time. As a result, there is a sense of separation between her spiritual self and her world.

HOW does an evil thought work? It falls upon the mind like a shadow, separating human consciousness from its grounding in universal awareness. When evil divides the mind in this way, obscuring its fuller nature, the mind loses its greater self and must cling to its material content. Human beings then become creatures only of sensual awareness, worry, fear, and division.

THE material world, as human beings know it, is a finite expression of self-limiting spirit. But spirit is *in*finite—i.e. not finite. So its self-limiting is necessitated for the purpose of placing limits on human awareness. In its fullness, spirit is bound by itself and no other. As such, it is filled with the grandeur of the unlimited.

THE object is to explain human intelligence in such a way as to demonstrate what its grounding in material existence might be. Initially, it is to show that human intelligence is not a privileged instrument standing apart from material being, but rather is grounded in it. This means that reason follows the laws of matter. It is utterly finite.

But reason also follows spirit, whole and holistic, where there are no discernible laws. There is only a boundless and indivisible unity. This is because matter, when experienced in the mind, and when apprehended within consciousness, is spirit. And spirit is not limited by matter, any more than human awareness is limited by neurons.

Human beings intuit themselves as having a free will because they experience their will within the unbounded unity of consciousness. Consciousness is not finite. It is indivisible. It is experienced as whole. Yet there are those who would say that there are only so many synaptic connections and that will and consciousness are products of these. Synapses carry forward the impulses of sense. These impulses may be conceived of as quantifiable.

How can this dichotomy be resolved? It is resolved holistically. For an organism, though material, experiences itself as a self-actuated unity. As such a unity, it is more than the sum of its parts. It is in this way that man comes to see himself as a living soul—unless he chooses to limit the term soul to a self-conscious physical being destined for annihilation.

So perhaps in some broad sense the definition may be extended further. It is possible to entertain the thought that a plant, a rock, the earth, or even the universe are souls. But in attempting to extend his thought beyond the self-awareness of a sentient being, a person cannot say what this means.

ENERGY is simply a concept for the human measurement of material change. But a spiritual dynamic, acting as the ground of material reality, may constitute a system of change so complex that no change can be measured within it.

THE concept of physical time is practically and experientially effective. But from a transcendental perspective, it is a superficial confection of the senses and the material mind.

THE dynamic of spirit is neither determinate nor indeterminate. It is change without reference to anything but itself. Such change is not an expression of physical energy. For physical energy is a creation of the human mind designed to account for physical change. But there is no stasis, no point of reference by which to proclaim the origin, character, or existence of spiritual change.

The dynamic of spirit is *in*finite in the sense that it is *not* finite. Metaphorically speaking, change in the dynamic is all change conceived at once, without passage of time. Thus no single change or set of changes can be specified. Nevertheless, in material terms, time and space are experienced and conceived as a continuum—a continuum in which points of reference have meaning. They are a continuum within which and in terms of which limited change is observed by human faculties.

In the spiritually dynamic state, unlimited and unspecified change is the fabric from which space and time are flung, like gossamer threads. Material reality, exhibited as present and past in human experience, is this emanation. It is an emanation projected within human awareness. Though it appears to be determinate, it originates in the spiritual dynamic.

In short, what is stated here is that change in the spiritual dynamic may be conceived of as unspecified, unlimited, existent possibility. To human awareness, it resembles the future. Material experience, on the other hand, is always thrust into the past. For the present is a mixture of the future and the past. It is the nexus of a future unfolding into a past.

What is anticipated is future. But any portion of it actually experienced is past. One can state precisely what lies in the past. Thus the past is determinate. Conversely, when future and past are considered together as one continuous, existent phenomenon, as they are in spirit, neither future nor past can be considered determinate. For they are both arising and arisen, without distinction between them.

This is because the future is unspecified. And the past is the future expressed. But because the future cannot be said to be determinate, the determinate character of the past does not imply that the future is determinate. It is therefore only itself determinate insofar as it is extant. For all that can be said of it is that it is simply extant within human awareness. Thus the fact that the future can be specified in the past does not mean that it is determined by the past.

So the spiritual dynamic, wherein the future dwells, is neither determinate nor indeterminate. It is unspecified within itself. But it is specified in what is generally understood to emanate from it, which is the past. Yet this past is only a manner of speaking. For it is an expression of limited human awareness. It is not a determined thing in itself but rather a product of time- and space-bound perception and thought.

FOR most people, dying is a fearful thing. Yet raccoons and birds do it. Like them, so will every human being. Young people go off to war in defiance of death. Does this mean there is something in life which transcends physical existence, which acts in defiance of its limitations? If so, what is it which implants both defiance and fear of death in the same being?

A cautious bird or squirrel feeding, watching for cats or hawks, is expressing the vulnerability of its physical nature both through its eating and its watchfulness. A bird may stake out a physical territory by singing. A rock dove displays its powers of flight for food and sex. These all appear to be materially induced behaviors. Yet there is a joy, an exuberance in this eating, singing, and flying which defies any mechanistic explanation. So the question is not, how does evolution work? It is, why does it work?

THE will to survive, to be, to overcome, etc. Sometimes it is referred to as the survival instinct. But what is meant by a survival instinct? Why should any creature wish to preserve itself any more than it should wish not to do so? Not to do so is far less work, far less painful, requires little intelligence, no cunning, and encounters no loss in valued circumstance, no enduring physical suffering, no permanently wounded sensibility.

So what drives living creatures to push forward into life, instead of conveniently dropping out of it? Why should the hare run so hard, squeal so loud, when pursued and captured by a fox or a coyote? There must be something in animal experience which strongly suggests that the individual ought not to perish either in body or (in human beings) reputation, something which contradicts the hard material evidence of death and decay, something which holds the attention of all sentient being.

That something is simple consciousness. Consciousness alone defies materiality. It cannot be counted. Its proportions cannot be measured. Nor is it divisible. It is simply present to awareness. It is awareness. It is at the heart of individual being. And it is that which is filled with the sensory and emotional content of experience.

So if that which contains experience may be said to be greater than the experience it contains, then is simple consciousness not greater than all the world sentient beings perceive and human beings think about?

Yet consciousness is often confused by human beings with its content. It becomes mixed with things of short temporal duration, things which perish. This confusion leads them into fear.

But consciousness itself demonstrates no proclivity towards perishing. It is not in a state of flux, as sensations and emotions are. It is a thing about which neither limits, nor permeability, nor lack of permeability can be perceived. It appears indestructible. It is this which the sense of self is, or ought to be, associated with.

Clinging to it, a person can stand in defiance of the weaker representations of the material world and that world's pitiable descent towards perishability and oblivion. Is not the awareness of self (in league with consciousness alone, which is its foundation) greater than the awareness of things external to the self?

Animals other than man, which also possess the faculty of consciousness, perceive that this is so. They do not confuse their inner being with their world. In truth, they do not think about it. And it is this simple unprejudiced character of their awareness which drives their perceptions and motivates their acts. When death comes, they perish materially in the midst of full living.

But consciousness must be separated from the perceptions, emotions, and acts of human beings. If this does not occur, all will appear to fly away in the face of death. For they are too much attached to the peripheral realm of immediate sensation to be reckoned with that which endures.

Nevertheless, death will have its way with every last individual, every last material thing. What comes into physical being must go out of it. But that which has caught up in this manner with its victim is only a lesser realm of material appearances. The greater realm, eternal consciousness, endures.

IT may be said that, in a certain sense, finiteness and infinity are one and the same thing. For they partake of one reality. And their mingling in that reality makes them one. But this encompassing view may be retained only in the sense that they are two sides of that reality. It cannot be held that they agree with one another within the single perspective of either one or the other.

For from a single point of view, reality must present itself as either material or spiritual, either finite or infinite. In other words, what this implies is that, for a proper meaning to be expressed in each case, there must be an exclusively material and an exclusively spiritual perspective concerning reality.

To understand this, a person must be careful not to confuse indeterminateness with infinity. Indeterminateness is finite. Infinity, brought within the same perspective as the finite, is in no way finite. It has no part in it, determinate or indeterminate. For infinity is that which is *in*finite—i.e. not finite.

Indeterminateness, on the other hand, is finitude extending toward but not arriving at infinity. It is analogous with a road leading to Paris. That road may come from the farthest nation. Perhaps even the furthest galaxy. It may run on indeterminately. But it is nevertheless a road *to* Paris only inasmuch as it is not a road *in* Paris. It is in this way that indeterminateness does not become infinitude. It merely approaches it.

MATERIAL existence is *being* in flux. Spirit is *being* in simple unity. It is also the awareness of being. For spirit is mind. But thought is not purely an expression of spirit. It arises from the interaction of spirit and matter. Thus it is a product of material perception as well as spirit. In this way, thought is not equivalent to spirit.

AN animal—that is, a sentient creature other than man—is spiritually whole. This wholeness comes from harmony. It is an integration of its being with its physical environment. The animal is superbly designed for this purpose through niche adaptation, instinct, and learning. Only extreme cruelty, environmental misfortune, or environmental disturbance can shatter this harmony.

But man internalizes so much of his external environment, and does so in a manner which is continuously variable, that the integration must be achieved largely within him. This is an ongoing process, a continual adjustment of mind. The price for this increased freedom of awareness is high.

All sentient life is conscious. In that sense it is spirit. For consciousness is spirit. But an intensely variable mind is a product of the dynamic of spirit. The more variable the mind, the more it must continuously seek harmony. So a human mind, with all its variability, cannot maintain harmony with the physical nature of its existence without reaching beyond it to spirit.

Spirit is unlimited and indivisible. It is an expression of unity rather than an expression of a division of parts, such as characterizes the material world. So, to become unified in its sense of self, a human mind must draw upon the unity of spirit. It is by this means that human beings integrate themselves with life. They conform to experience. But in internalizing it, they also make it conform to them. They create a spiritual unity of it. They may do this poorly or well. If done poorly, they lose their sense of integrated being. If done well, they find wellbeing.

NATURE, when looked at in part, say from the perspective of one of its creatures, can be seen, by turns, as fascinating and cruel. But when considered as a whole, it can be seen as a calm but intricately complex expression of the inscrutable dynamic of spirit. It is full of mystery and harmony. It is visible, tactile, compounded of known relations. Yet in its full integration, it is incomprehensible.

If the first kind of nature excites, wounds, and intrigues, the second kind elevates human minds into a state of peace and joy. It does so because human beings can only find wholeness and freedom within themselves when they relinquish any divisive and oppositional state of mind. Contemplating nature as a whole encourages a person to focus upon his own inner spirit, which is one, unlimited and indivisible. This leads to a sense of the unity of all things.

But the analytical instrument of the material world is the rational mind: a divisive and oppositional tool. It is designed as an instrument of survival, therefore of enmity and cunning. Its analytical, hence divisive, focus in the service of physical survival authenticates an elevation of the material view over the spiritual view.

Thus the material view becomes all important and confirms the expression of spiritual being in terms of the material being known by the analytical mind. For this reason, it is difficult for that mind to look back to its source. For the material realm is the realm of the senses. It is not the realm of the unity of pure conscious awareness. That would be spirit.

Because of the urgency of the messages received from a divisive world and the demands of the senses, human beings protect and provide for themselves in that world. They become blinded by this realm of the senses. These senses belong to the realm of the material. But the material is a creation of spirit. Nevertheless, by obscuring its own origin in spirit—that is, its origin in the purity of conscious awareness—the material mind becomes a denier of spirit.

To live in the material, that mind must think in the material. Immersing itself in it, the mind finds it to be a realm of constant worry and agitation. To live in wholeness and peace, the mind must recognize spirit. As its own pure consciousness, spirit is closer to it than the beating of its material heart. People know this is so. But they have trouble reconciling the two. The demands of the senses are overwhelming. So they give in to the one and lose the other.

HUMAN beings comprehend everything they can know through the mind. They cannot intellectually fathom anything other than through the mind. Now this mind, which takes every individual through his daily course of living, is by its essential nature orderly. It is the form in which the material world is perceived, thought about rationally, and discursively communicated. So, if any apparent disorder is encountered in the physical world, the mind is referred to for a remedy. But it is not the material mind alone that is referred to.

Insofar as the mind expresses itself in terms of logical thought about the material world, its character is clear. It is rational and discursive. But the mind partakes of a dynamic it does not directly perceive. It is an eternal spiritual ground, not unlike human consciousness, but filled with a creative potential which extends beyond the content of material awareness. Though the method of it cannot be materially understood, it is also this which communicates to the human mind its material awareness in time and space.

This immaterial ground of awareness is unknown to the material mind. The material mind has no insight into the spiritual origin of its materiality. But the material mind's perception and understanding of the material world is nevertheless challenged by the experience of its own consciousness. For that consciousness is greater than the material content which is thought to be its full complement of awareness.

So it is in light of this greater awareness, which is felt but not understood, that the ideas of the logical, discursively thinking mind are periodically critiqued, broken down, and restructured by that mind. For it is aware of more than it knows. Thus it continually strives to reach beyond its own structures of perception and thought.

Without the intervention of an immaterial experience of conscious awareness, human beings could not think creatively. The material mind could not escape the box of its limits. On the other hand, though the free modification and association of ideas of a creative will resembles spirit, these creative operations do not penetrate the veil of consciousness, which stands looming and opaque before the material mind.

For unlike spirit, human consciousness registers only the material. Beyond that, it is empty of content. So the human mind, though inspired by the breadth and mysterious depth of its own consciousness, must double back upon material perception and thought to form what is new. Thus it builds toward what it cannot see, using only what it knows.

CHANGE never takes place in either space or time alone. It always occurs in space *and* time. To speak of change in time alone or in space alone is an abstraction. The physical universe is an environment of dynamic change, in which space and time are inextricably interwoven.

It is good to remember this and not assume that to precipitate space or time out of this dynamic whole is to arrive at reality. On the contrary, to do so is to depart from reality for the purpose of analyzing or measuring it.

If it is understood that the physical world is a dynamic unity, and it is understood that an examination of its constituent parts is something momentarily precipitated from it by the mind, then it is possible to see that the dynamic unity is something immeasurable and indefinable. This is because adding up the analyzed and measurable parts does not yield a return to the original dynamism. A static whole is not a dynamic whole. It is an entity without life.

Spirit is life. When a person enters the world and, as a living being, becomes a dynamic unity in himself, he becomes a living soul. Form whence he comes is not the question. Man to himself is spirit. But to another he is a patchwork of parts. He overcomes this problem of material alienation through a process called empathy. That is, he seeks to understand another being like himself as a dynamism like himself.

Yet a living soul is a dynamism within the greater dynamism of the world. One does not dissolve into the other. Nor are there multiple dynamisms. Rather, an individual person is a focal point, a single perspective of the whole, which whole is centered in his consciousness. Because death and undisturbed sleep do not enter into conscious experience, they are not part of the spiritual, or dynamic, reality. They are not because they are not centered in awareness. Such conditions are unknown. They are arrived at by analysis and implication.

Spirit is the dynamic, the one and only dynamic, which is expressed through every conscious being. What appears to be material is a precipitate of dynamic being. A stone is a part of someone's reality. It is a part of everyone's reality. That reality is a material precipitate from the dynamic being of spirit. It exists in awareness.

FOR a human being there is only one focal point for reality: individual consciousness. Everything else is an abstraction from that viewpoint. This is not solipsism. It is an understanding of how human beings conceptualize both themselves and their world. The most abstract theories in physics, metaphysics, epistemology, and mathematics take their initial departure from this perspective and have their final resting point in it as well.

That is why Einstein could not accept the "spooky interactions" of early twentieth century quantum mechanics. He understood that the ultimate reference point for any theory is the individual human mind, and that that mind is an instrument which cannot function without a sense of order. This need for order is something which, no matter how seemingly independent of human will and action the material is in which it is sought, it is referenced to the human apprehension of that phenomena. It is how human beings *must* see things.

For instance, arithmetic, as Gottlob Frege pointed out, is grounded in the orderly logical operations of the human mind. But he does not go beyond these operations, thus leaving them in an original state of disunity. It is Kant who suggests a more fundamental unifying synthesis. Without such an underlying synthesis both for logical analysis and for human perception of the world, there could be little ground for any correlation between human thought and human action in the physical world. Arithmetic would not apply to anything in that world.

The same is true in religion and in the political realm. There is always some kind of correlation between the mind and the reality it contemplates. In religion, anthropomorphic conceptions of a god are formed because it is a human center of awareness which is being related to this being. The god may be more or less anthropomorphic. But something of human character is always in the conception.

For only like can be related to like. Otherwise, there is nothing but differentiation. So it need only be remembered that any religious ideas and doctrines, any elaborate descriptions of a god, are no more than human concepts designed to answer human problems. They are not final descriptions of a transcendent reality. This, of course, does not deny the possibility of the existence of something transcendent.

All religious ideas are structured in this way. Even the more abstract Hindu and Buddhist notions of a transcendent immateriality out of which being should arise are anthropomorphic in origin. These latter concepts are a good deal closer to a description of the state of human consciousness alone than they are to a person's isolated sense of herself in a material world, such as is found in the descriptions of an anthropomorphic god in the Semitic religions. But they are nevertheless spun out of the stuff of some aspect of human awareness.

In the present Western sector of the world, the individual is the focal point of political reality. This is the value and meaning of Western democracy: a recognition that the individual (particularly the individual in terms of natural and civil rights) is the source and limit of political governance.

No doubt this perspective can be abused. And the idea of individual rights can rise to such a pitch of emphasis that it weakens or otherwise harms the community. But it remains true that it is the individual which is the fundamental reality. The community is an abstraction from the individual.

Of course all political systems, both ancient and modern, are in their daily, lived character strikingly similar, be they founded upon the democratic, aristocratic, or monarchical model. This is because in everyday practice they are all reduced to a single pattern, which is that they are inevitably refined down to varying institutional configurations within which the few always find a way to manipulate the many. This is why historically, and with a good deal of frustration, humankind continues to repeatedly cycle through these three principal systems.

This continual overturn of political systems, particularly in the history of the West—moving from lesser to greater individual freedom to lesser freedom again—results from the fact that human beings refuse to ground their public practice on a fundamental understanding of the role of a more comprehensive human awareness in human interrelations.

The role is that there is but one universal spirit, fragmented by individual centers of consciousness. Continually ignoring this role and refusing to recognize that it has universal points of view which cannot be ignored, a myopic perspective on life is created. People fight against their common interest.

For example, if in her dealings with another person, an individual can only see her own immediate needs, and if furthermore she persists in limiting herself to a narrow perspective of subordination or control relative to that other person, she herself becomes a helpless, struggling speck of flotsam in the daily flow of events.

But if she troubles herself to seek and, having found, keep ever present in her mind principles grounded in a larger human vision—while nevertheless recognizing the human origin of that vision—she frees herself from the passing moment and accidental place in which she finds herself.

Such a narrow viewpoint as the one in which she fails to do this is what causes her, causes so many people, to plod unconsciously and repeatedly in the traces of egoistic competition, resulting in manipulation of the less cunning by the strong, who devote every nerve and fiber of their being to the development and exercise of cunning strategies.

Thus it can be seen that in political and ethical matters "human centered" should mean centered in a greater fullness and depth of the human perspective. A person should be conscious that she, in a unique way, shapes the world. That world is a human creation, but hopefully a human creation of spiritual depth and interconnectedness. Human beings become its blind, helpless creatures only when they forget this.

IT is impractical to support a definition of the empirical which would place it entirely on the side of sense experience and in opposition to a transcendental ground of knowledge. For the nature of consciousness cannot be approached through the senses. Consciousness is transcendental. And it participates in both knowledge and sensory experience.

On the other hand, the human race is unquestionably a product of the earth's biosphere, as it exhibits so many close analogues in its behavior and physiology to other forms of life. So it is reasonable that this observation should preclude consideration of anything which might appear to be present in human nature but wholly absent from any other life form. It applies to such seemingly unique human traits as reason and a faculty of spiritual awareness.

If reason and spiritual awareness are present in human beings, then they must at least be potentially existent in other life forms. Human beings differ from other forms of animal life in the emphasis which has been placed on the rational process. But this emphasis is a matter of degree, not kind. Nevertheless, its impact has been huge. For it has made humankind the dominant species.

So, in light of this distinction in human beings, and in consideration of its potential relationship to other life forms, what should be practiced is a form of empiricism which is more inclusive of the whole of life experience, both actual and potential. This is to say that an empirical approach must include a consideration of more than what the senses alone can reveal.

It should include the experience of consciousness, as well as recognition of a fundamental behavioral characteristic which could serve as a point of origin for the development of reason. For both consciousness and the senses are involved in making reason possible. The one serves as a ground of abstraction, while the other provides a material basis for both the matter and the structure of the reasoning process.

What is most important is that this enlarged empirical approach should be extended across the entire spectrum of sentient being. Animals are conscious as well as human beings. For both consciousness and sensory perception are components of any one unified experience of sentient life. Thus that experience must be understood in terms of general laws of nature which apply to all life forms capable of a varied and mobile response to stimuli, where choices must be made and alternative actions put into effect.

It is certainly evident that the faculty of reason is present in varying degrees in what are generally referred to as the higher forms of animal life. But it may be assumed as well that it is at least potentially present in those lower forms which do not appear to manifest anything approaching it.

Thus it can be assumed that the human capacity for experience and response, or such a capacity in any other life form, must be seen as a construct of nature. But what is nature? It can only be construed as something material which is grounded in spirit. Reason, arising both from matter and spirit, may, therefore, not be as much exploited by other life forms as it is in human beings. Or it may not be exploited at all. But it does exist within them all as a potential for adaptation.

In other words, a more developed capacity for reason might have become actual in other life forms had additional conditions conducive to such an adaptation been present for them in a measure equal to that which has influenced the development of human beings. There are many paths to species fulfillment. Not all these paths lead to a higher intelligence.

But where it has been most favored, the faculty of reason has included powers of abstraction, such as those used in general language-based conceptual classification, as well as the more structurally integrated conceptual classifications informing arithmetic, geometry, and the science of logic. In addition, and perhaps most interestingly, the power of abstraction has generated an evolving concern with the ground of conscious existence itself. This is the quest for an understanding of universal being.

In casting about for a name to attach to the particular orientation of thought expressed here, a *philosophy of common experience* comes to mind. Nothing more is meant by this label than an emphasis on the unity and universality of living experience, specifically in animals, but probably at least potentially in plants as well. For all life experience is communal in that it is grounded in one reality, a reality that is material yet arising from spirit.

Thus organic reality is both spiritual and sensory. For this reason, a biological designation for it cannot be reductionist in character. Physical science alone, as it is presently conceived, cannot limit an understanding of life to a mechanistic view. For in its dynamic development, biological life is underpinned by spirit.

It is spirit, or the unity of consciousness, which explains evolution's forward press into more complex forms and ultimately toward a form which can make a quest for a unified understanding of experience, both material and spiritual. This unified understanding approaches, though it does not equal, the unified comprehension which emanates from creative spirit and brings about the overall process of life experience. But the influence of consciousness and its drive towards unity remains critical. For, left without this spiritual impulse, natural selection could only be conceived to run about in circles. Matter alone cannot exhibit such an orientation or concern.

For conscious life in particular (as opposed to plants), there is an awareness and a response to stimuli which is at least in some measure an expression of choice not governed by blind instinct or a physiological reflex. Certainly an ant, and most probably an ameba, must own some governance over its actions. Or it would likely perish.

The awareness shapes the response. And the limited options for response shape the rational or proto-rational structures of that awareness. In other words, though the structures of reason and instinct are material, they are formed within the parameters of an interaction between conscious awareness and material circumstance.

For even in matters of an animal apparently confined to closely following instinctual patterns, no response to environmental circumstance which it can make is entirely blind. There must be a flexibility of choice, however narrow. And where such a faculty of choice rises to powers of abstraction in rational beings, it derives this power from the resources of its spiritual, or conscious, awareness.

THE role of spirit, or consciousness, in inducing the power of abstract thought and in fomenting an innate sense of unity has consequences which reach far beyond those of the immediate powers it confers. For it shapes humanity's evolutionary development in a way which would not occur were this characteristic not ever-present. To understand it in evolutionary terms, one must consider the whole of the biosphere as a single organism.

Just as in a human body the head has powers not given to the hands or feet and vice versa, so humanity acts as the head and eyes of nature. Accordingly, it may be understood why some organisms devolve. They devolve toward a niche they will fill in the body of nature. So, assuming nothing egregious should occur which would remove humanity from the earth, it can be assumed that humanity has found its niche. And its development in that niche continues.

What is this development? It is a move toward an increasing internalization of the environment. That is the say, the human mind is empowered to create an ever more sophisticated internal map of its world. The reason for this is that a sense of unity in the mind, arising from the unity of consciousness, seeks order and unity in its intellectual efforts.

Now this map is more than informational. It is not a matter of there being a fully complete and consistent knowledge of the world. For reason is an abbreviated language. Though necessary in seeking consistency, it cannot give completeness to human awareness. Something more must be added to function in combination with reason.

That something is emotional intelligence. This is as much a part of the acquisition of wisdom as right principles. And it is gleaned from experience over a lifetime. This is not only the lifespan of an individual, but the lifetime of a culture. It is not only the lifetime of a culture, but the duration of humanity.

It is here that suffering plays its role. For the suffering of the race enriches its understanding. The mistakes made by individuals and cultures are not important. The injuries brought about by an apparently indifferent universe are of little enduring consequence. All contributes to the completeness of the whole.

Slavery in America produced unspeakable wounds in individuals and the nation. But in the long years of recovery, there has been a deepening of understanding of the human condition, which would otherwise not have existed. The same can be said for wars and the displacements of peoples. Humanity learns the hard way.

Emotional intelligence is gradual and cumulative. It is a layering of good and bad experience encountered over years. It develops best in reflective minds and over the long development of a culture. Thus it brings with it an enriched awareness which discursive reason alone cannot compass.

No one can say what is in the mind of universal spirit. Finite beings know only what spirit gives. Neither can anyone say what is in the enriched mind of an individual, least of all the individual herself. Yet it is these resources she will draw upon in her increasing wisdom. Likewise, a culture, a world, grows toward completion. Insofar as is possible in finite beings, matter transcends itself in this way and becomes spirit.

WILLIAM Wordsworth was an English philosophical poet who lived from 1770 to 1850. He was a Romantic. To a Romantic, imagination was a form of reason. Romantics were democratic. They were interested in things like emotion, sympathy with disadvantaged people, nature, and colorful description. Most importantly, they turned to a study of the human heart. It would seem that to them the human heart included the mind as well as the emotions.

There are two fundamental elements which enter into all human thinking. One of them is free imagination. The other is reason, a systematic structure in which human thinking is arranged into specific classifications. The structure linking those classifications is determined by logic. Probably the most impressive logical system created by man is mathematics, which is an internally ordered system of thought. That is to say, it is a system ordered within itself with little or no reference to anything else.

Most importantly, it is logical in its development. Logic works with concepts, within which imagination has already done the work of grouping, dividing, and classifying properties. Several important branches of mathematics work with quantitative concepts. So quantities and magnitudes (a variation upon quantities) are the properties of their concepts. These take the form of mathematical units and the numbers which are composed of them. Quantitative concepts are simple, precise, and susceptible to a rather complex development of relations.

So when used as a structural pattern for a systematic representation of the physical world, mathematics simplifies and rigidifies the physical relations. This is to say it creates a pattern of interlinked concepts based on quantities and magnitudes. In doing this, it develops a reliable and predictable form of discourse, which can be widely shared and understood.

But there were those who doubted the supremacy of logic in any form. The Romantics looked around and saw the messiness of human institutions and individual relationships. They were not at all sure these things could be put into a simple logical order. Many Europeans of Wordsworth's time had good reason to be reinforced in this doubt. They had witnessed the bloody, chaotic French Revolution and the even bloodier conquests of Napoleon.

Now, before an understanding of Wordsworth or Romanticism can be achieved, the question must be asked, what is the element of the faculty of thought that Wordsworth and others like him came to favor? That, as has already been stated, was imagination. For to a Romantic, imagination was a form of reason.

But here is a problem: can imagination alone make value judgments—i.e. judgments without rational principles? Or can it get along with relatively few of them, at any rate? For example, if it is decided that human nature is fundamentally good, what knowledge can this be based upon? Other imaginative intake from experience? If there is no precise imaginative measure for human nature and human ideals, then maybe something other than imagination should be sought as an instrument of discernment.

But the Romantic eschewed principles drawn from other principles ad infinitum. He was inclined to say that the conscious mind itself could fulfill this role with all its complex of reasons and emotions, giving equal priority to both. Yet are the emotions measurable? What about individual reasons, or principles, which are held to be valid without reference to a rational system?

How much of this rather loose human thinking is true discernment? Perhaps the foundation of human awareness must be logically complex after all, rather than predominantly imaginative and freely referenced to feeling and random principles. So, in response to this doubt, the Romantic found that the highest form of imagination must be awareness itself. Thus its discernment was conditioned by its universal perspective.

The philosopher, Jean Jacques Rousseau, an originator of the Romantic view, believed that people were naturally good, or, more precisely, that they were naturally innocent. He thought that what had happened in the decadent social order of seventeenth and eighteenth century France and other European countries was that they had corrupted human nature. How had they done this? They had brought it about largely through the magnification of human vanity, or egoism.

If, as an example, today's world should be carefully examined, it would probably be noticed that people do a great deal simply to impress one another. Their cars, their homes, even their clothes are often acquired with this in mind. But more importantly, many of their habits, their ways of thinking about themselves and the world around them, are influenced by social conformity and ego. As civilizations have become more complex, intricately structured, and layered in terms of social class, these traits have become so complicated, they cannot be clearly seen by the unreflective mind.

People cannot recognize that they are being driven in their motives by false values and unwise behavior. What are false values? They are values based on vanity rather than natural motives. A person might naturally want to work simply and sincerely at a simple occupation, leaving himself time to enjoy his family, simple honest friendships, and the natural world around him. But instead, he is caught in the competitions of vanity. So he spends his time working a job he does not like so he can buy a flashy car, big house, and rich clothes.

Because he lives this life, he comes to believe in it. And eventually he begins to judge others by its standards. In this way, people put pressure on each other to promote and continue the false life. What is worse, the competition makes such a life more and more complex. Soon one is lost in it. A person does not know why he is doing what he is doing.

He does not know his motives have been turned out of their natural course into a false life. He has lost his innocence, innocence being defined here as naturalness. Or to put it another way, innocence is the expression of emotions based on actual circumstances, not those created by the complexities of an artificial human social environment.

Wordsworth, among others, was deeply influenced by Rousseau's ideas. So much was this the case, that he came to think of the city as a place that corrupted the human soul and spent most of his life living in the rural Lake District of northwestern England. He lived there so he could be close to nature, which his poetry is full of, and close to other people who were living close to nature: farmers, small tradesmen, and sheep herders. He knew these people were not without their faults. But he believed their closeness to the natural world and to simple emotions kept them from going to extremes and losing sight of who they were.

The philosopher Immanuel Kant believed the human mind organized the phenomena of reality. This put the human mind at the center of nature. Such a view put the human mind in a position where the Romantics could argue for its close link to nature. An argument strictly from the senses could not have done this.

But an adopted perspective which said that the human mind itself is involved in the structure of reality could. However, the unique distinction the Romantics, and thus Wordsworth, contributed to this view—the one that distinguished them from Kant—was to emphasize imagination as a sympathetic and universally comprehensive faculty linking human beings with the natural world.

Imagination in this role is more of a correlative than a creative faculty. It does not establish the order of nature. But it does help a person to see the world in ways that reflect his own spirit. It creates a sympathetic emotional relationship between him and the natural world. Moreover, if universal spirit is understood to be the source of the natural world, then this understanding can lead to an imaginative sense, rather than an intellectual knowledge, of the location of spirit's universal oneness in both nature and the human spirit.

A person can then feel or experience that oneness, if he imagines himself as spiritually grounded and being at the center of his own physical and mental experiences. He is looking out upon reality from the perspective of spirit. Spirit is universally within him and within all that he experiences.

He can also experience himself as momentarily separated from, or elevated above, other things, while yet remaining connected to them. For they proceed from his conscious awareness and can be momentarily set aside in contemplation of that awareness. Long before the Romantics, mystics, both Eastern and Western, had discovered the simple unity of a conscious mind which has been temporarily emptied of its content.

It is human awareness that links human beings to the essential oneness of nature. The unity of this awareness is the unity of all things. In other words, awareness, or consciousness, is the spiritual ground of itself and of being in general. But this spiritual oneness is not immediately apparent to a person. For nature at first glance may appear divided and full of opposition.

But beneath this fragmentary appearance is a oneness of all things grounded in a single state of being. It is much like the oneness of all things in human experience: the unity of human consciousness and its content. That is to say, all things are experienced to exist in a universal harmony.

But this is denied by the deceptive report of the senses, which appear to separate the individual from the wholeness of his awareness. Nevertheless, upon reflection, the individual knows himself to be part of a greater harmony. Accordingly, the universal oneness found in an individual and simultaneously in nature is what is meant by the term God.

All things are thus coordinated in a single system of nature. Since in any system the parts are conditioned by the whole, each of them has a specific function in relation to the other parts. And together their relations express the whole. But also, the whole expresses the unique character of each of its parts. All is in one and one is in all because spirit, the ground of all, is indivisible and one. So, through an imaginative association of unrelated things in surprising ways, a general feeling of connection between them and to them can be produced.

Say a person were to think of a flowing stream as having some relation to a lark, its purling waters and smooth rhythmic sound resembling the flight and song of the bird. The two ideas could then work together in a previously undiscovered way, the unifying imagination operating in their midst. Thus an association is made between stream, bird, and mind and found meaningful.

In this way, a connection between the oneness of spirit in an individual and the oneness revealed in the world can be recognized. The two things associated above were in the physical world and seemed to be unrelated to anything but themselves. But they were related in imagination by a human mind. And the relationship was discovered to be meaningful. Meaning is a human power. Its character is to unite.

So this power of association, which is imaginative, and the emotion of connection with the world it can create, are what is meant by the Romantic faculty of higher imagination, or comprehensive awareness. Imagination thus becomes a mystical power which can connect a person to the being which underlies and permeates all things. And it can make him one and harmonious with that being.

UNIVERSAL spirit is a dynamic of unlimited possibilities and unfathomably complex relations which are beyond any human reckoning. Yet if universal spirit were to convert itself into a material expression which might be grasped by the human mind, that expression would take the form of a static, indeterminate, space-time continuum.

Such a transition would be as though the brilliance of the sun were gathered into the refracted light of a glass prism.

Such a continuum would also not be all there is of spirit. It would be all that is pertinent for man's existence and understanding. Thus the continuum would form an interrelated web of relations, out of which the experience common to all human beings would emerge. Moreover, it would lend itself to human understanding. For the human intellect would be so conditioned by the continuum as to possess a means both of apprehending and building upon its relations.

But the total continuum could not be an expression of any one individual human experience. For in its static material state, all expressions of change would coexist within it. This is something which they do not do in individual human experience. Rather, the human mind experiences change sequentially. In addition to this difference, there is the indeterminate character of the continuum's totality, which could not be grasped by human intelligence.

Now individual human consciousness is also spirit. It is grounded in universal spirit, as being one and the same with it. But it is much reduced in phenomenal inclusiveness in comparison to the continuum which purports to be a material expression of universal spirit. For, when understood in comparison to the continuum, an individual human being's capacity for experience exhibits even greater limitations than the continuum. These limitations arise from the ever-changing temporal character of human experience: its sequential apprehension of change. Thus human awareness would constitute but a single facet of the prism which is the material expression of the mind of spirit.

This prism is clearly a simple image. And in many respects it is inadequate. For it does not exhibit the material relations of the continuum. Nor do its facets express the complexity of an individual human awareness. Nevertheless, it has been introduced to serve a purpose, which is to represent in a pointedly elemental way the material expression of the spiritual dynamic and its relationship to human consciousness.

For given the fact that so little is known of spirit in its immaterial character, it would be impossible to account for anything but its immediate impression on the human mind. That impression is consciousness. There—i.e. speaking of consciousness itself and not its content—everything in the way of immediate experience is made present to human awareness. But nothing in the way of human knowledge can be gained from the fact of consciousness alone. It can only be derived from the content of consciousness.

Thus it is the content of consciousness which supplies the substance of knowledge. For it is this which is tasked with presenting the finite relations of material experience to the finite mind. Material experience is not only finite in its spatial relations. It is delivered to human consciousness in finite increments of time. Thus, unlike consciousness itself, the material continuum falls within human experience in a manner which can be grasped intellectually.

However, human consciousness in its insistent immediacy remains obstinate in its opaqueness. For its direct impact on the mind is all that can be understood of it. Thus, since consciousness is spirit, spirit is also incomprehensible to the mind. So the human mind is confronted with an irreducible dichotomy between that which cannot be intellectually known to it—i.e. consciousness—and that which can be intellectually grasped by it. The latter is the content of consciousness.

It should be stated again for the sake of clarity, that the material expression of universal spirit does not constitute the entire mind of universal spirit. It is merely that portion of it which is focused upon the domain of human experience. This is not an individual domain of experience, but a collective domain encompassing all individual human states of consciousness. Thus it is in this way that the greater material domain functions as a prism within which the lesser material content of each individual human consciousness is but a facet.

Accordingly, when an individual human consciousness is taken up in discussion, as opposed to all individual human states of consciousness conceived collectively, universal spirit should be understood as spirit focused upon a limited perspective. In fact, it is not a limited perspective only, but a perspective which is a deliberate act of self-limitation on the part of universal spirit. It is this which is an individual human awareness. To recur once again to the image of a prism representing the material domain, it is as though spirit were self-confined to looking through one facet of that prism.

Human consciousness is limited because it is confined to material awareness. In addition, it is more strictly limited by time. Thus human consciousness is acutely aware of both spatial and temporal limitation. Moreover, as a being intellectually confined to such an awareness, a person, in his own view, simply is this awareness and the limited world of which he is aware. For his experience cannot encompass the completeness even of the material world, as universal spirit can be understood to do. There are but portions of the material world available to individual human experience as they are revealed in the unfolding of time.

So a human being is clearly bound up in material limitation both spatially and temporally. Yet in spite of this, he remains aware of the unlimited spiritual ground of his being. This is not an intellectual apprehension, but simply a sense of the unconfined nature of the ground. He does not know its character. But he knows that it is the source of his awareness.

This ground lies within his consciousness. But he does not know the ground, other than to recognize its self-limited expression in human consciousness. Thus, if he is meditative or deeply reflective, he regards his consciousness as his true self. Though it is mysterious to him in its workings, it is a self which transcends material experience.

Accordingly, in contradistinction to the material view given above, the meditative or reflective person understands that his true self is not his material self. In addition, he recognizes that the content of his consciousness is a world transmitted to him by means of his consciousness. But his human consciousness does not itself create material experience. Rather, it acts as an organ of transmission of that experience to his awareness.

Thus it can be understood that within human consciousness is to be found the origin of its content. This origin of the content of human consciousness, which is the true creative self, is by no means the material self as recognized in the daily course of human existence. Nor should the origin of material experience be understood as a direct product of the limited consciousness of human awareness. Rather, this origin is to be found in self-limiting universal spirit, the creative ground of being.

For the content of human conscious experience is a projection of the dynamic of universal spirit, which is the ground of human consciousness. Upon the passing of the content of human consciousness into human awareness, it is structured by mind. But that mind is prior to human awareness. Only the mind which apprehends this structure as experience is human.

Because the human mind is unable to intellectually comprehend the spiritual dynamic, it is limited to the structured content which the spiritual dynamic presents to it. Thus the human mind receives the structured content as it is, building intellectually on what it receives. But since what is known to human awareness is given through consciousness, and thus (in spite of common appearances) not external to that consciousness, material reality can be understood as, in a sense, a product of human awareness.

This would clearly imply a solipsistic view of reality, were it not for the greater dynamic of universal spirit, which coordinates the various facets of the prism of material being. In this way, the material experience of each individual human awareness is synchronized into a single common reality. Thus a number of individuals may have an equal number of different experiences. But such is the family of resemblances between these experiences that the whole is intellectually common to them all.

Yet when it is viewed in this subjective light, the human mind may appear to be the immediate creator of its own experience. For, when human experience is viewed in this manner, it is spiritually occluded. This is to say that the mind cannot penetrate beyond itself, since it cannot see the workings of universal spirit. Thus, in its self-regard, it ostensibly becomes a self-creating mind.

Such a subjective perspective is opaque due to the unapproachable character of its spiritual ground. So, for experience to be more fully grasped by the human mind, human understanding must not limit itself to a spiritual approach. It must entertain an opposing material view as well. For neither perspective will fully comprehend the matter. But the two together will closely, though imperfectly, encompass it.

Thus the order of reflective thought can be reversed. For, in practical terms, an origin independent of the mind can be attributed to the content of consciousness. From this perspective, that content would be considered as given to the mind by sensation. It could accordingly be understood as something standing apart from human consciousness. This is a strictly material view, an outlook which is maintained in modern empirical science.

Material experience thus becomes an objective realm distinct from subjective human awareness. As such, it can be taken as a principal point of reference. Given this view, speculation would begin with a sense of the limited and the physical. For the content of consciousness is finite in character. But as a consequence of such a view of experience, individual human existence must also be conceived as limited and material as well.

Building from this perspective, the human intellect becomes an organ strictly limited to a material understanding of itself. It ignores the origin of consciousness, other than to speculate upon its grounding in material relations. Thus it discovers experience to be finite in all its observable particulars.

Consequently, logical relations readily present themselves for discovery. For logical relations are finite in themselves, even when concerned with matters of transfinite speculation. Following a refinement of this reasoning faculty, causal relations, which were initially acknowledged independently of one another, are systematically integrated. Thus, in its attempt to broaden its grasp of empirical relations, the mind infuses causal relations with a logical certainty.

Consequently, they become laws upon which predictions can be based. It is in this way that bodies of scientific knowledge are built up.

Evolutionary theory is one of these sciences. And it is by means of it that human mental processes can be understood as having been developed, at least in part, by means of natural selection. That is, the human mind's rational properties can be accounted for in material terms, insofar as reason may be understood to follow a logical progression.

For example, an indicator / response conditioning in animals was first proposed by the Russian scientist, Ivan Petrovich Pavlov. For he experimented with this behavioral characteristic as it is found in dogs. Having located it in dogs, an inference could then be made concerning other forms of sentient life, particularly the higher forms.

Once understood in this broadened context, which includes human beings, the characteristic can be made to serve as a means of accounting for the emergence of cause-and-effect reasoning in humankind. Cause is in the position of the indicator. And effect is in the position of the response. As an indicator calls forth a response, so a cause calls forth an effect. But it need not end there. For, in addition to having established such an important link between a simple behavioral phenomenon and a mechanism of thought, the next logical step is to note that the indicator / response relationship also supports logical implication.

Thus, if it is understood that A anticipates B, as the scent of a rabbit indicates nourishment to a predator and governs its response accordingly, this is what is meant by an indicator / response relationship. Pavlov's ringing of a bell, and the salivation which demonstrated the dogs' anticipation of an expected appearance of food, together constitute a laboratory fabrication of this behavior.

So it is not difficult to infer from the foregoing that, should this indicator / response experience form in certain cases a necessary relationship wherever encountered, without any alteration in the character of A or B, and without alteration in their proximity to one another or sequential occurrence, then it can be assumed that A not only anticipates B. It causes B. Thus it can be seen that causal thinking is grounded in the indicator / response experience.

Following this insight, the mental process of logical implication lies but a small step beyond.-For logical implication, like cause and effect, follows the pattern of the indicator / response relation. It is a matter of something being anticipated in consequence of the appearance of something else. For to state that "if a bell is rung, food will follow" is to assert that if A occurs then B must follow. In other words, A not only anticipates B. It implies B. So logical implication can be understood to reflect the indicator / response experience as well.

Thus it can be seen that these mentally apprehended relations, both causal and logical, are grounded upon an anticipated outcome, such as would be the case were they to be encountered in experience. This outcome is presumed to follow some particular circumstance, either as an effect or by logical implication. In its simplest indicator / response form, such a recognized juxtaposition of one experience with another is a trait commonly encountered among a great diversity of sentient creatures. Its elevation to human thought is accordingly not a leap, but a progression.

But in spite of the importance of reasoning in human thinking, spirit cannot be accounted for in this manner. For consciousness cannot be deduced. Nothing can be known with certainty to precede or act as a ground for it. In other words, the immediate experience of consciousness does not arise from anything prior to it in experience, let alone material experience, however tentatively such a link may be made, such as between brain and mind.

Nor can consciousness be ignored or empirically dismissed as an epiphenomenon of physical processes. For without it, there could be no means of adequately accounting for intellectual abstractions. Without these, empirical knowledge of a complex theoretical character would be impossible. In other words, such knowledge is composed of logically interrelated concepts. And the human mind cannot form these concepts without a reliance upon its experience of consciousness as a tool instrumental in forming mental abstractions.

Consciousness is such a tool. Thus it is more than a simple platform of awareness. This is so because conceptualization demands a unity of specific properties under a definition: a dog is defined as having such-and-such characteristics which make it a dog. Consciousness is a unity. Thus it is consciousness which is the fundamental experience of unity in human experience. This experience of the unity of consciousness is what is brought to bear upon all the other recognized unities of experience, including the development of concepts in the mind.

Accordingly, a sense of unity initially arises from the experience of consciousness within the mind. It does not arise outside the mind. Rather, it is imposed as a fundamental means of organization both inside and outside of the mind. In this way, it is involved in both perception and thought, particularly conceptual thought. This is to maintain that it is *a priori*. It is therefore not *a posteriori* in character.

Perhaps, if their subsumption under a unity were to be overlooked (which cannot truly be done), the mental formation of imaginative images might be understood in accordance with a simple association of properties. But not so the mental formation of concepts. Here the role of unity cannot be ignored. For concepts are specific combinations of properties.

The mental formation of a concept requires a precise sense of the unity of certain properties under a definition: a dog is such-and-such, no less and no more, every pertinent detail of the such-and-such being accounted for under the definition. Of course, the important point to be made here lies in the phrase "pertinent detail."

For if the definitional implications of a concept were to be followed out, it would include other definitions. Thus, if it is maintained that *all dogs are mammals*, the definition of mammals leads to definitions of warm-bloodedness and mammary lactation. Warm-bloodedness leads in turn to a definition of metabolic internal heat regulation, etc.

So, when understood in terms of these implications, a conceptual unity is a unity which is an indeterminate string of such unities. Even a definition not drawn from matters of fact would submit to this rule. For example, the concept of an equilateral triangle leads to questions concerning angularity and line. And what does it mean to assert that "a line is a breadthless length," as Euclid does in Definition 2 of Book 1 of his *Elements*? What is a breadthless length?

So, however complex may be the relations of properties taken to the nth degree, the fact remains that a concept is not this string. Rather, it is a matter of certain properties being necessarily involved in a combination which pointedly excludes other properties. That exclusion is an arbitrary expression of unity. It does not delve into the endless string of definitions just pointed out.

The definition of a dog held in contradistinction to that of a cat or a bird makes this clear. For it is neither a cat nor a bird. And what it is not is as much its point of emphasis as what it is. For if the strings of definitions for dogs, cats, and birds were to be followed out at great length, the definitions would converge in meaning, causing the difference between them to become less and less prominent. Thus each of the original definitions would lose its precision.

Hence the precise limitation of definition which is involved in any concept, as opposed to the loose and variable association of properties in an imaginative image. Now the sense of unity which makes this type of collective limitation possible belongs to consciousness alone. For the content of consciousness is always in some sense a collective unity. Thus, when the conscious mind focuses on a concept, it emphasizes that collective unity of pertinent properties to the exclusion of all others.

Let us leave this line of thought. To put a consideration of these matters of spiritual priority in a different way, let synapses and networks of neural interaction be considered. In accordance with a material view, their workings may be supposed to be liable to chemical or surgical derangement, thus affecting the content of consciousness. This has been carried out in practice. But it indicates only a simultaneous occurrence. For a definitive causal link between the material brain and the state of consciousness remains undetermined.

This is why a rational explanation of both consciousness and its content can flow from spirit to matter, but not from matter to spirit.

Nevertheless, the difficulty in the latter case does not invalidate the general idea of material reality, insofar as human experience is concerned. For a material assessment of human experience, which explains only what the mind can intellectually apprehend and not how it does so, is complete within itself. But this point of view does require that an understanding of the character of consciousness be set aside.

The fact that the character of consciousness presents a problem simply indicates the intellectual limitation of human awareness. But what is important to note is that human awareness encompasses more than intellect. Human beings are aware of both their consciousness and its content. The problem is that they cannot explain the former.

An explanation of the character of consciousness eludes the intellect. For consciousness is spirit, not matter. And the human intellect is confined to a material understanding. For this reason, human experience may be described as a materially limited dynamic which is grasped by a materially oriented intellect. But these two are enclosed within a greater spiritual dynamic, figured forth by consciousness. Just as consciousness contains its content, so the greater spiritual dynamic is the ground of all.

So once again, the human mind must be understood as materially limited. For, both in its capacity for experience and in its articulate understanding, it is confined to considerations of finitude. On the one hand, the material expression of universal spirit, which is the matter of human experience, may be intellectually apprehended by the human intellect. This is to say that it may be imagined by the human mind. But only limited portions of it can be figured forth by human reason. Thus the intellectual apprehension of material experience is less comprehensive than the full material expression of universal spirit.

For these reasons, when the attempt is to understand man spiritually, he is conceived as universal spirit expressed under focused circumstances. These are circumstances in which universal spirit limits itself to each individual human consciousness. Thus the human mind is fragmented and unidirectional in understanding as opposed to the unified, multidirectional mind of universal spirit. This multidirectional mind may be expressed in terms of the material continuum, which provides the matter of all human experience. But as spirit, it extends far beyond this material expression. For it transcends any form of finite representation.

Thus, when conceived spiritually, man must be understood to be a direct expression of spirit. But when conceived materially, as he generally conceives himself, he is not a direct expression of spirit. In his mind, he is but a small material presence immersed in an all-encompassing material world. Beyond this finite, yet indeterminate, world is a void. There is limitation, division, and death. It is all that is open to him.

Consciousness and Mind

IMAGINE a drop of water put into a well. The drop of water is human consciousness. The water in the well is universal spirit. It is often thought that spirit dwells in people. But it is more a case of their dwelling in spirit. Once the drop of water enters the larger body of water in the well, it mixes with and becomes indistinguishable from it. So then to speak of human consciousness is to speak of universal spirit.

THE investigation of human experience cannot be materialistic. For materialism reviews the operations of the mind within an assumed sensory framework, whereas the senses themselves are experienced within consciousness. This leaves consciousness unexplained.

THERE is no mystery of the human mind. The only mystery lies in the heart of nature itself.

A MIRACLE is that which does not accord with a present conception of things. Were an iron ax head to float, people would be amazed. But if ax heads had always been known to float, and this fact had long since been incorporated into a rational construct of reality, they would be no less surprised to see one sink.

MEN and women of genius are not necessarily smarter than other people. They have simply learned to focus their intelligence. Making a carefully directed use of imagination lies at the heart of this focus (e.g. Einstein, Monet).

THE human intellect is not immediately grounded in nature. Rather, it is grounded in the way the human mind works. But it has a rough parallel in nature because human beings and the way they think are products of nature. Thus its effectiveness. But as human beings are a derivative of nature, it is reasonable to assume that they would be more limited materially than nature is. Accordingly, they are more limited mentally as well, insofar as the material content of their thought is concerned. Consequently their thinking does not encompass all that is nature.

ALTHOUGH learning can both support and build toward the achievement of insight, insight is quite different than, even opposed to, learning. For it contains an element of the spontaneous. It reaches into the unplumbed depths of experience and a personal response to that experience, which is greater than any functioning of the analytical mind.

TRUTH is like the unbroken continuity of a mathematical line. It can never be partitioned with any degree of finality. There is always a nearer and nearer approach, but never a conclusive analysis.

THE mind is a function of body and spirit. That is why it cannot escape the limitations of the body, yet is elevated above it.

THE physical appetites, such as the need for sex and food, occupy an important position in life, just like breathing or the elimination of waste. But they do not distinguish a human being from a dog.

ALL forms of sentient life possess simple awareness, or consciousness. What differentiates them is the apparatus through which they take in and process information about their environment. If a raven or a coyote should produce amongst its kind an individual of unusual capacity, it is unlikely that human beings would recognize the fact. This is because the perceptions and priorities of the animal in question are arranged differently from those of humanity.

MUCH of the history of Western philosophy takes the form of an opposition between two contrasting views. The one is idealist, centered in the mind. The other is empirical, centered on the input of the senses. But it should be no surprise if anyone should discover that these opposing views are interrelated.

When mind thinks, it constructs the whole of its thought with the materials of the senses. Even simple consciousness is thus understood as an entity within the whole of the sensory realm. Yet to be apprehended at all, the sensory realm must be submitted to the structuring mind. So to argue for the otherness of nature on the one hand, or for the otherness of mind on the other, is to attempt to draw a line where no line exists.

Mind is inevitably understood in terms of matter, even when a reference to its origin in matter is omitted. And in the same sense, matter is apprehended as a product of mind without reference to its origin in mind. Yet such is the human dilemma that it is only because an arbitrary line is deliberately drawn between the two, now here in this place and now there in that place, that any sort of discussion of the issue can be established.

HUMAN beings are in possession of two transcendent modes of awareness: a sense of self and a sense of the immortality of the self. Neither is derived from the content of consciousness—i.e. sense impressions. Both are derived from consciousness itself. The sense of self is fundamentally a recognition that all thoughts, pains, and joys belong to something which is not those thoughts, pains, and joys.

Thus the fact that these thoughts, pains, and joys are presented within an individual conscious mind is what strengthens the sense of an individual self. And sensations of external things give the individual self local color. But consciousness, that empty, clear-sided fishbowl without limit or divisibility, is what grounds the sense of self. From this, an awareness of immortality can be seen for what is. It is the sense of unlimited, indivisible being.

UNIVERSAL love, or agape, is often thought of as an emotion. But it is inevitably accompanied by a particular state of mind. It is possible that that mindset should be so enlarged that it should be one in which the universal oneness of all things is recognized and given its fullest realization in each individual being.

But this is not how the human race normally functions. For in each individual, the world of his experience and how he relates to that experience is determined by the manner in which he perceives and organizes the data of life. Unfortunately, this is naturally carried out in discrete units, in bits and pieces which form the material view of life, the pieces being assembled into ideas, the ideas into a general sensibility.

Consequently, the individual perceives himself to have been born into an inescapable fragmentation of sensation. In this state of mind, his sensations appear to be separate and individual. That is to say, so many sensations make an emotion. So many emotions make a person, isolated and different from any other person. So many properties make a part. So many parts make a thing, separate and jostling with the next thing. All of these perceived limitations are finite and perishable.

As a result of such a fragmentary perception and an even more fragmentary understanding of the experience which is revealed by it, each individual is overcome with a sense of the divisibility, separateness, and perishability of things. So every person comes to see himself as a limited being which is in competition with all other limited things, living and inert. He is not only limited, but cut off both spatially and, most frighteningly, in time.

But this view is not the inevitable heritage of humanity. Rather, it is a pastiche of impressions wrought by a superficial experience which is determined by the sensual content alone of conscious awareness. If a person were to shift his view to a consideration of consciousness in contradistinction to its content, he would obtain a different input.

He would perceive that consciousness is like a great, glass bowl in which the sensory contents of awareness can be viewed but not the bounds which hold them. He would see that neither the limits of consciousness nor a divisibility of it can be determined. Only the content is divisible and limited. For it is composed of what are understood to be perceptions. But consciousness alone is the condition of awareness, prior to all its content. It is an undifferentiated unity, indivisible and one. It is spirit, the ground of all that is, is known, or can be known.

Such a view comes from looking inward into the ground of awareness, rather than outward through the sense impressions. It is a focus upon the core of oneself. This is to say that an individual's own person is the only material entity which can be looked into at its very core. It is an inner, not an outer, perception.

This core is consciousness, spirit, which is, as stated above, unlimited and indivisible. Furthermore, it is only by means of the mental state of empathy that each person discerns in the emotions and actions of others the reflection of a consciousness which resembles his own. Thus empathy is his guardian against solipsism.

To a lesser extent, this phenomenon of a grounding in consciousness can also be recognized in other sentient life. Moreover, the fact that it is not seen in plants and nonliving things does not convince the mind that their core being is not in some way the same. They simply lack the means of action which would function as a medium of expression between that core and the outer world. They neither think nor feel. But this does not indicate that at the core of their nature there is an absence of that which either is or, at least, can be a means of such things.

Spirit, being indivisible, must be one and the same everywhere. That which is whole and complete in one person must be whole and complete in the totality of things, just as it is wholly present and complete in *each one* of those things. If each person understood his fellow human beings in this manner, he would know him or her to be the full expression of one being, the being which is himself.

Thus he would say: That man or woman is one with me, one with all things. How can I do otherwise than have a high regard for such a being, as I do for myself? A fellow human being has not only this spiritual wholeness, but a moral faculty of awareness and sensitivity in expressing it, such as I have. Whatever his apparent failings, I too have apparent failings. Whatever my apparent glory, she too has this apparent glory.

THE unity of consciousness is the ground of the sense of self. Consciousness having unity, consciousness being also indivisible and unbounded, it provides a sense of the indestructible self. At least, it does so until the human mind begins to measure its existence by the *contents* of its consciousness. These contents are finite, ephemeral, destructible, mutually competitive, and mutually annihilating.

But returning to the unity of consciousness, the mind discovers transcendence, indivisibility, and the all-pervading character of spirit. Consciousness is spirit. And as such, it is the indivisible ground of material being, bringing all things together in one, yet fully manifest in each individual thing.

Thus it unites all existence, leaving nothing without its foundational presence. In doing so, it spares human awareness from a sense of its own destructibility and, in such a way, relieves it from an annihilating will. Since it exhibits a lack of ephemeral weakness and suggests no need for a mutual competitiveness, it is the only certain basis of a mutual respect.

SPIRIT is the core of individual being. Every human being has this core. Without it, he or she would not exist. But humanity does not do well with the spirit because fear cuts it off from such an awareness. To live in the spirit, to find and maintain a sense of his own ground of being, a person must be able to see past the material, divided world reported to him by his senses.

He should have a sense of the wholeness of things, which he finds within the unity of consciousness, the contemplation of his own undivided inner nature, and the recognition of the universality of this undivided nature as it is made present in the spiritual contemplation of all things.

But the material world, which limits a person through sense perception, seizes upon his attention and allows him to fall into fear. Fear permeates his being. And in one fashion or another, self-preservation becomes his obsession. From that point on, he can no longer see the wholeness of things—their unity. Thus he is unable to have confidence in the spiritual ground of his being.

WHEN a master carpenter makes a chair, he does not exercise his entire skill as a carpenter in making it. For this reason, the chair does not reflect all the rules, or laws, of carpentry which are stored in his mind. In the same way, in the universal spirit's creation of the universe, it can reasonably be assumed that the spirit does not necessarily exercise the full range of its creative intellect. So the laws of the universe are not the laws of the mind of universal spirit, but only a reflection of some portion of them.

Likewise, if the idea that man evolved is accepted, or if man is in some other similar way thought to be a creation of this universe, there is no compelling argument for assuming that his reason, which is a product of natural development, is a mirror image of the laws of the universe. For only those laws which are required for his survival ought necessarily to be represented in his reason.

So looking back upon the universe and attempting to discover the hand of universal spirit in its design would seem rather futile. Human beings are, after all, twice removed from the mind of universal spirit. In this way of thinking, an overall intelligent design can be suggested but not proven. This is because science can only measure what the human mind is capable of experiencing, which is what the human mind is able to perceive and conceptualize. Nothing more.

REASON is not a faculty drawn from the heavens, but from the earth. The human mind is not the mind of universal spirit. It is limited. For man is subordinate to nature in his material being. And thought is material inasmuch as the structure of reason is concerned. Even the power of abstraction relies upon nature for its material.

It is no more than this: A similarity of function in many kinds of chairs can be seen by the limited and pluralistic mind. From that multiplicity, a limited unity, the idea of a chair in general, can be drawn. But such a generalization does not in any way indicate a transcendent universal. It does not express an unlimited unity.

The idea of goodness in men is also drawn up in the same way. It is abstracted from a collation of individual and limited goods, then combined with an expectation of what are deemed to be favorable circumstances to which a general goodness might lead. But this does not indicate the existence of a universal good. It merely speaks of a widespread good.

So given these limitations, is there any one thing which does transcend the natural? There is. It is an experience of the unity of spirit. This experience is to be found in consciousness. It is in consciousness that limitless, indivisible being in the midst of limiting circumstances is found. Here there is unity of spirit, where everything else is division and separation.

Everything known to man is contained within his conscious mind. So that consciousness encompasses everything he knows or can know. Thus it is greater than everything known to him. For everything is enclosed within it. And everything is shut out of existence when consciousness is deemed to be gone. Were no one conscious, there would be nothing to be conscious of. Likewise, the most expansive representation of a universe, rendered either by numbers or imagination, is no greater than the mind which contains it.

So the idea of a universal, all-encompassing oneness can be obtained from the experience of consciousness and from that alone. For oneness is the generalized character of consciousness. It is this oneness which is combined with the lesser abstraction of a limited, but not universal, goodness that is found in the material experience of life. In this way, the idea of a universal, transcendent goodness arises.

Does such a simple origin of the idea of spirit and universal transcendence imply that there is no god and therefore no eternal life? Far from it. For consciousness is not simple. It is a mystery inadequately expressed by material means. It is the greatest of miracles because it is so ready to hand and yet is not understood. It stands above empirical investigation. Science is carried forward within it. For in the human experience of it, and it alone, something other than the material is encountered.

At best, it might be held up in equation to the material. For it can be said to be another equivalent realm. Or it can be understood as a different way of looking at the same thing. In this dualistic view, reality becomes a two-headed coin. One face exhibits the material, the other reveals spirit, both sides making one coin.

SINCE there are limits to human understanding, it should be reasonable to assume that the god of the philosophers and theologians, insofar as that god is logically understood, is a limited work of the reasoning mind. Like an idol built with hands, this god is a human creation. So it bears the limitations of human awareness.

But there is also direct experience, by means of which the god may in some sense be apprehended. Most believers in the biblical god, if they are truly believers, have carried on a relationship with their god, which might be called a dialog. In this way, since there is a communion between such persons and their god at some level, their faith becomes experiential.

The exploration of a person's inner life can also be experiential. And it can lead to an expansion of belief in something transcendent. If a person cannot definitively assert with Socrates that there are eternal ideas in the mind, she can nevertheless contemplate the mysteries of her own thought and consciousness. And these mysteries may free her mind from the strictures of material experience.

For example, from this examination she might observe that associative thought, which is imaginative thinking, has a quality of unlimited play and expansion. Also imagination, when in the act of contemplating consciousness itself, experiences a sense of the unlimited. For pure consciousness alone has no material bounds or limits. And this sense of the unlimited is strengthened by a knowledge of the indivisible character of consciousness as well (i.e. indivisible as opposed to its content).

So for the purpose of illustration, the associations of imagination might be called analog. This is in contradistinction to the discrete character of reason, which takes a logical, or digital, form. For, in the sense in which the word analog is used here, the meaning encompasses not only a discrimination between two things by difference, but an awareness as well of their unified character as expressed in their similarities. It is a discrimination and awareness which is unfettered by rules of thought. Thus it can view the same phenomenon in a number of conflicting ways.

In the case of imagination's awareness of the unified character of things, a crude example might be a recognition of the grouping of cat varieties into one species, or of different species into one genus. But if this grouping is held in place by a definition stating the precise character of a species or genus, then the grouping becomes a classification. As such, it is an instrument of reason. And reason, in its formation of discrete definitions, cuts off the free play of associative thought.

The human mind possesses reason for the sake of its relationship with the external world. Because of reason's role in shaping that world for the mind, it casts perception into discrete forms. Thus there are determined objects. And specific sensations are labeled for the organizing work of the mind.

But imagination is different. It functions to expand the range of rational thought by breaking free of logical thinking in order to add new concepts to a train of thought. And it seeks to perform analog functions entirely apart from reason, such as in art or mental reverie. For the operative power of imagination is associative thought, which is free and unencumbered by definitions.

Imagination is, or can be, an instrument of exploration into the unlimited inner world of the human spirit. If a person finds such a world to be unfathomable—if she cannot explore the fullness of its domain—she may nevertheless use imagination to extend the ineffable quality of the unlimited to those things she does understand—to all things, in fact, since that which is unlimited must by definition encompass everything else.

PEOPLE often speak of the "heart" as opposed to the "mind". It is not difficult to determine what mind is. It is reason, imagination, and memory (the latter two considered without reference to feeling). But what is heart? It is certainly not a simple organ. Rather, it is the seat of the emotions. Much feeling goes into the idea of heart.

When closely thought about, it is found to include unconscious proddings and impulses, as well as what is generally attributed to mind. So the heart is a larger faculty than mind, something which is referred to at times as sensibility. An understanding of a poem, music, or a painting is an expression of the heart, not the mind alone. For it is the heart which makes possible an understanding of life.

HOW does evil work? It falls upon the inner mind like a shadow, separating it from its grounding in universal awareness. The term "inner mind" is used because it is not the attentive mind but the sensitive mind which is spoken of. This may appear to be a reversal of terms. For the sensitive mind is not sensual. It feels *itself*, not its content. But when evil falls upon it like a shadow, obscuring its fullest nature, it loses something of that fullness and must cling to its divisive content. A person then becomes a creature only of sensation, fear, and worry.

THE hope is to find a common underlying basis for both cognition and conation. What fundamental process might be responsible for both the way human beings think and the way they will, feel, and act? This is not psychologism because it is pre-psychological. It is something which must be considered as prior to human awareness.

For instance, if natural selection is assumed to occur, there must have been from the earliest origin of life a will in every organism to preserve itself. That will must, as it were, predate the living organism.

Otherwise advantageous traits could not be passed on. And evolution would be meaningless. This consideration would include not only sentient life, but plants, though volition in plants would refer to their organizational tendency.

So where does this will originate? If it is said that it is itself selected, the problem presents itself that natural selection cannot effectively occur without a will to self-preservation being already present in the organism. Thus one must look beyond natural selection to determine in what manner it might have originated.

This approach would have to explain logical, rational processes on the one hand and motivational, striving, affective processes on the other. They could not be accounted for together. For the two distinct processes are clearly differentiated from one other. Nor can it be thought that one is derived from the other. So a third, more fundamental foundation for both must be considered. That foundation would enter into each process without any reciprocal relationship between the the two processes being required.

SUPERSTITION is the uncritical acceptance of a belief. For this reason, superstition implies a neglect of reason. A pure superstition would be a purely unreasoning acceptance of a belief. And a pure rationality would be the acceptance of a belief only on the condition of reason. This leads to an unacceptable dichotomy because the human mind is always positioned somewhere between these two extremes.

There is always some element of uncritical acceptance, even in something as rigorous as a mathematical proof. For, if nothing else, such a proof requires an acceptance of the reliability of a logical system of deduction and of the truth value of its terms. Likewise, there is always some element of reason in the uncritical acceptance of a belief, since the believer must think that it is in some way reasonable or convenient to hold such a belief.

IT is important that human beings should not privilege logic as an end in itself. If humankind is to be understood as a product of nature—

i.e. as a result of evolution or as a member of the biosphere—then there must be a physical basis for the existence of human logic. This implies a psychological explanation for the origin of logical structures, regardless of how new, strange, and different that psychology may be.

THE primal categories of logic are existence, nonexistence, greater, and less. These are mathematical concepts: unity, zero, addition, and subtraction.

LOGIC, insofar as it is formal in character, is a science of quantification. For it focuses upon the precise relationships of terms without regard to the substance of those terms. It merely asserts a degree of inclusion or exclusion. The material embodied in the terms comes from experience and imagination. For this reason, it can be seen that reason is barren without imagination.

THERE is a close relationship between causal thinking and logical thinking. To think logically is, in a sense, to think causally, as is illustrated by modus ponens: If A then B. A therefore B. For this reason, human beings do not think logically without using causal relations.

ALBERT Einstein is reputed to have said that imagination is more important than reason. This is true. Imagination does all the creative work of the human mind. Every new idea comes from imagination. Reason—i.e. logic—is the mind's indispensible agent of organization. Not the invention, but the forward progress of ideas, depends upon this faculty.

Only by forming images into concepts and setting those concepts into a rigorously structured relationship with one another can the mind see where to go in its formation of new ideas. But those ideas must begin as images in the imagination. For it is here that the ferment of creation takes place.

REASON relates ideas to one another. But it is imagination which creates ideas.

REASON is not infallible. It cannot plumb the depths of physical reality or inner truth with certainty. But it is the only defense of an independent mind and personal integrity an individual has. To surrender this to any form of authority is spiritual suicide.

THE observation has been put forth that most logical thinking should be considered to be synthetic. For it is not only generally the case that several independent propositions brought together may lead to one conclusion. It is also the case that no single one of these propositions contains the conclusion. But this would appear to be a myopic approach.

It is necessary that an analytic apprehension of the circumstances linking all these propositions in a manner which would produce the conclusion must exist in the mind of a thinker in intuitive form. For one does not, as it were, tighten a screw into a void. At the imaginative level, which is prior to any reasoning process, thought is inherently unified. It is not a mechanistic process in which disparate means fortuitously approach an unforeseeable end.

THE human proclivity towards classification can cut in many directions across matters of fact, which partake of what John Stuart Mill refers to as the "fundamentum" lying at the root of logical predication. However, it is not the fact which constitutes this fundamentum. For fact partakes both of the nature of things and of the way they are arranged, or classified, by the human mind.

The nature of things alone is the fundamentum. But how can anyone ever be sure she is in possession of it? Due to the inevitable interference of classification as a means of the intellectual apprehension of facts, the human mind always finds itself in possession of the hybrid nature of facts rather than its being in possession of the fundamentum. So it is never on irrefutably certain ground as to the character of the truth. This is why theories—philosophical, scientific, etc.—are always being augmented, reduced, transformed, discarded, and otherwise modified.

THE problem which exists in understanding physical nature does not lie in anomalies found at the microphysical level, as in quantum mechanics. Rather it lies in the human mind. For human beings have, both as a matter of convenience and of necessity, grown accustomed to seeing the world in a digital manner. In other words, ordinary concepts concerning the world are built around discrete entities.

But physical scientists are coming to understand that the world is in fact analog. It is a continuum. Thus there are no truly discrete entities. This insight is assisted by an increased understanding of the human practice of concept formation and of the mathematical basis of physical science. Both result from mental processes. And both involve discrete thoughts. For both general conceptualization and mathematical science are built upon a foundation of identities and otherness. The identities suggest continuity. And otherness suggests discreteness.

Let mathematics alone be taken as an example. Mathematics differentiates between identities, such as between the ones in 1 + 1, or between the equalities 2 + 3 = 5, thus creating an otherness between them. The numbers 7 and 8 are also identical (or similar) in that they are composed of identical units. And they are other (or different) in that they are composed of different quantities of units.

This way of making distinctions, but simultaneously retaining a relationship between two concepts, is a convenience which was developed in the structure of mathematics in recognition of the human need to operate among discrete entities. For thought cannot advance where such distinctions are not made. So, in mathematical science, there is a recognition of both similarity and difference, of combination and independence, and of continuity and discreteness. Each of these properties expresses identity and otherness.

By these means, mathematics has been developed into a bridge between the practical necessity of human existence, which is a need for a recognition of discrete entities, and the fundamental nature of things, which demands a recognition that discreteness is a human device. In other words, nature, unfiltered by the mind, is amorphous.

Thus mathematics stands as one of humanity's most remarkable compromises between nature and itself. For it is an effective logical paradigm designed to establish a workable link between the limits of raw sensory experience and those things which the human mind wishes to make known to itself within that experience.

But the fact must not be overlooked that, where the human mind draws up the continuous into classifications of discreteness, it cannot conceive the entire fabric of the continuous whole of human experience in discrete terms. Consequently, there are likely to be contradictions, or anomalies, in what it conceives as matters of fact, even though its logical expressions in relations of ideas appear to be consistent.

A PERSON knows what a thing is. She knows what the absence of that thing is. But does she know what nothing is?

FOR all anyone knows, there is no such thing as chaos. Order is the only reality the human mind is able to conceive. For, even if it were the case that there is such a thing as chaos, the human imagination could neither represent nor describe it. A person might attempt to imagine the explosion of a bomb into a myriad of fragments. But any attempt on the part of the imagination to represent the scattering of these parts must place them in relation to one another. That relation is order.

TO imagine that nothingness can be described is to assume that a total vacuum can be perceived. For what is represented in the imagination must be given, at least in its sensory elements, by the senses. These elements may be rearranged by imagination. But they cannot be invented. Only their recombination can be invented.

What can be seen, or what can be imagined to be seen, without light? Is there touch without extension and resistance? Science has never proven the existence of a total vacuum. Neither have philosophy nor poetic imagination been more successful. For how can something be understood which is represented only by what it is not? If there truly is a space that has nothing in it, humanity, considering its present faculties, would be the last to know about it.

But someone insists, "I can imagine a totally empty space left behind by what was once there." But it is only the removal of the something which is imagined. And the absence of something does not imply its replacement by a nothing. It does not leave an empty place where nothingness prevails. This is the essence of insights expressed in Henri Bergson's *Creative Evolution.*

IMAGINE the perception of a three-dimensional universe without time. What would be its character? It would be discovered that time, which is so important to human awareness in the ordering of events, is also the instrument which most severely limits a person's view of the world. For without time all things would be present to him at once and not sequentially.

This is because time expresses limitation in much the manner that space does, establishing focus and order through progression, while space preserves identity and distinction through separation. But the limitation of time is imposed upon the structure of space in such a way that the former subdivides the latter, not into contiguous units of being, but rather of coming into being and going out of being. In other words, that which would be simply existent becomes that which shall be, is, and was. From this it may be seen how it is that time is a fourth dimension which alters and limits the first three.

HERE is a consideration. In Eastern thought there is a concept which can be labeled the eternal moment, or the eternal now. This bears some resemblance to Nietzsche's eternal recurrence. So, for the sake of a close comparison, let a moment be defined in terms of eternity, thus establishing a reciprocal relationship between the above concepts.

If eternity, by definition, has no beginning or end, it might be visualized in terms of the circumference of a perfect circle. Since there is no starting or ending point on the circumference, and no distinction between any of its parts, no point on that circumference can be indicated as a fixed reference for the whole.

Now let a point be designated on the circumference. It may then be referenced in relation to its closest or more distant neighbors. But the overall position of both it and its neighbors cannot be fixed on the circumference. This characteristic is also true of any other point on the circumference which might be chosen. For the circumference not only has no beginning or end. Its indistinguishable parts cannot supply a fixed point of reference in relation to the whole.

Any point may be chosen. But where it is in relation to the whole cannot be determined. For, there being no beginning or end point, it cannot be distinguished by position. And there being no point of independent distinction other than that of a random selection, the selected point is indistinguishable from any other point in any terms other than its selection.

Let time be considered to be eternal, or at least indeterminate, as has been said and as it generally is thought to be. It follows from this and the above circumstances that a designated moment of eternal recurrence may be fixed at a position in time and yet may be anywhere, and thus everywhere, in all time. It may be referenced to its nearer or farther neighbors in time but not to all time. In this way, the eternal recurrence can be seen to resemble an eternal moment.

When designated, it becomes a moment which is fixed as a reference point in such a way that all other moments are understood in terms of it. But conversely, though all the other moments can be individually understood in terms of that one moment, the one moment cannot be understood in terms of all the other moments collectively. For how many such moments are there? It cannot be known, though any of those moments may be randomly selected.

Thus, for example, arises that collection of moments which a person normally defines as his life. They may become a reference point for each of the other moments of time, all of these moments being understood in this way as an extended expression of his being. For they are all individually referenced to him, near or far.

But he cannot, in turn, be referenced to all time as such. For, in relation to all time, the individual moment, or any such designated collection of related moments, is, when taken together as as single unit, an indeterminate moment. An indeterminate moment like this can be defined as a specified moment within a greater indeterminate field since, if not specified, it would not be a moment.

But as the field within which it is contained is indeterminate, the moment is likewise indeterminate, since it cannot be fixed anywhere within that field. Thus, not being localized, it may be said to cover the whole range of time, as it may appear anywhere within it. This is what makes it an eternal moment.

THERE is no such thing as energy. There is only change and the quantitative expression of change. What is needed is a theory of mind which makes sense of this fact.

THERE are no distinct increments in change. One may choose a frame of an event and compare it to another frame of the same event. But change, like time, is seamless. The frames are arbitrary isolations of phenomena.

TWO things make life worth living: beauty and love. Beauty is the recognition of truth. In art it is a recognition of truth in the midst of an emotional and sensual affirmation of life. Love is a recognition that that which is contemplated and held in the heart as being of supreme importance is, in fact, a necessary complement and equivalent to one's own being. The Good Samaritan had such love for a stranger when he recognized in that moment by the roadside, here was one like himself.

IT is a strange paradox that language, the very tool with which human beings think, can be such a clouded instrument for expressing that thought. It has been said that naturalness and a simple clarity of expression are the mark of a well-oiled, thinking mind. Perhaps. But one wonders at the deep intuitions and profound reasonings that are never conveyed to the world due to the lack of a suitable instrument.

THE greatest impediment to an understanding of the character of spirit is the human tendency to use modes of thinking which belong to matter. Extension, duration, limitation, quantity, etc. belong to a physical world. No one can be certain as to how to apply them to spiritual ideas.

Nevertheless, the effort is made because these things are all the mind has to work with in forming ideas. There is nothing wrong with this, so long as it is remembered that any conclusions reached by such means must be considered tentative. For it is better to grope in darkness with inadequate lighting than to abandon a search for meaning and understanding altogether.

MOST thinking is non-rational. It involves a rapid association of images driven by impulses. These images are almost instantly weighed, evaluated, and compared to reach a derivative impulse-driven image generally thought of as a decision. It may be a decision for a course of action or simply for a way of understanding something. It is only after this process has been completed that the mind looks back and unconsciously organizes its thought into a logical structure.

But human beings, so much more than any other animal (so far as is known), have capitalized on logical structures and built them into mighty theoretical edifices. Thus thought, in this rational form, becomes the backbone of human culture. It can be preserved, passed on, and understood as a common language of awareness.

Nevertheless, the mistake of believing that this makes human beings categorically different from other forms of life should not be made. Human beings have specialized in casting their perceptions into logical forms of thinking in the way a cat has specialized in teeth, claws, and a flexible spine.

IMAGINE an ordering of the sensations of touch without reference to the four other senses: sight, hearing, smell, or taste. The only sequences in time would be the pressures felt at the fingertips and the internal effects of the organs. Any representation of space would also have to be constructed from these sequences of touch as well as distances being determined by sequences in the internal effects of the organs.

And any presentation of space in the mind would be sequential in its representation. For thought follows action. Following sensation, the mind brings ideas into focus one at a time. Such a representation of space would have to be at least two-dimensional (length and breadth) to account for the individuality of things. Otherwise, they could not be conceptualized as separate from each other, yet simultaneously existent.

But would there be a third dimension? The answer is yes, for this reason alone: that human beings might conceptualize themselves as a separate existence. For it is only in the act of mentally withholding from all others those sensations equated with the self that the division between objective and subjective awareness can be accounted for. This produces depth, or separation from that which is already two-dimensional. Hence the experience of space as it is known to the mind.

THE human mind has a narrow range of focus. Let it contemplate three apples. Let it try to visualize all of them at once. It cannot be done. The mind goes to the left, sees two, then—roughly—those two (somewhat faded in focus) are visualized against the one on the right. That is the best that can be done.

But as if that were not enough, the mind cannot see even two objects entire. It sees their proximate edges, the remainder being somewhat faded in focus. What does this reveal? It is that the mind has a single clear capacity for division: a partitioning of something into two parts. All other complexity is a compounding or abstraction from this.

So what about the question of unity? There is, of course, a unity of consciousness. But that is a unity without bounds—without a clear sense of limits. And it is indivisible. Nevertheless, if the mind tries to visualize a single apple as an indivisible unity, can it visualize the thing entire? Again, not with much detail.

Thus focusing on details brings the discussion back to that fundamental division into two parts. The mind can see a stem and a generality of the rest of the apple. Or it can see a blemish and a faded stem and remainder of the apple. It is quite striking how narrow the range of mental focus really is!

IT is impossible to perceive without an involvement of the capacity for perceiving. So, as Aristotle pointed out in his essay on the soul, the organ of thought and the content of a thought can be interpreted as one and the same thing. To obtain an understanding of this idea, let us imagine someone's hand holding a rock. We will further suppose that the hand alone is that person's organ of awareness.

To facilitate this example, we will also say that person's eyes are closed. So, while feeling the shape and hardness of the rock, his attention shifts from his hand to his awareness of the rock. While focusing on the rock, he is no longer aware of the hand which holds it. But it is still a hand through which he is aware of the rock.

The mind perceives and thinks in the same way. It focuses upon a perception or a thought and does not concentrate on itself. Thus it takes the form of a perception or a thought. But it can nonetheless focus on itself. It can concentrate on itself as a consciousness which is aware of something: that something being a perception or a thought. So it is alternately the thing perceived and the perceiving thing. The mind is in this way inseparable from its perceiving and thinking.

CAUSAL thinking and the power of making logical transitions in thought both have their origin in consciousness. Consciousness, therefore, should be understood to be more than a backdrop for experience or a passive participant in experience. It is an integral part of human experience. For it enters into the human thinking capacity as a means of understanding experience.

This is to say that consciousness is not simply experience itself. Nor is it a passive receptacle upon which the events of experience are registered. It is active. For it enters indirectly into the apprehension of experience under the guise of an intuition of simple unity. This intuition is not consciousness itself.

Rather, it is derived from the experience of pure consciousness. This is to say that the intuition of simple unity is a product of consciousness experiencing itself as a simple unity. Thus, when the mind focuses on a set of mental phenomena, the intuition provides a basis for an experience of the unity of those phenomena.

From this mental foundation, the human capacity to unify, subdivide, and classify is derived. In other words, an intuitive apperception of unity among mental phenomena, which is both limited and modified by means of a shifting of mental focus, leads to a recognition that more limited unities may be encompassed by larger unities and that larger unities may be subdivided into more limited unities. It is this simple insight which provides the mind with a starting point for classification.

But because the mind thinks linearly, it often fails to notice this. To say that A = B and B = C, therefore A = C, is to say that A, B, and C refer to the same unity. Without an underlying sense of unity, such thinking would not be possible. For A, B, and C are unities which are brought into further unity with one another. Also, to say that A causes B, or again to state the proposition, if A then B, is to assert that the unities, or classifications, A and B are individually fixed within a greater unity which is the causal or propositional statement.

Thus there is a unity underlying either statement. Both of these statements, as statements, are based on the intuition of unity. The entire statement is a unity. Accordingly, both statements are (by indirect means of the intuition) founded on the experience of that simple, indivisible unity which is pure consciousness. Pure consciousness is consciousness without consideration of its content.

It is this intimate link to the unity of consciousness which provides the well known feelings both of causal and logical certainty. For these causal and logical relations are unifying functions. The sense of certainty is further strengthened by the fact that consciousness is the ground of any knowledge of being. When omitting a specification of the accidents of any known thing, substantiality is established. That something, no matter what, can "be" is something known only to consciousness. For what can possibly be known outside the sphere of consciousness?

Consciousness is the ground for an awareness of whatever should constitute a specific manifestation of being. That manifestation, being specific, is finite. Thus, whatever it may be, it is material experience. And material experience in all its complexity of sensation and relation is apprehended solely within consciousness. It is unknown outside it.

So let us return to the role of the intuition of simple unity. To employ this intuitive sense of unity, which is derived from the experience of pure consciousness, is to use the intuitive sense of unity as a unifying instrument for perceptual awareness and as a classifying instrument for conceptual thinking about such experience.

Thus the intuition of unity is consciousness employed as a means of mental focus. That which is focused upon is the specific portion of the content of consciousness upon which consciousness centers its attention. The focused upon content thus becomes the full content of consciousness. This process affirms that what is known through consciousness is both consciousness and its content.

Moreover, consciousness has some control over the extent of its content in terms of focus. Consciousness is therefore knowing. And what can be of greater certainty in knowing than the fact of something knowing itself—i.e. of consciousness focusing upon itself as the instrument of awareness?

So what could provide a greater sense of certainty in reasoning, than to relate whatever is thought about, not only to the *unity* of consciousness, but to consciousness itself? If the perception or thought is, it is because consciousness is. And if the thought is unified, it is because consciousness is unified. Consciousness does not change. Only its content undergoes change. Therefore, consciousness is not material.

It is spirit. As such, it is the means by which the material is experienced. But understanding this offers no insight into why things are experienced in the particular character and order in which they are. For the order of material experience which is made present within the mind is an order which transcends its presentation. And its conceptual apprehension is in large measure dependent upon that order.

Nevertheless, as it is presented to the mind, it is known only to the mind. That a similar experience appears to other minds in a manner which is, in some measure, coordinated among them can only be referenced to that which lies within the depths of mind itself, beyond the range of human understanding.

TRUTH does not exist in intellectual terms. It is a point beyond the horizon of the human mind at which the mind always aims. But the mind will never get there. That is, truth will never be arrived at intellectually, though human sensibility—heart and will—may encompass it. Every theory, scientific or philosophical, ever devised by the mind of man, has fallen short of a comprehensive explanation of experience.

This is because experience is difficult to conceptualize. When it is divided into discrete units for the purpose of quantification (as in mathematics) or classification (as in logical discourse), something indefinable evades analysis. This is because experience is holistic in character. It is more than the sum of its parts. For it is a sum of parts which are complementary but independent of one another.

The best example of the indefinable character of experience can be seen in a work of art. Is such a work no more than a mechanical sum of its parts—one thing added to another, or one thing determining the character of another? Why is it that a person can look at a Rembrandt painting repeatedly with careful attention but never fully comprehend or describe it? Is the situation any different with a Cézanne?

Now consider something as mundane as a house. Insofar as its relationship to a human being is concerned, to list its parts or describe their combined working is meaningless. So, if a person wanted to express what a house truly was for a human being—i.e. what it is for—only a statement of its human-oriented function would do. But such a function is not quantifiable. For it is something which relates one thing to another without a causal connection.

The linkage between a house and its human purpose is an idea in the mind of a person. Aristotle referred to this idea as the "form" of the house, a plan for what nails, lumber, bricks, etc. could become. And he considered such a form to be a cause. He believed the idea caused a person to build the house.

But this form is not a cause in any physical sense. For a physical cause is an efficient cause. An example of an efficient cause would be a billiard ball striking another and moving it. A hammer striking nails into lumber, fastening them together in framing a house, would also be an efficient cause. But the idea, or thought, of it would not.

The function of a house is to provide shelter for someone. A person can materially cause a house to come into existence. She can procure lumber and nails, etc. and build it. But the idea of the house, which exists in her head, cannot be said to have caused anything. For the relationship between an idea in someone's mind and an action which appears to put the idea into effect is not demonstrable.

The person has willed the house, to be sure. And she has provided a pattern for its construction. But neither the idea of the house, which is this pattern in her mind, nor the willing of it, which is a complex of emotions linked to the idea, have caused it to come into existence in the concrete and material sense of an efficient cause.

Even if a very close relationship between certain chemical properties and nerve impulses in the brain and the idea of a house which they accompanied could be demonstrated, it would be impossible to demonstrate with certainty how a thought caused the house. The brain process would have to be materially divided into its component parts (nerves and chemicals). Then how they interacted chemically and electrically could be seen.

But the idea would have vanished from this analysis. At best, the idea could only be said to have an analogous relationship to the brain process. It was concurrent with it. For perhaps, by means of careful observation, it could be temporally linked to it in occurrence. But the two could not be united by means of efficient cause.

This meditation is a reflection of the duality of human experience. The inward and outward aspects of that experience are seemingly in cooperation. But upon close examination, they also appear to be in opposition, since they cannot be physically linked. That is why truth as a purpose or an idea can exist in human experience. But as a conceptual program, uniting all of experience with irrefutable logic, it cannot.

HUMAN beings are a species of animal. They are a product of nature. Any response a person has to the physical world, including both sensory representations of physical experience and the constructions of her intellect, is a product of that physical world. To begin with, her sensory representations are fragmented, leaving responsibility for their integration to her intellect.

Yet her intellectual response to the physical world is no more than a template thrown over it, a template which is entirely a product of the physical world but not a full expression of it. Hence the problem of the thing-in-itself, the noumenal world which stands mysterious and unapproachable beyond phenomenal awareness. Can the gap between these two realms ever be bridged?

Humankind are conscious beings. Is consciousness thinking? It is not. It is simple awareness. Then what is thinking? Assume that thinking is a process by which an organism internalizes environmental relations. If thinking is defined in this way—that is, simply as an internalizing process—then included under such a heading would be much that is not considered thinking.

The processes involved in the absorption of nutrients, metabolism, and growth are means by which an organism internalizes its environment. Can a plant think? It cannot. Yet it internalizes its environment. The movements of an organism require the absorption of energy. For movement expends energy. These movements include plant growth. That growth is environmental displacement, not unlike animal movement. Movement is change. So energy absorption is an internalization of the power to produce change.

Organisms take that power from the physical world and place it at the disposal of themselves. Thus an organism can move itself. It can create change of place without an immediate reliance upon something else first imposing that change upon it. It internalizes change. A person does the same. She can walk of her own free will. And she can pause to build a fire.

A bird can follow a migratory route, build a nest, or care for its young without having been taught. Is this thought? It is instinct. But instinct is frozen thought, thought in slow time. For it can be modified. New habits may be learned, such as a new migration route. And these may be acquired as instincts passed on to future generations until change is needed. Most importantly, this transition in frozen thought may be accomplished in a few generations. Slow though it is, it is much too quick to be considered a product of random variation.

But what exactly is meant by higher thought: reasoning? Many animals appear to reason in varying degrees. Human beings reason in complex ways. Their thinking is sometimes multilayered and rich in surprising convolutions. It is not unlike the unfolding of a flower bud or the logarithmic spiral of the shell of a chambered nautilus. Such reasoning aspires to encompass the complex relations of a universe.

Reason itself then is at issue in any discussion of the internalization of environmental conditions. While most organisms appear to specialize in internalizing this or that group of environmental relations, human beings specialize in the process of the internalization of internalization itself. This is what is called higher thought. And it is a capacity which is generally designated by the term, human thinking.

Hence the disappointment concerning some animals, which appear to reason in varying degrees but fail to make a *point* of doing so. What further complicates the issue is that such a large proportion of humanity also refuses to do so. For most human beings, reasoning is simply a means of altering the environment and not a deliberate means of organizing environmental relations within themselves. For most, it is not an instrument of wisdom. Thus higher thinking is exercised by only a few. Yet these few have become the definition of the race. Because of this, human beings call themselves reasoning beings.

At issue here is an examination of how the reasoning process might have come about. But the investigation should not be carried out through time. There is not sufficient leisure to pause to examine the development of the species, Homo sapiens sapiens. That is a project for anthropologists and evolutionary biologists.

These investigators may determine how it is that humanity came to specialize in concentrating its efforts on the process of internalizing environmental relations, a process called thinking, or, more specifically, reasoning. Such a study might focus on the accumulation of adaptations until the process of accumulation itself becomes the focus of adaptation. For reasoning in its more practical mode is a passing in review of a person's adjustments to her environment. At this level, it is an abridger of physical acts.

But what is of concern is the mind of humanity in its present state: an approach to wisdom, but not a fulfillment of it. How is this mind to be understood? Can it be found out in its depth by a person looking into herself? Is it by looking into her own mind that a person discovers both the things which she knows and the means by which she knows them? Keeping this search focused on the idea that these two things must be intimately related, it may be possible to come to understand each in terms of the other.

For this reason, neither mind nor nature should be enthroned at the expense of the other. Mind is not prior to nature. Neither is nature prior to mind. Nature is a product of mind. And mind is a product of nature. Where is a human mind to be found but in nature? What is it inextricably linked to but nature? Yet how else can the physical world be known but through the mind? Thus, in this final sense, the physical world is a product of mind.

None of this is an attempt to specifically support the idea of a creator god. Nor is it transcendent in its reach. Nor is it a pantheistic interpretation of existence. Neither is it a denial of these. This is simply an effort in the direction of greater honesty, or sincerity of heart. For human beings know very well that they are material beings.

Yet they sense within themselves—and ultimately, by extension, within all things—an immaterial ground of being which is concurrent with the material expression of being. How else can they explain consciousness? So, in fact, each is an expression of the other—consciousness of matter and matter of consciousness. But neither is contained within, or limited by, the other.

If the physical world were contained only in minds, it could not be accepted as existing in itself. And if consciousness was no more than an epiphenomenon of matter, individual existence would have no meaning. Independent being at any level would be an illusion. Thus, since it is unacceptable to deny the reality of the physical world or the reality of the individual person as a knowing, willing being, and since a duality of mind and matter offends the human desire for a single unified explanation, a person must plant her feet firmly in both realms and allow them to bear up a single weight.

HOW might human reason have evolved? This has already been briefly suggested. But for a closer look, let a single element of reasoning be taken into consideration. That is the *causal* relation. In the relation of cause and effect, a cause is said to produce an effect. This is its empirical character. For it can be observed. It asserts that a billiard ball striking another billiard ball causes the reaction observed in the movement of the struck ball.

But David Hume pointed out that the *power* of a cause to produce an effect cannot be demonstrated. It can only be noted that a certain cause regularly precedes a certain effect, as in the movement of a struck billiard ball occurring time and again after a striking ball makes contact with it.

However, if Hume is right, this establishes the relationship of cause and effect as something other than empirical. For what is observed cannot be demonstrated. Causal relations do occur. But one is left asking: *why* do they occur? All that can be said is that a recognition of the relationship between a cause and its effect exhibits a strong inclination of the human mind.

Given the many kinds of physical experience which regularly occur in this fashion, human beings feel compelled to believe in causal relations. In addition, the relationship of logical implication—as in modus ponens, *if p, then q*—bears an uncanny resemblance to empirical cause and effect. In fact, it becomes all the more uncanny when one considers that a belief in the cause and effect relationship is attributed not to physical experience, but to the mind.

So Immanuel Kant attempted to remedy this problem by supposing that there were twelve categories of the mind which determined the phenomenal structure of the manifold of sense received by the mind. In other words, Kant was asserting that the structure of human experience is a product of the human mind, not an expression of an independent reality. The causal relationship was accordingly one of the twelve categories which determined this structure.

But he also went on to suggest that the laws of the mind might well reflect laws in the mind of a transcendent being. This suggestion is an indirect conclusion of the present writer, gleaned from Kant's ethical position. For, if the commands of reason are morally justified in an afterlife, as he asserted, then reason, or something very nearly like it, must be understood to transcend the present life.

Thus its commands are recognized by a transcendent being in the afterlife. And in light of this conclusion, a belief in the validity of the causal relationship could be supported on transcendental grounds, since the general category of causation in the human mind, particularly in light of its close affinity with logical implication, would be a necessary support for the laws of practical reason which govern moral behavior and which are recognized and rewarded by this transcendent being.

However, there is probable evidence for another source of the faculty of reason, which was mentioned earlier in this book, and which is much more theoretically modest and practical. It arises from the following. The Russian physiologist, Ivan Pavlov, conducted an experiment in which dogs were conditioned by the ringing of a bell at mealtime. At the moment of their being fed, a bell was rung. The dogs would salivate as they proceeded to eat.

After much repetition of the association between the ringing of the bell and the presentation of food, the bell was rung but no food was given to the dogs. In spite of this fact, the ringing of the bell was sufficient to make the dogs salivate. This was considered a demonstration of a conditioned response: the dogs salivated because they associated food with the bell's ringing. Since the bell ringing and the appearance of food had repeatedly occurred together, the dogs had become conditioned to salivate on hearing the bell, due to an expectation of food the bell aroused in them.

Now an extension of the train of thought aroused by this research readily arises in a curious mind. It suggests a question: what if a dog were a wolf? Could a similar instance of conditioning then be discovered in the natural state of the wolf? Of course, it turns out that it can. For it can be easily imagined.

A person may be led to construct a simple thought experiment. She can begin this experiment by considering how a mother wolf feeds and educates her young. At first the mother wolf eats her entire kill, carries it in her stomach whatever distance her hunting has taken her from home, and regurgitates it at the den for her pups to consume.

But in time the pups need to learn to hunt for themselves. For they must be fitted to survive on their own. So the bitch begins to bring home an unconsumed part of the kill. She lays it before the pups. They learn to eat the animal, say a rabbit, in its natural form. They taste and smell it. These experiences are stored in their memories.

Later, when they begin to forage for themselves, they may come upon the scent of a rabbit or similar game. When they do, they will remember the positive experiences associated with that type of scent. Thus they will pursue the scent and possibly kill a rabbit or some other game because an association of such a smell with a good meal is stored in their minds. This is nature's version of the conditioned response: a smell can bring about the satisfaction of a meal. As it turns out, the association is critically necessary for survival. So it is reinforced in the mind of the wolf.

Now let a human being become the object of investigation. Could not the same sort of thing occur in this case? Could not the indicator / response relationship (like the smell / food conditioned response of the wolf pups) help in a human being's survival? What if this person is a creature who has also gained control of her imaginative faculty in such a way that she can use it not only to project immediate goals, but to project distant goals?

In other words, she can extend various associations in her mind in a systematic process called reason. A suggests B and B suggests C, etc. Granted this is a simple description of reason. But it is the basis for the more complex forms of the faculty. At any rate, given her control of her imaginative process, the person involved can extend her train of thought indefinitely and do it all in her mind in a single effort.

But let the process be kept simple. The goal is food, or the satisfaction of immediate hunger. Now the person can simply *imagine* the rabbit in its hiding place because someone or something (like a book) has told her about it and suggested its nutritional use. She has never hunted before. But she is quite hungry and is presently in possession of no other food source.

So she can decide to go looking for the rabbit, prepared to ensnare or kill it, and calling upon whatever knowledge she has of its behavior. This knowledge has possibly also been gleaned from books. So she has become convinced that if she carefully takes advantage of what she has learned about a rabbit's behavior, she will likely secure a meal for herself.

At this point, she is clearly reasoning. Or at least it can be said that she is making associations in a deliberate and regularized pattern. She thinks: if this, then that. And if that, then something else, etc. in a growing chain of thought. In other words, she is putting into practice the mental conviction that one thing follows from another.

Thus the indicator / response relationship becomes both the pattern for logical implication and the cause-and-effect relationship. For the overall pattern of her thought is governed by a simple relation: rabbit results in meal. In thought, it takes the form of: if rabbit, then meal (with, of course, a few intermediate steps). Or in a very real physical sense, the presence of a rabbit causes the subsequent presence of a meal (with, of course, the same few intermediate steps).

And all the steps in her mind which are inserted between these two ideas—all the steps which will secure her the rabbit as food—follow the same *one-thing-will-bring-about-another* pattern of the original relation: rabbit results in meal. So to follow such a pattern of thinking looks a good deal more like an instinctive mental process than a transcendent power of the mind which reaches beyond ordinary experience. It is instinctive because the indicator / response structure for recognizing these relations is already present in the minds of both wolves and human beings, not to mention a number of other creatures.

It is, in fact, a natural inclination of the mind which both the person mentioned here and the persons who informed her of the rabbit and its use have in common. It is an inclination which they all have in common with the wolf and the dog. Though, of course, it should be noted that the people can do much more with it. They can elaborate their associative faculty into an extensive reasoning process.

So to reiterate the process, let its pattern be repeated in a little more detail. It has been noted that this person feels hungry. So, due to certain things she has learned and stored up in memory, she thinks of the pleasing possibility of a rabbit as food. This motivates her to gather the necessary tools and go on a hunting expedition to secure it.

It is in this frame of mind that she calls up the image of a rabbit stew, which she has recently heard about, and says to herself, “That is the food I need to assuage my hunger. For a rabbit will cause my hunger to go away.” She remembers where she has seen rabbits on several casual walks through woods and fields, and knows from her books where they are likely to hide and what they are likely to do if she goes in pursuit of them.

In other words, she recalls details of their behavior which she has been informed of. She is able to use these images in her mind to project an outcome favorable to herself. So she "reasons" that, if she does certain things in relation to the called up images and presently imagined behavior of the rabbit, she will be able to follow a sequence of very likely events, one following another in predictable order, and kill the rabbit to have a meal.

She has reasoned, or done something very similar, using cause-and-effect relationships stored in her memory. These cause and effect relationships are essentially indicator / response relationships. So, by means of her control of imagined scenarios, she has combined a number of such relationships into a single train of thought. Her object is to produce a predictable result.

THE finite cannot be conceived without the infinite. And the infinite cannot be conceived without the finite. Imagine space as a void with no stars, planets, etc. Place a chair in that space. How large is the chair? Is it the size of a human thumb or the size of a sun? With nothing to compare it to, the answer cannot be given. Again, what is its shape? This becomes vague, uncertain. What is its purpose? The question is meaningless.

If a person were to focus on the parts of the chair, say its legs, it would seem that she would have some idea of their shape and function as she compared them to other parts of the chair. But overall, the parts of the chair are too few. And their modes of comparison are few as well. For example, the legs of the chair could not be considered as legs. For legs are not a concept which originates with chairs.

Nor could they be considered as supports. Supports for what reason? There is no justification for assuming gravitation and weight. The legs of the chair would have little more meaning than the protrusions of an ameba have in relation to a giraffe. Thus a comparison between the few parts of the chair would render the parts insignificant, nearly shapeless, and meaningless.

It might be observed that the seat of the chair is only two thirds as long as the legs or the back. But the only instrument of mensuration is the seat, back, and legs. To measure something against half again its length, when there is no other means of comparison, is no easy matter. How does a person get a sense of the half? She is obliged to guess. And she has no idea of halves anyway. For on what basis would she have developed it?

It should be noted that even the person contemplating the situation is not an object of comparison. She is an unembodied mind. So, without any form of reference but itself, the chair is incomprehensible. Consequently, due to this lack of reference, the chair loses definition and meaningful shape. It becomes formless, or nearly formless, matter. It ceases to exist in any significant way.

The implication here is that there must be more in the way of reference than the parts of the chair alone. But what must be further understood is that a finite enumeration of any kind is not sufficient. For where the enumeration, or iteration, of finite things terminates, there is a void. However, the enumeration of finite things does hold insofar as the things enumerated are empty spaces, as well as physical objects. For empty spaces are not voids.

Physical objects are extensions. And empty spaces are extensions between extensions. For they are bounded on all sides by physical extensions, however remote their boundaries may be. Even outer space gets its definition from the bodies found within it. And insofar as it may be considered finite, it must be tacitly assumed to be bounded in some way.

If it is considered to be infinite, this is only a detached, indemonstrable supposition. When the concept of infinitude is used in this way, it really means indeterminate, or innumerable. It is to say that the boundaries of space cannot be determined. They cannot be reached, even by imagination. But surely they are out there somewhere.

Thus it is not an empty space, but a void, which is the problem. Where a void purports to play a role in the foundation of anything, meaning cannot be anchored. For, where a void is contiguous to an existence, both the existing thing and its function are incomprehensible at that juncture. The portion of the entity which is contiguous to the void cannot be fixed. It cannot be defined. For it is bounded by nothingness. And nothingness cannot be a boundary.

A chair suspended in open space is bounded by the extension of space around it. For the space must be assumed to be bounded. But a chair in open space, where the space is understood to be a void, is different. It is different even if the chair is bounded by a void on only one side. This is because the void-bounded portion of the object, and thus the object itself, cannot be articulated. So it cannot be determined to exist.

Consequently, the entire object is undone, as well as all other finite entities contiguous with it. For they become parts of the greater grouping. The chair is itself a part of this grouping. The chair has an uncertain part, making the chair uncertain. The uncertain chair in turn makes any contiguous object uncertain. This is because it forms an uncertain boundary with it. So the imagination must conclude that they all drift, as it were, into the void which is understood to form a part of their physical being.

In other words, this relationship with nothingness being incomprehensible, all objects involved in it, directly or indirectly, dissolve entirely into the nothingness which is a constituent part of their collective being. For the situation is unlike that of arithmetic, where nothing added to something leaves the something intact. In this case, the nothing is not added. It is the thing, or an inextricable part of it. Thus the whole thing is nothing.

So since no object can be bounded by a void, it is necessary that, for any one object to possess meaningful shape and function, there must be an indeterminate, or potentially indeterminate, supply of objects poised in interaction with one another. This is a type of indeterminacy which is generally understood as infinite.

It is like the concept of infinite space cited above. Though in truth, *in*finite simply means *not* finite, as the word indicates. When the concept of infinity is understood in this sense of indeterminate, it refers to an innumerable array of finite and articulate entities, the completion of which array is inaccessible to experience or concrete imagination.

That is to say, this necessary but inaccessible whole provides a context within which measurable, definable objects are recognized. For they are observed within an unlimited and incomprehensible plenitude of individually measurable and definable objects. This means that, for the finite to be conceived, there must be, at least potentially, an infinitude of finite things.

Why is this so? It is so because things are articulated by one another, whether they be physical objects or the objects of thought. Inasmuch as they are articulated, they are defined and understood. But it is not the case that one thing is only articulated by its constituent elements, by its closest neighbors, and by its function among other things.

These elements, neighbors, and function are themselves articulated and defined in the same way. The process is necessarily unending. And when this does not appear to be the case in human perception or thought, it is subtly presupposed, as in the case of outer space mentioned above. For there can be no genuine void in human awareness. To suppose such an absolute nothingness is to suppose a world unformed.

Of course, within the human mind an illusion of one finite object as measured against another finite object can be created without an apparent reference to the infinitude of other such objects. This is because both consciousness and memory supply that reference, even when it is held in abeyance in the mind. They provide the shadow of a backdrop of an infinitude of finite entities.

Within the context of conscious awareness, there is the ground of a reference to the infinite. For, within the unlimited bounds of consciousness, an indefinable number of material things and relations may possibly occur together, even if they are not all specifically represented in the mind at the moment of consideration of some of them.

This is so, even if it should be observed that they *cannot* all be represented in the mind at any moment of consideration, due to the limiting role of mental focus. It is nevertheless the range of their possibility. For consciousness is unlimited and could contain the unlimited were there no focusing of the mind, both voluntary and involuntary. As for the the role of memory, it is the recollection of other things and of the experience of an ongoing encounter with the new which supplies the raw material for this unlimited range of possibility.

But it is not only the case that the finite is understood in terms of the infinite. It is also the case that there must be the finite in order for the infinite to be conceived. This latter situation again arises from the fact that the word "infinite" simply means indeterminate. It means innumerable. So it is in effect a negation. It is that collective circumstance the constituent parts of which are individually finite, but which in total cannot be numbered. Thus the negation is the *in*determinate character of the whole.

There is no other means of conceiving the infinite in finite terms, other than to conceive the innumerable. For, at any possible point of intersection, the indeterminately great and the indeterminately small reveal themselves to be finite. For example, no matter what number in an indeterminate list of natural numbers should be arrived at by counting, it and all that comes before it are both individually and collectively finite. There are therefore no physical or conceptual examples of the infinite in the sense of the not-in-any-way-finite. Consequently, the material infinite is simply a negation of the finite in terms of enumeration or extension. It is nothing more.

So without both the finite and the infinite (in the sense of the indeterminate), an experience or conceptualization of anything actually existing is not possible. An unlimited finite context of awareness must always be involved in the conceptualization of the finite. This indeterminate form of the unlimited is the infinite. For what is the experiential infinite but that which is indeterminate and therefore not finite in terms of enumeration?

On the other hand, that which is limited is that which has been made articulate to the mind by means of the unlimited. For it is endlessly bounded by other things, which are themselves bound in turn. So a physical object, or a thought insofar as its content is concerned, is that which is limited by that which is limited: a physical object by other objects, an object of thought by other such objects of thought. And the limiting thing, being limited in itself, is also limited by another entity which is limited.

The progression is unending. A person may speak of another person's first and last thoughts. But this distinction pertains to a temporal sequence of the thought, not to the character of the thought content. The thought content is potentially interconnected with all such content. To be material content, it cannot be otherwise.

So this finite / infinite duality of meaning is why the finite and the infinite are inseparable. But what is the ground of this relationship? For clearly the relationship is a mental phenomenon. Given that sensory perception, insofar as it can be experienced, is ultimately mental, there can be no doubt of this all-encompassing mental character concerning all of human awareness. Thus the phenomenon turns out to be nothing more than an interplay of consciousness and mental focus.

Within the unlimited potential of human consciousness, there must be something actual, something to be focused upon, something finite. For the human mind would have it so. That is its character in expressing its own limitation. This is the case, even if that something is no more than the effort not to focus on anything, as in the transcendental exercises of a mystic. Such an effort is something. It is a specific effort which is concentrated upon. Thus it is finite in its articulate expression. It can be visualized as an effort, thus becoming a thing. In becoming a thing, it materializes as a mental object, an object of mental focus.

In other words, consciousness must be conscious of something. For to be conscious is to be conscious of. The mind must focus on something. Thus, although consciousness in its potential admits of an unlimited possibility of inclusiveness, it must articulate the limited. It must focus, thereby limiting its own possibility of inclusiveness.

Consequently, focus, or the attention of the mind, requires finitude, a finitude within the infinitude of possibility. So it is in this way that consciousness and focus are the two principal characteristics of the human mind. They work together. They are inseparable. Either one implies the other.

IT is notable that when something transcendent like Plato's eternal ideas or the eternity of a transcendent being is spoken of, there is always a reference to time and not space. For both the ideas and the transcendent being are held to be eternal. But other than an assertion of their transcendence—i.e. their not being in this mutable world—their location is not an issue. This indicates time's fundamental, intuitive role in human awareness.

Space, which is the physical structure of this world, is for the human mind a construct of time, a weaving of physical dimensionality out of sequential experience. A human being initially learns to experience space within the context of time. In the earliest years of a person's life, the sequential character of sensory experience provides a ground for the mental structuring of space. And in maturing years, it again provides a means for the subsequent conceptualization of space.

This conceptualization is a person's intellectual analysis of spatial experience. The structure of this experience has early taken shape in his mind. Both processes, sensory and intellectual, are mental. And both take place within the context of another aspect of experience, that of personal duration.

Sensations come to the mind sequentially, well before they are recognized as having a physical location together or apart from each other or apart from the mind. The child learns first that there are sensations. Then he learns that they come separately, that there is a before and an after. He also discovers that they are either inseparable from his person or exist apart from it.

In the case of those sensations which he has determined to exist separately from himself, he learns that they may be understood to occur in this or that relation to one another, together or apart. This is the beginning of his awareness of spatial extension. For individual associations of sensations are recognized as spatial extensions.

The identification of a group of associated sensations as constituting an individual extension results from the fact that the separate groups are themselves closely associated with one another. Thus they are found to be contiguous to one another and to empty spaces enclosed by them. This contiguity gives both the associations of sensations and the enclosed spaces extension.

For extension is what distinguishes them from one another in close and simultaneous existence. Thus simultaneous extension lends them physical existence as objects or parts of objects. Changes among these simultaneous extensions bring about the empty spaces between them. The empty spaces are enclosed by the sensation filled extensions. When apprehended together, the sensation filled extensions and the enclosed empty spaces constitute a general perception of space.

So what makes the recognition of space possible is the recognition of extensions. And the recognition of extensions arises when the sequential nature of time is brought together with an intuition of unity. The intuition of unity is derived from the experience of the simple unity of pure consciousness. It is this intuition of unity which allows for a recognition of associations of sensations as individual extensions. For it is what unifies groups of sensations which appear before the mind in a close temporal sequence.

The fact that there are extended empty spaces between physical extensions arises from the configuration of the whole. The ongoing existence of change—of extensions modified in their sensory properties or coming into existence and going out of it—is what necessitates the existence of these spaces.

Now to assert that the intuition of unity is derived from an experience of the simple unity of pure consciousness is to say that it arises from the mind's capacity to direct its attention to varying amounts of sensation appearing within the content of its consciousness. Thus the mind alters the focus of its overall range of consciousness.

Consciousness is a unity. And the mind's attention brings that unity to bear upon whatever falls under its focus. In this way, the mind is capable of establishing a unity in whatever material it chooses. Such a unity can be the unity of an image, of a concept, or of a collection of images or concepts.

For example, the conscious mind may become aware of a bowl of fruit sitting upon a table in a room. Initially, the bowl, the fruit, the table, and the room may be held together within the mind's focus. But having regarded this scene and developed a more specific interest within it, the mind may then narrow its attention to a single piece of fruit among the fruit within the bowl. The other fruit, the bowl, the table, and room are now excluded from the frame of consciousness.

The mind directs its attention to those sensations grouped together in the perception of a single apple, affirming their association in that one object. Due to the narrowness of this focus, greater detail is observed. So the mind holds within itself a close image of the apple. For it has focused its attention upon the apple alone.

But it might be that a pear also occupies the bowl containing the apple. The focus on the apple momentarily excludes any sensations which are associated together as the pear. Nevertheless, these sensations could appear in the mind directly following those of the apple, as the mind subsequently moves across the larger scene which was originally in its greater purview.

Now sensations appear before the mind sequentially. They appear in the stream of time underlying all human experience of the material world. So all this activity of the mind, enlarging and narrowing its focus, is not truly its own doing. For the stream of time controls the appearance of sensation.

But for human awareness, this point of view is not possible. Were it to occur, it would appear to negate the role of will. For will is in truth a subtle process underlying the flow of sensations in time. It does not belong to the conscious person within the realm of sensation. Rather, it lies below sensation at the level of spirit.

Thus it reaches far beyond what is thought of as human will. This is a level generally unknown to human awareness. So the material mind invents a human perspective, assigning the will to itself. And that is why, when the matter is being discussed from a human perspective, the mind's actions are referred to as its own.

In human terms, it is memory which is generally referred to as the means by which the mind enjoys its range of free play, as it appears to move independently through various series of closely associated sensations—i.e. from object to object. Thus, in the example given above, the mind appears to shift its attention from the room, table, bowl, and fruit together to the apple alone, then to the pear. Yet while narrowing its focus, it seems able to maintain an awareness of all the other things it has encountered.

The mind *appears* to be able to do this by calling upon memory. The word "appears" is used here because it should be remembered that this discussion assumes a material human view, not a transcendent spiritual view. So, in this way, memory is introduced. And the sensations of memory, in addition to the more immediate sensations, are understood to complete the combined character of experience.

Moreover, the mind may perform a similar operation while thinking piecemeal about an experience, the entirety of which has already occurred. Or it may simply hold to a compound image or set of images drawn from the past experience. These complex functions each appear to involve recall from memory.

But given the more transcendent view of spirit and its underlying role, this effect of memory is to be attributed to something deeper than the human mind, or at least to something deeper than that expression of mind which is known to human awareness. For memory, when understood in its transcendent character, is nothing more than a direct construct of sensory experience. It is given in the stream of sensation in time.

In other words, the same sensations as originally appeared before the mind appear again before the mind. But due to the presence of other accompanying sensations, an association with which relegates the now repeated sensations to past experience, these repeated sensations are assigned to the role of memory. Thus these sensations, like all others, are actually prior to individual human consciousness and will. For the sensations of memory are in fact a part of the general ordering of sensation.

Thus the human sense of time, which involves allowing memory to be a repository of the past, is not the same as the more fundamental sense of time which supplies the original movement of sensation. Rather, it is a form of time which is both derived from and causes a human sense of the self, with that self's seeming involvement in the flow of general sensation. This self, to be a self with an autonomous sense of its own will, must have a before and an after which are independent of the before and after of the original flow of sensation.

For the human sense of time appears to move in parallel to the original flow of sensation, placing some of that sensation in the individual human past, some in the present. Thus arises the role of memory as a means of accounting for the past. So this duality of time can be understood as a human sense of time riding on the back of time's fundamental role in the revelation of sensation. In childhood development, that fundamental role is soon obscured and forgotten beneath the human sense of time.

So the human sense of time is something which is created by the human mind to provide a convenience, which is the mind's need for a sense of autonomy. Thus it is separate from the general flow of sensation. For, without the human expression of time, a human being could neither organize an autonomous sense of self nor view itself as able to move about effectively in a physical environment of experience.

But as the underlying foundation of time is prior to—i.e. more fundamental than—the organization of human experience in terms of physical space, the objective physical world, which is an expression of human experience, cannot precede this fundamental time in its affects upon awareness. So the sensations brought forth from memory are not what they appear to be. They do not reach backward in true time. Rather, they are a reiteration within the flow of this time.

What appears to be a repeated experience of sensations, when they are drawn from memory subsequent to their initial appearance in direct experience—in other words, what appears to the mind as a recall from memory—is an appearance in the stream of time of roughly the same association of sensations as have previously appeared in the stream of time and been attributed to direct experience.

Now the term "roughly" suggests something different. So, to put the matter graphically, the mind's attention may at first pass back and forth between an apple and a pear, initially appearing to draw from experience the association of sensations involved in each. Then it may appear to draw both associations of sensations from memory, so as to bring the two pieces of fruit together as existing together in space.

But what is actually occurring is that the association of sensations for the apple and the same for the pear each appear one after another in the stream of time. At first, they appear as direct experience. Then they appear again with other sensations interspersed among them, say sensations expressing an effort to draw them from memory.

These added sensations make the original sensations appear more distant and faded than when they were regarded as sensations of direct experience. For the newly included sensations of effort to retrieve them from memory function like a veil, giving memory a character of less immediacy than immediate experience. Thus these added sensations of effort and the reiterated sensations of whatever is supposed to be recalled together give the apple and the pear an appearance of arising from memory.

Again, all sensations initially appear within the fundamental stream of time. Which is to say that they are associated with one another within the experience of time. Some belong to this association, others to that, as in the case of the apple and the pear. Each sensation within an association of sensations appears in close sequence with the next. Likewise, each full association of sensations also appears sequentially with the next in the stream of time. Hence either the direct experience or the apparent memory recall of first the apple, then the pear.

But as has been observed, this appearance of sensations within the stream of time, particularly in regard to memory, can be overlooked. Such an omission would be the point of view of a conscious human being. Thus will is seen by the human mind as its own agent, rather than as what it truly is: something beyond human awareness which controls the stream of sensations in time.

It is strictly from this human perspective that it can be maintained that the human mind is responsible for its focus. For its own will is felt to guide the determinations of its attention. Thus, as described above, it would be the intuition of unity which is understood to make possible a working of the temporally associated sensations into separate integrated extensions. The extensions are recognized as physical objects, or as parts of those objects. For, when that which is extended is divided into parts, the parts are extended. And of course, that which is composed of extended parts is itself extended.

When temporally associated sensations function together in this manner, their sequential character, and the application of the intuition of unity to them, creates in the mind both the independence of one object from another and the recognition of a contiguity of those same objects—i.e. their appearance together as separate and distinct entities. This contiguity of objects becomes the structure of space.

Seen from this same human perspective (and not that of the underlying stream of time), the specific order of this contiguity of extensions in space is also a result of relations between the extensions, particularly relations of change. These relations will, in varying degrees, present themselves as independent of human will, though they are in fact controlled by will in the underlying stream of time.

Such relations are resemblances, differences, and, most importantly in regard to change, the relations of cause and effect. As stated, all these relations are initially determined by the order of sensations in the flow of time. But this origin is not registered in human awareness, at least not beyond its earliest stages. What is registered is the spatial structure of objective experience, a modified sense of time derived from the changes which occur within it, and the subjective structure of thought.

So the result is that, in what often appears to human awareness to be a mysterious distinction, certain extensions are perceived as objective in character and others not. For objective extensions do not resemble thoughts, in that their relations are in varying degrees independent of human will. Whereas the relations of thought extensions in the mind clearly appear to be subject to human will.

Thus, in contrast to the independent relations of objective experience, images and concepts in the mind are produced in a manner similar to, but distinct from, those in the objective physical realm. For, inasmuch as they are similar to objective experience, thoughts are composed of associated sensations. But inasmuch as they are products of the mind, they may be greatly modified from objective experience. Accordingly, in the physical world a horse is a horse and a narwhal is a narwhal. But in the mind their properties may be modified and recombined to produce a unicorn.

In this way, they become extensions in the mind. And because the sensations in thoughts appear to be drawn from and represent sensations within the extensions of space, thoughts are initially closely related to physical experience. In fact, the most faithful of these images and concepts closely represent physical objects and events.

However, as stated above, they are also occasionally subject to varying degrees of reworking in the mind and may become quite abstract, idealized, and generally distanced from physical experience. These processes of abstraction and idealization are carried out by means of the same intuitions which are involved in perception.

In fact, all thoughts are products of the intuitions, of which two more, the intuitions of plurality and totality, will be described below. These will complete the total number of intuitions. In general, what the intuitions produce are thoughts. For an articulated perception does not occur without mental imagery.

Moreover, the sensations of perception are given directly to awareness in the flow of sensations in fundamental time. Thus, not only are mental images thoughts composed of sensations. These images are necessary for any sort of articulated perception. This is true of concepts as well. For they are thoughts derived from images. So it is mental imagery which constitutes the initial act of an articulated perception. And it is mental imagery which lies at the heart of all mental activity.

It is possible, of course, for a perception not to be articulated. But such an inarticulate sensation plays very little role in mental life. For it to play a more important role, one more important than a mere stimulus, or sensory impression, the mind generally combines it with other sensations to produce an image. If it does not do this, then it associates it with images, as when the sensation of a sudden brightness or shadow is associated with the various effects of light.

However, mental imagery need not be confined to visual imagery alone. For there is the imagery of sound, taste, smell, and touch. Moreover, the perception of an emotion or of pain is figured forth in the mind with great clarity, though with little or no representation. And such experience may appear again in what is generally understood to be memory. But here it will be accompanied, even aroused, by an associated imagery.

Now, when thoughts are considered as thoughts, what distinguishes them most from physical experience is that they are not contiguous. They are only sequential. Nor are their relations independent of the human will in the way objective experience is. So, in spite of thoughts being considered as mental extensions, they are not physical extensions. Rather, thoughts are representations of physical extensions. Thus the physical extensions are objects of thought.

These objects of thought have no extension in themselves. But they represent physical extensions and the relations which occur among physical extensions. Consequently, thoughts can be considered extensions by means of their acts of representation and by the fact that they are distinguished from one another in terms of their sequential appearance before the mind. Nevertheless, in the realm of thought there is no actual physical space.

Viewed in greater detail, this is how the process works: The sequential character of experience is initially recognized in the flow of sensations in fundamental time. These pass before the mind in early infancy, prior to the mind's organization of a material world. This is, of course, prior to the child's recognition of a self in such a world. So this primitive recognition of the sequential character of experience occurs within what might be called a domain of pre-consciousness. By pre-consciousness is meant that portion of human consciousness which is not registered in maturing human awareness.

This is not unconsciousness in the Freudian sense. It is not an awareness hidden behind a veil of ego. Rather, it is prior to anything which might be identified with an ego. In other words, it lies beneath the structure of both the objective realm of physical experience and the subjective realm of thought. It precedes their development. And since it is these which are involved in the formation of a sense of self, it is prior to that sense. Though present to the mind of an infant, it fades increasingly out of view with the maturing human mind, until it is lost altogether.

Now let this flow of sensations in the fundamental stream of time be brought under closer scrutiny. It may be that on some occasions individual sensations, like green and blue, are so closely associated in sequence as to appear to be combined into one sensation, such as turquoise. Even so, when in such a combination, they may yet be singled out by means of mental focus and concentration of attention. This may be done in such a manner that the green and blue can still be separately identified. So it is that the mind develops a sense of separateness and division among individual sensations.

Thus, as there is already in the mind an intuition of unity, which provides the mind with a power of the recognition of unity, there is added to this a recognition of the character of distinct separateness. So, as a result of repeated usage, the two faculties together form a second intuition. By means of this second intuition, any one sensation in company with another or others in the mind can be clearly delineated. Each individual sensation constitutes a separate unity. In this way, a plurality is created.

Again, a recognition of this plurality is repeated in many cases. So, in time, the practice of such a recognition is freed from any particular application in the mind and becomes a general intuition. And it is this intuition which establishes a capacity for clear articulation, not only of the individual sensations, but of the existence of individually recognized associations of sensations. Hence the beginning of a recognition of extensions.

All sensations occur within the unity of consciousness. Whatever lies within the focus of consciousness takes on the character of that unity. So, when only one sensation appears within the mind's focus, it is perceived as a unity. Therefore, a sense of plurality can arise only when more than one sensation occurs in consciousness in a separate relation to another, where each is recognized as a unity. Thus the close appearance of two sensations in the mind, in which they do not appear to be one.

So if the appearance is close in character, but not too close, the two sensations act by virtue of their individual limits to distinguish one another as individual sensations. In this way, not only plurality, but finitude is established. The individual sensations are two unities, demarking one another as limited, individual, and separate. This is how the intuition of plurality arises from a sense of separateness working in conjunction with the intuition of unity.

Furthermore, there is a third intuition. This is an intuition of totality. It comes about in a similar manner. For it is a product of a fully operational intuition of plurality working directly in conjunction with the intuition of unity. Accordingly, this combination makes possible a recognition of a *unified* plurality. Thus the first two intuitions work together in forming a third intuition, which is the intuition of totality.

This third intuition renders possible a unification in consciousness of separately recognized units of sensation. They become more than a plurality. They become a unified plurality, which is a totality. Moreover, this unified plurality, say an extension, may be compounded with other extensions into a greater unity, as in the parts of an object. And even greater unities may be compounded of such as these. Thus a soil is built up of individual grains of varying dimension. And from this a prairie is composed of multiple soils and the ecosystems upon them which are built up in another way.

Accordingly, in its simplest form, a totality is initially little more than an association of sensations considered as a unity in itself. This unified and individualized association of sensations, particularly where there are a number of them combining into different properties, forms a physical extension or a mental representation in the form of an image or a concept.

In this way, the whole becomes a unified plurality which is extended and takes up the character of a physical object or a thought. Beyond this, a multiple of associated objects or parts of objects may be recognized, as has been set forth with the example of the soil and the prairie. And to be recognized in the mind, these physical objects become objects of thought, displaying the same characteristics of extension without physicality. So the list of possible combinations into greater and greater unities is endless in both the physical and mental realms.

But as mentioned above, a series of sensations may in some cases result, not in a totality, but in a melded unity. This is a very close association between sensations, an association so close as to render them nearly indistinguishable from one another, and in some cases absolutely indistinguishable from one another. These constitute such a blending of sensations as is found in a color like turquoise or in some other single property of an object.

For an example of a property other than color, there is the flavor of a ripe apple. This property expresses together sour, sweet, and other sensations in a manner which makes them nearly, if not at times completely, indistinguishable from one another. It is in this way that those sensations in closest association with one another, within a greater association of sensations which constitute an object, will make up the individual properties of the object.

These things having been observed, it can now be stated without reservation that there are but three intuitions of the mind: unity, plurality, and totality. These intuitions, singly and in various combinations, render possible all mental operations. And as for the fundamental character of time, it is a necessary condition for any mental process to occur.

For without it, there would be no mental content. There would be an awareness, but an awareness of nothing other than awareness itself. Therefore, there would be nothing for the mind to perform its operations upon. Thus fundamental time is an autonomous operation of the mind, rather than an intuition.

There remains the issue of subjectivity versus objectivity. Only as a result of the fact that a perceiver does not control the appearance of some sensations which are systematically linked together in his mind, but which he may nevertheless manipulate in certain ways as objects in space, is he given a reasonable, but never certain, assurance that an objective realm corresponds to his subjective recognition of these objects and this space in his mind.

This differs from a person's subjective control over his own thoughts. For he may freely alter the composition and order of elements in his thoughts. And those thoughts, being sequential but not contiguous in character, do not occupy physical space. Therefore, their relationship to one another is not in any way independent of his will, as is characteristic of the objective realm.

But the uncertainty remains concerning the nature of objective experience. Hence the problem of accounting for what has become known to philosophy as the thing-in-itself—i.e. the objective existence of a thing subsisting independently of a perceiving mind. It is in varying measure that this appearance of an independent subsistence carries its sensations outside the will of the perceiver. For there may be a manipulation of physical objects, implying control by the subjective will. But the specific character of their relationship to one another is subject to autonomous rule.

For example, cause and effect, likeness, and difference are such relationships. Cause and effect may be manipulated to effect change, thereby altering relations of likeness and difference. But such changes must be carried out systematically and not arbitrarily. Thus the role of will is inhibited, even where it is permitted to operate. Yet this means that it is also permitted to operate, even while being inhibited. Thus there is a subjective involvement in the objective. And this subjective involvement, however constrained, lends doubt to objectivity.

Moreover, in spite of the fact that objective sensations do appear in certain ways to be independent of a person's will, it is nevertheless the case that they are known to him only in his mind. This is the principal cause of the uncertainty of an objective existence independent of the perceiver. For even an object's independence from the subjective will of the perceiver does not guarantee its physical existence outside his mind.

However, due to its exclusively subjective nature, the existence of fundamental time is never doubted in this way. The flow of change in material experience may appear to be independent of the perceiver's will, where that will is understood to be an expression of his human mind. But as the fundamental temporal flow of sensation is prior to the mature human level of consciousness, he is not aware of it and its true association with will. Rather, the time he comes to recognize with increasing precision is the product of an intellectual deduction from the sequential processes of physical change.

So never does the same problem occur with the experience of time as occurs with physical objectivity and therefore space. For, not only is fundamental time prior to space in human experience, and thus prior to human awareness, it is prior to all but the most elemental experience of sensation.

Thus its unshakable foundation in human awareness. Likewise, experiential time, though derived from objective experience, is based upon an observance of change, rather than upon a concern with what is changed. Thus it is reflective of the immutability of fundamental time, from which change derives its direct origin.

For this reason, a thought concerning the character of a transcendent being does not initially concern itself with where that being is, but only with the idea that that being is for all time. However, it does eventually dawn upon the speculator that that being must be somewhere. If there is a transcendent being, such a being would appear to demand a location. So where is it? Hence the transcendental reappearance of the issue of space. Even though that space may be conceived or imagined to be different from the space rendered familiar to human understanding, it is nevertheless a derivative of that construction.

Science's Origin in Mind

ALL profundity lies in simplicity. If the theory is complex, it is not profound.

COMPLEXITY in observation results from complexity in one's approach to a problem. Increasing complication is inevitably an indication that a search for a simpler solution should take place.

REASON is a product of nature. But what is nature a product of? Can anyone measure it with reason to find this out? Can an eagle soar beyond the air which sustains it? This is not to disclaim the advances of science. It is only to insist that science is an ongoing adjustment of humanity to the intellectual limits of the human condition. It is not a path towards absolute truth.

PROBABILITY in science is the mathematical equivalent of soft determinism in philosophy. Soft determinism mimics freedom, while probability mimics rigor. There should be honesty about this. Probability supplies only the appearance of certainty. It cannot achieve it.

IN a certain sense, the standard model in quantum physics resembles the Ptolemaic system. They are both highly complex systems that work well on a practical level. But by their very complexity and practical utility, they impede any radical new approach to the problems they represent. It took more than a millennia to overcome the Ptolemaic view of the heavens.

THE Ptolemaic theory was not wrong. It was a theory that was so generally adequate in portraying what could be seen in the heavens, the human mind could not progress beyond it. So beware of the standard model in modern physics. Both these ideas—the Ptolemaic theory and the standard model—appear to have been or to be massive agglomerations of minute adjustments. It is best to be wary of any such a flexible but over-weighted theory, lest it turn out to be intractable.

THE object of physical science is to work with dynamic relations, not with a static condition. Thus its focus is on the concept of energy. But the energy of physical science remains a materially limited concept. Beyond that is the unfathomed ground of conscious experience.

ENERGY is change. And time is space structured by change.

THERE is no such thing as energy. What is actually measured in terms of energy is change through time in the properties of substances extended in space. The observed change is quantified for the convenience of a future manipulation of the process. But unfortunately, the quantification is often treated as though it were itself an extended substance.

TO declare that energy is simply a concept for change is not to be deliberately naive. The complex relations underscored by the scientific ideas of work, force, and energy are sufficiently understood by those who employ them. But to make the statement that energy is no more than another word for change alludes to another matter. It reflects a concern with something other than the business of doing physics. For it applies where there is no need to control some aspect of the physical world or accurately predict its occurrences. Rather, what is desired is an understanding of how human consciousness relates to its content.

WHAT is energy? To consider energy is to consider the relationships of things in space and time. These relationships involve changes, which are explained by means of the concept of energy. There are different kinds of relationships, to be sure. Thus there are different kinds of energy: electrical, mechanical, thermal, etc. The problem lies in inadvertently substituting a term defining changes in relationships between things for a thing in itself. Energy is not a thing.

If the more complex issue of light should be brought into consideration, it would be appropriate to point out that light is a compound concept. Insofar as it is observed in its physical *effects*, it is matter. For it is a property of things which are observed. The light presumed to lie upon any particular thing is experienced as a property of that thing. On the other hand, insofar as this property of an object is referred to as an effect of something acting upon the object, it is light energy. Easily said. But is the energy of light ever really observed?

Take the example of a darkened room into which light is presumably introduced. To assert that something can be seen after the introduction of the light, when that something could not be seen before, is not to speak of the light. It is to express a relationship between the seer and the thing seen. The light supposed as not being present and then present, expresses a relationship between the seer and the thing seen. The thing is not seen in one instance, then seen in a different instance.

As another example of such a physical change, take an apple. When dropped into a glass pitcher filled with water, it is thought to become distorted. The energy of light in this and the above cases is simply a means for expressing a change in the relationship between the seer and the object seen.

The change is attributed to the effects of energy, in this case light energy. For otherwise, such an observation in the changes of light is simply a description of altering properties of a thing. As properties of a thing, light or dark and one shape or another shape are no different than sweet or sour.

But because of a proportional regularity which can be observed in the relations of things which change from one state or set of properties to another, the relations between the two states or sets of properties may be expressed quantitatively. Thus in experience a person moves from a thing not seen to the thing seen. Or from a thing seen to the thing not seen.

Or from a thing seen to the same thing seen differently. And each of these changes will be uniform in its relations. Should any such process of change be repeated in the same circumstances, it will be the same in its relations. Hence a regularity in quantification and the origin of the concept of energy.

ALL combined perceptions brought before the mind are referred to as things, be they direct physical impressions, or independent imaginative representations, or conceptual. In fact, for anything to be meaningfully perceived or thought about, physical perceptions must enter the mind combined as an image, where they may be transformed into a different image not understood to be encountered in the physical realm, or where either an original image or a transformed one may be translated into a concept. Thus every image or concept, however transformed or abstract, can be referred to as originating in an encounter with something in the objective physical realm of experience.

So any alteration in what passes before the mind from one image or concept of a thing to another, however original the images or abstract the concepts may be, is what is accounted for by change. This is true even of changes in the perceptions of objective experience. For, to be meaningfully perceived, they are registered in the mind as images.

Likewise, any supposed event, involving a series of images, and which is recognized in the mind by means of a transition in thought from one image to the next, is yet a relationship between things. This is so even when it is a strictly conceptual relationship, such as the following. If p then q. Let p be affirmed. Therefore q. For concepts are images under strict definitional rule.

In this particular sequence, which involves a type of change, p and q represent either things, or states of things. They, or their prototypes, were first encountered as something in experience. Then they were abstracted from that source and generalized. In any case, both perceptions and thoughts take place in the mind in the same manner.

And such a related series of thoughts is quantified mathematically when it is understood to represent physical change, and when it is held to be proportionally uniform as an expression of that change as repeatedly observed. When this is the case, such a physical relationship is conceptualized as an energy relationship.

IN physical science, the wave concept describes energy in terms of space and time—i.e. wavelength, amplitude, and frequency—while the concept of point mass gives it a locus in space and time but leaves it devoid of either. For, in the latter case, the energy is considered only as originating in a point mass, as between two extended bodies. The mass, not the magnitude (or extension) of the bodies is what is significant.

Examples of the former would be electromagnetic phenomena, sound, or ripples spreading from a stone dropped into water. An example of the latter would be gravitation as understood by Isaac Newton. Einstein's conception of light as a particle, or photon, notwithstanding, to mix the two descriptions of energy and think them somehow the same is to form a contradiction.

IN science there is no such thing as absolute truth. It is not necessary for a scientific theory to be true to be effective. It need only gather the greatest amount of experimentally verifiable data under the most clearly integrated and least complex set of laws. When more data can be gathered under a theory which expresses a system of fewer and less complex laws, the new theory replaces the old.

Atoms and their particles, such as electrons, do not need to exist to be useful for explaining various phenomena in chemistry, physical science, and electronics. However, they do provide a mental picture, a construct which, if carefully integrated with other useful models, can be expanded upon as experimental evidence and theoretical sophistication increase. So, until there are better models, these will remain.

THERE is a peculiar quality of unimaginative overreach in modern science. It derives from the belief that science is firmly on the path of absolute truth.

SCIENCE is a beautiful body of knowledge. It need only be remembered that false and inappropriate values should not be attached to it.

THERE is no such thing as a lack of underlying unity in thought. An example would be as follows. Each of the concepts of sameness and opposite requires an implied element of similarity—a field of shared meaning for any ideas within its purview. This is rather obvious with the concept of sameness. For one object resembles another by means of shared properties.

But with the concept of oppositeness, it is also true. Take existence and nonexistence. According to the law of the excluded middle, to assert that a thing either is or is not is to imply no alternative to a yes or no response to its existence. For existence and nonexistence are opposing conditions.

But how can opposing conditions be spoken of if there is not any common ground between them? The common ground in this case lies in the overall question of existence. A non-existing thing is simply a reference to an existing thing. It is the existing thing which is said to not be existent.

So it is with any thought structure, any logical progression. There must be an underlying unity. And this has interesting implications for the realm of the subatomic. What it says is: The question is not whether or not nature is causal. The question is whether or not it is logical. If a person is going to think in a satisfactory manner about natural processes—that is, if she is going to think with some degree of continuity, sufficiency, and completeness—she is going to have to assume there is an underlying unity.

If she does not find it, if experimental evidence appears to belie it, then she must reexamine her preconceptions. Did she enter upon the experimental process with the right theoretical framework or with a correct understanding of the nature of the phenomena under consideration and of the apparatus used to observe them?

WHEN an effort is made to understand flux, or the physical realm of universal change, it is the human mind attempting through its material view of things to understand their underlying dynamic. Modern physics has moved closer to this dynamic in its attempt to describe change in terms of force or energy. In fact, it has been moving increasingly toward reducing its concepts of force and energy to the pure relations of mathematical expression alone.

But the problem with this is that change, not a material substance, is what is being reduced to a mathematical protocol. Force, energy, and mass are not material substances. They are expressions of relation. These relations are found in the human mind, though they are recognized as operative in the material world. The material world is the realm of objective experience.

But as science probes deeper into the material realm, it approaches the original dynamic from which the material is expressed. This dynamic is spirit. And it is presented to human awareness in an original stream of sensation. The stream of sensation is the time-limited human mind. But these sensations are an expression of the spiritual dynamic. However, they are not the dynamic itself. Thus the relations of the dynamic are not those of the material realm.

If the human mind were not limited in its capability by seeing the world only through time's agency, it would perceive the dynamic immediately. Or to be more exact, it would perceive an all-encompassing material expression of the dynamic. Time would then be seen for what it is—a mode of relating things through an unfolding process of change. For two states of change cannot be concurrent in human awareness.

If a person could hold together in his mind all the constituent elements of the material expression of the dynamic, seeing all its relations of change at once, that person would have arrived at a condition of pure knowing, though it would be a knowing limited to the material. Pure knowing in this sense is the material expression of the spiritual dynamic as seen through the perspective of an all-encompassing exhibition of its relations. In other words, it is a material view which is not sequentially limited by time.

This is the view of things which the physical concept of a space-time continuum attempts to approach by means of an integrated web of mathematical relations. But it is a view which is insufficient. For it must ultimately be trans-relational, since there is no ongoing change to define any relations within it. Such a view is a static view. It is therefore devoid of the concepts of energy and mass.

THE way a spoon looks in a glass of water as opposed to the way it looks out of the glass. If the theory of refraction is ignored, or any other supposed explanation, then the spoon exhibits two realities. So the question is, which is the true nature of the spoon? A person would likely choose to give the spoon out of the glass priority in importance because nothing like water or glass stands between that spoon and his perception of it. Thus the spoon out of the glass is his simplest perception of the spoon. Therefore, it is given priority.

Not so the subatomic world. Who has directly experienced it? There is always an intervening apparatus for observation. And it is inevitably accompanied by a string of explanations. For example, it is expected that a certain subatomic particle should behave a certain way. Yet sometimes it behaves another way. In explaining such an anomaly, does anyone have a sound experiential sense of what that particle is as compared to what he has of a chair?

There is a theory, its terminology largely derived from macrophysical experience. And the conceptual components of that theory stand between an observer and what he is trying to observe. Thus the extended theory composed of those components does not quite fit. Perhaps it is because the original theory, when applied to macrophysical phenomena, was being applied without sufficiently close observation. Certain subtleties that appear even in the macrophysical world were overlooked. At the microphysical level, they have come glaringly to the fore.

Theory is a product of the human mind in its material mode of analysis. If this material mode of analysis should be the problem, then perhaps a different mental approach is required. There must be some kind of a relationship between human consciousness and the subatomic world which renders a strictly material analysis inadequate.

So human consciousness would in this sense be a mediating environment between the observer and what is observed. For the role of consciousness could not be ignored. Consequently, subatomic material phenomena are experienced through the medium of consciousness in such a way that they must be understood in its terms. The material phenomena must in some sense be spiritualized.

Analysis and the limitation, division, and comparison of material things which make analysis possible are the means by which the physical realm of space and time is perceived and processed by the human mind. So, regardless of whether or not the material world should exist on its own terms, the finite material realm of space and time is of the human mind's own making. For, inasmuch as such a realm is comprehended by that mind, it is a mental representation.

Conversely, the unity of consciousness is boundless and indivisible. It is a transcendent realm which, when considered in itself irrespective of its content, takes the mind beyond the finite material realm of space and time. In this spiritual realm, nothing is divided, nothing has limitations. Thus the spiritual unity of consciousness is an absolute in which no analysis is applicable. This is why it transcends the finite material world. For there is no finitude in a realm of spiritual unity.

It would seem that it is for this reason that causal anomalies exist in the subatomic world which cannot be explained in the usual way. For what is observed is an expression of both consciousness and material observation. Thus any attempt to probe into the subatomic world transcends space and time at least in part. And all the categories by which things are measured, recognized, and placed in some sort of causal order become confused.

In other words, a question arises: if the material relations of space and time are transcended by the mind, even if only in part, must not the observed phenomena be located outside these relations? They will partake of the realm of spirit, or consciousness. So how can anything in an all-encompassing and unifying oneness be definitively determined? Inasmuch as it partakes of the immaterial it cannot. There is a material uncertainty in this spiritual crossover precisely because there is the participation of an absolute unity, which is not a condition under which the material can be conceived.

An understanding of the mechanisms of the material world is based on analysis. Analysis implies limitation. And limitation yields definition: this is such-and-such as opposed to that which is a different such-and-such. So any apparent indeterminacy characteristic of subatomic phenomena is a result of the human mind having—at least in part—penetrated beyond the material to a realm of absolute, unlimited unity. That absolute, unlimited unity is consciousness, or spirit.

It is a realm of pure consciousness, an environment of human awareness where the tools of intellect, which are analysis, limitation, and definition, are inapplicable. Though causally incomprehensible, this situation can nevertheless be bridged with mathematical probability, just as gravity could be mathematically described by Newton without his defining it.

But in doing this, a bridge is being created which reaches from solid ground into mist. The bridge itself holds. So it can be used to build lasers, just as Newton's formulas can be used to journey to the moon, Mars, or beyond. But what the mist actually represents may never really be understood by means of intellectual analysis. Thus the Buddha experienced spiritual unity. But he never defined it. No mystic ever has.

THERE is a curious recurrence in physical science. A component of the formula for the surface area of a sphere ($A = 4 \pi r^2$), which is radius squared (or distance squared), appears more than once in scientific relations. For example, there is the inverse square in Newton's law of universal gravitation ($F \sim m_1 m_2 / r^2$). And it appears again in Coulomb's law of electrical force ($F \sim q_1 q_2 / r^2$).

So it would seem that the implied conception of space, as extended from any particular point of reference, bears a relationship to the idea of an expanding spherical surface. For, given the inverse square, the greater the distance, the larger the spherical surface a particular force must be distributed over.

What is of interest is that the distribution of a force calculated from some point to another in all directions, all such directions being equal and thus equivalent to radii, would describe the area of the surface of a sphere. This may seem too obvious to deserve mention. But its interest lies in what it reveals about the human mind's role in both the perception and conceptualization of space. It appears that the limits of the human mind are inevitably involved in the mind's discoveries concerning the physical world.

THE diminution in gravitational force at any distance from a body considered as the origin of that force is proportional to the force being spread over the surface of an enlarging sphere. The force diminishes as the surface of the sphere is expanding away from a point lying at its center and the center of the volume of the body.

THE formula for the surface area of a sphere is $A = 4\pi r^2$. The use of pi in this formula reflects the fact that the sphere's surface is spherical. In other words, it is circular at all points. This is demonstrated by the fact that any intersection between a plane and the sphere will describe the circumference of a circle on the plane at the locus of intersection.

The radius of the sphere also expresses a similar function to that of the radius of a circle. For it extends from the center of the sphere to its surface, just as the radius of a circle extends from its center to its circumference, which might be thought of as its outer surface. So, when computing the surface area of a sphere, the fact that the radius of the sphere is squared reflects a relationship between the area of the sphere and the area of the planar surface of a circle—i.e. the area within the latter's circumference. For to find that area the radius is also squared. It is as if a sphere had been flattened to the two dimensions of a circle.

What is of interest here is that if a force, like gravity, were to be calculated as spreading outward from a point in three-dimensional space, it would decrease at any specific distance from its point of origin in accordance with the inverse of the square of the distance. In effect, the force is dissipating throughout three-dimensional space. This universal three-dimensional distribution and uniform decrease in strength of the force can be represented by the expanding surface of a sphere.

It is as if to say that the force has to be distributed over more of a three-dimensional area in accordance with its distance from its point of origin. So the force's relative strength would be that of any point on the surface of a sphere, the points of which occupy the three dimensions of space, and all the points of which are at the same distance from its center. Hence Newton's inverse square law for gravitation and the fact that the electrostatic force between two charges also obeys an inverse square law in distance.

This relationship between the calculation of force at a distance from its point of origin and a calculation of the enlarging surface of a sphere suggests that the two formulas are related and that they are both products of the way the human mind thinks. So a question arises. Is the human understanding of both mathematics and physical science more a function of the mind than of the senses?

SOME of the anomalies encountered at the quantum level have had a shadowy, overlooked existence in classical physics. But they have not been dealt with. For example, in relation to matters of uncertainty and entanglement at the quantum level, it is possible to suggest that these issues either exist, or potentially exist, in the classical physical realm.

Is it truly possible to know at once the velocity and location of any projectile? Is the motion of a projectile, however minute the time segment under consideration, not an ongoing change of location? If something is moving, its precise location cannot be determined. For its location to be determined, it would need to be in a state of rest.

This would appear to involve a contradiction. For how can movement and a state of rest be the same? And what about instantaneous velocity? Since time and distance are necessary constituents of velocity, what would an instantaneous velocity be with no passage of time and no distance covered?

The two closely related concepts which this example exhibits are distance and location, an indisputably important set of concepts in classical physics. So perhaps the problem separating the two levels of physical science lies in these concepts, which are so much taken for granted where they have been employed for centuries. Whereas, they are more recently introduced at the quantum level.

For example, if two photons of a decaying pion of neutral charge are observed in a laboratory to be flying apart, opposite in every respect, thus behaving like one superimposed system, then why, in spite of experimental observations, should it be assumed that there is any distance between them? There is simply a *distinction*, expressed in the experimental results as an apparent ongoing change in distance.

Distance lies between two locations, with other intermediate and uniformly contiguous locations uniting these extremes. Conversely, location is distance from another location, even where there is contact between the two locations. Moreover, distance is necessary to any concept of motion, which traverses a chain of contiguous locations.

Thus distance and location are inseparable. When one of these concepts is employed, the other inevitably lies hidden within it. So two identical and opposed aspects of one thing could only express individual distinction by means of separate location. And a difference in location implies distance. Moreover, a change in distance illustrates the distinction.

Distance and location play a ubiquitous role in physical mechanics. They underlie the structure of causal relationships. One thing cannot cause another unless they are differently located, contiguous in some way, but not overlapping. So, if these concepts should be what establish a ground for causal uniformity at the classical level of physical science, could it be a misapplication of the same concepts which results in an interpretation of anomalous behavior at the quantum level?

This problem of a shifting role in terminology may have been overlooked because the phenomenal relations being observed at the classical level were relatively crude. And the concepts were tailored to fit that crudeness. Perhaps it is the case that these concepts of distance and location need a greater refinement for use at the quantum level. Or perhaps they do not apply.

Moreover, the surrounding conceptual language used to describe such matters at the classical level may also have been fitted to the same crudeness and will not function comfortably at the quantum level. It is in this light that a closer scrutiny should be applied to distance, location, and related concepts.

For it should be understood that distance, and consequently location, are, in their most fundamental classical sense, concepts designed to individualize contiguous extensions of a visual and tactile variety. They are the means by which the human mind makes distinctions between objects.

That is to say, they determine relationships between objects in geometrical space, a space recognized and expressed in terms of the human senses. So it should be asked, does this geometrical space apply in the same way at the quantum level? What distance is there between the left and right sides of a dimensionless electron, photon, etc.?

So it may be that these concepts do not apply at all where it would seem that they are, in fact, meaningless—i.e. where particles are not extended objects. For it is not clear that certain fundamental particles, such as electrons, have dimension of any sort. And if they do not have dimension, can it be maintained that they have a location, even a statistical location?

Is location not a factor of dimension, or dimension of location? As dimensionless entities, quantum particles are reduced to expressions of relation, not to something which can be related. An electron is a relation of forces, or of one force to others. The relation varies dynamically in various contexts. But it is still a relation.

So it may be that it was in this way that, when the conceptual apparatus of macrophysics was brought into microphysics, it broke down at the microphysical level. This breakdown, or unfitness of the concepts for their extended role, was due to the fact that reducing the application of the original language to extremely subtle distinctions undermined those very concepts, particularly those of space and a general notion of causality based on changes in spatial extensions. For these cruder concepts did not fit the new subtleties. Yet it was presumed that they should be retained in some manner.

The reason for this problem is that language in any form is incapable of encompassing the whole of reality. There is always something outside of its range. So in its specified use, it not only must be, but is tailored to fit a less than universal field. But when this restriction of range is ignored, a disparity between the language and its phenomenal reference will become evident in extreme applications. For the language cannot then be used to adequately describe the observed phenomena.

The problem then extends to quantitative relations. What this means is that the proportional relationships which are understood to hold between the original concepts do not accord with those which are observed in the new and indirect sensory phenomena. This disparity results from the fact that the new phenomena are subsumed under older concepts whose meaning and interrelationship is inapplicable to them.

In other words, the relationship between the classical concepts and the relationship between the quantum phenomena should both be expressed in some mathematical form. But a logical consistency between the mathematics employed in the classical application and the mathematics which might have been employed in interpreting the experimental quantum evidence cannot be established. For there is a disparity of applied meaning which governs the quantitative relations in each situation. So statistical reasoning becomes a necessary substitute for mathematical rigor in the latter case. This disturbs the causal thinking mind, but does not impede technical progress.

To extend matters further, it can be argued that the anomalies in the quantum sphere occur regardless of experimental method or the language used to describe them. In addition, it can be insisted that these seemingly strange occurrences are ontic and not merely phenomenal or conceptual. It can also be assumed that nothing conceptual or mathematical can be done about it. But if such assertions are made, then certain questions ought to be asked in support of them.

For as long as these questions remain unanswered, they insinuate doubt. In other words, they will continue to trouble minds which seek logical consistency in thought. Such minds want to know: is reality causal or is it statistical? If it is statistical, this raises implications concerning the reach of human understanding. Perhaps overmuch statistical thinking will become so cumbrous as to impede progress at some future time. So, if possible, this doubt must be firmly removed from consideration.

The questions are as follows. Are these anomalies truly inevitable? Or are they a result of biased observation and interpretation? In other words, are they or are they not the outcome of a particular observational approach which is already tainted by the conceptual apparatus which accompanies it, creating the unwonted results?

And if not, the anomalies must exist throughout the physical realm. So why were they overlooked in classical physics? Surely both classical and quantum physics must share a logical consistency. For it is not likely to be the case that the former should turn out to be nothing more than a crude and inaccurate expression of the latter, as is sometimes presently postulated.

THE law of inertia is an hypothesis, the conceptual foundations of which are ideal. Moreover, its two propositions would seem to be mutually exclusive. The first proposition states that if something is in a state of rest, it will remain in a state of rest until a force imparts motion to it. The second proposition states that if this something is in uniform motion, it will remain in uniform motion until its motion is altered by another force.

This law of inertia freed modern physics from the physical anthropomorphism of the ancient and medieval worlds. Or did it? Are human beings ever free from anthropomorphism? Through whose mind are they going to analyze the world, if not a human mind? Through whose eyes do they see the universe? Of course, the universe cannot be seen, but only portions of it, the mind of the perceiver projecting the whole through imagination—that is, through an assumption of a final unity for all things.

Now the principal question is this: is there such a thing as a state of rest? For both propositions do involve background material which is posited as being in a state of rest. For something to be in a state of motion, it must be in that state relative to something else which is in a state of rest. Thus, for something to be in a state of uniform motion, this relationship must be its defining condition.

Furthermore, it might be asked, what is the character of a relative state of rest? This is a question raised by the concept of multiple inertial systems, each system depending upon a different point of reference. Whatever the point of reference may be, it is to be assumed that there is an integration between all inertial systems. Hence the Lorentz transformation, which provides a means of making a transition from one inertial system to another.

Since time and change lie at the heart of human experience, any state of rest must occur in a universe which registers an ongoing process of unfolding time. This time, though differing in its measure between inertial systems, is ubiquitous, linking all states of motion and rest. Moreover, the experience of time necessitates that there cannot be a state of rest everywhere. For time implies change, which involves motion.

Now, if a person should look out upon her world in act or imagination and see something at rest, she would generally recognize that something as positioned against an unvarying background in its immediate vicinity. That is to say, the something which is at rest would be at a specific and unvarying near or far distance from something else which is also at rest. This is assuming, of course, that a reference point is not simply chosen as a state of rest relative to other things in motion and without reference to anything else not in motion, as was the case when the earth was considered to be the center of the universe.

So it is true that one thing alone could be said to be at rest, if there were no other stationary reference and other things in its vicinity moved. But to fix its position and state of rest, some of these moving things must move away from it in a uniform manner. Such circumstances would establish its relative state of rest. Thus the object at rest would not appear to need a reference to anything else at rest. But this is a somewhat illusory condition because the uniformity of motion in those other things does itself imply a form of rest.

What this means is that there is in each of the uniformly moving objects but one kind of change: a motion which is unvarying in character. In regard to any other possible change (or motion) affecting any of these objects, the object in question must be assumed to be in a condition of rest. Thus it does form a background of rest to the original object at rest. And of course, the original object at rest provides a background of rest to it.

Accordingly, if a person sees or imagines something in uniform motion, she posits it as moving against an unvarying background: either an object at rest or another object in uniform motion. Were the background object to accelerate or change direction—without any other point of reference but the original moving object being involved—the acceleration or change in direction could be attributed to the original moving object.

But were the background object understood to be moving in a uniform motion relative to the original uniformly moving object, the original uniformly moving object could be posited as being in a state of rest, its motion attributed to the other. (No further mention will be made concerning acceleration or other changes in motion, since they would merely complicate matters without changing the fundamental character of these relations.)

Thus, given this reciprocal relationship between uniform motion and rest, the difference between the uniform state of motion and a state of rest lies in the uniformly varying distance or distances between the moving object and whatever object or objects form a stationary background to it. For, as regards motion, these distances are in a state of continuous change.

This state of continuous change renders positioning the moving object vis-à-vis its background an impossibility. For, however precise the observation, the moving object changes position as it is being observed. Whereas the coordinate relations between an unmoving object and its background—i.e. between two unmoving entities—do not change.

This difference in the capacity of an observer to position a moving and an unmoving object is due to a subtle contradiction between the concept of motion, which is continuous change, and the concept of a state of rest, which involves no change. They are not compatible mental representations. And the reason for this lies in their mutually exclusive character. Change accords with objective human experience. Rest does not. It is subjective, an hypothesis which is ideal, or strictly mental, in character.

This problem expresses the uncomfortable position in which the human mind finds itself in regard to the two propositions of the law of inertia. For it represents a single property affecting one proposition which does not affect the other. Thus, under less than the strictest scrutiny, the two propositions appear to exhibit a condition of intellectual compatibility which does not hold between them.

The two propositions of the inertial law provide that there should be either movement or locality in the forms of uniform motion or rest. But there cannot be both in the same object simultaneously. Thus there can be no definable bridge between the two states. There is either the phenomenon of change involved in a state of motion, or there is an absence of it in the state of rest. It is this which creates a vital and disturbing distinction between the two states.

Now change occurs with motion, but not with a state of rest. For motion is change. Moreover, time is based on the observation of change. So motion is observable time. And time does not stop in the human universe. So, even if the mind should contemplate an object at rest, time would presumably continue. But in stating the specific conditions of the inertial law, this is not the case. For, within the "state of rest" portion of the statement, time is abstracted from that state.

In framing this law, the mind appears to objectively posit a state of rest involving no motion. But in truth, while it appears to posit the state of rest against a fixed objective background where nothing in the immediate environment of the state of rest is in motion, it is in fact positing the state of rest subjectively against the changing stream of its own thought. In other words, the changing stream of thought provides the motion which supports a real world environment for the state of rest. Time is thus present, but removed to the realm of the subjective.

Change is motion, however circumscribed and apparently stationary its affected elements may appear to be, as in the subtle alterations of figures on the face of a digital clock. For the figures seem to change instantaneously, but do not. There is a gradual movement in the transition from one number to the next.

In addition to the observation that this change is motion, is the fact that all change is motion. Moreover, a relative motion between two sources of change is the measure of time. Thus time is motion. Of course, this does not mean that a motion can always be observed. It may be either too quick or too slow.

Nevertheless, change is motion. And time is observable by means of change. Thus time is motion. Accordingly, it is the changing stream of thought which subjectively imparts a temporal character to an immobile object set against an immobile background. That temporal character is the durance of the state of rest. This durance is not objective, but in relation to the mind.

That is, the time involved in the state of rest is relative to the thought stream, but not to the physical circumstances in which the state of rest is posited. It is therefore subjective in character. This subjective registering of time is what retains the all important presence of durance in respect to the objective domain of the law. But as time is nevertheless not considered within the objective statement of the inertial concept of a state of rest, the law is ideal rather than experiential.

Now it is only because an objective realm is set apart from the subjectivity of the mind, that an inertial law of uniform motion can be objectively put forth. For its relations are not subjective. It is an objective law. But the situation is not the same concerning the inertial law of rest, which objectively assumes no change. It is not relevant whether there *could be* change elsewhere. No change is posited within this portion of the law of inertia.

Yet there can be no such thing in human experience as no change. For that would imply no passage of time. Thus arises a problem of mutual exclusiveness in the statements of the two separate propositions of the law of inertia. They are mutually exclusive because, while one of them accepts objective change, which involves an inevitable passage of time, the other ignores it.

So it is the human mind which anthropomorphically frames these apparently conflicting statements. First it posits the moving object and the objective conditions of its background in a manner which involves motion, which is change. That motion is its registering of time. So, by doing this, it posits time in an objective manner.

But then the mind shifts its involvement in stating the law of rest. It does this by abstracting time from the objective situation, bringing it into a subjective condition by omitting any objective indication of change, or unfolding time. Having done this, it posits the objective conditions of the motionless object and its background in a manner which does not involve objective time.

So finally, in conclusion to this discussion, it may be further noted that both propositions of the law of inertia are rendered ideal in character. For, upon closer examination, it can be seen that both states posit a stationary background which is presumed to be in a state of rest. Were an attempt made to logically establish the state of rest of the background material, it would lead into the same ideality. Thus it can be seen that the entire inertial hypothesis is based on an ideal concept of a state of rest.

The whole issue may best be understood in the following manner. A computer on a desk appears to be in a state of rest vis-à-vis the desk. And vice versa, the desk appears to be in a state of rest vis-à-vis the computer. But if a person considers the minute particles of each, she may seriously conjecture that some or all of them are in a state of change—i.e. motion. Thus the relationship of rest between the computer and the desk is only apparent. It is an idealization.

It may be further conjectured that many other things besides the computer and desk are in a state of general flux, or change in all directions. For that is the character of experience. Thus the reciprocal relationship between these two things (the computer and the desk), on the one hand, and the general flux, on the other, is not one of rest. Nor is it one of a uniformity of change. Therefore, can it be maintained that a condition of rest should in any way be held valid for the computer and desk?

Quite the contrary. In human experience, there is universal change. And rest is a mere appearance. For the fundamental character of the general flux is that time, which is change and motion, pervades all things. If this were not so, some things would be without time. Though given the multiplex character of such change, a uniform measure of time could not be deduced from it.

Therefore all things undergo continual change in their mutual relations. And anything supposed to be otherwise is a result of seeing only a very limited part of the whole and abstracting time away from that appearance. Consequently, it is appearances alone which may be held to be in a state of rest.

IT is said that hope springs eternal. But why? What is it which in the midst of an oppressive cycle of events, urges an individual on when she ought to give up? Is it the survival instinct? If so, why should any creature want to persevere, let alone survive? Is it evolution? But how did evolution select what was originally not there: the desire to be there? And how could it have selected anything at all without that desire? There is more to the human spirit, to the animal spirit, perhaps to plants, than a material explanation can reveal.

TOTAL instinct is no match for the infinite variability of environmental circumstance. Thus all sentient life, even an ant or an ameba, has some independent awareness which it can freely act upon.

A HIGHER organism responds in its development not only to environmental pressures and the physical constraints of internal necessity (i.e. to its genetic makeup), but also to an organization individually peculiar to itself. For the whole creature—emotions, senses, nervous system, and whatever lies yet unseen by the eye of science—is a mentality. Thus it is not an empty box full of diverse, unrelated traits, but a container enclosing a unified inclination which, while developing, shapes the evolving course of its behavior.

So if temperament—the inner dynamic of the individual creature—is involved in natural selection, how large a role does it play? One need only conceive of an animal disposed by curiosity, sensual impulse, and an overall inner compulsion to interpret and interact with its environment in varying degrees which are relative to its individual character.

This is sufficient to suggest a recognition of the importance of the organism's unique inner nature. The interaction between experience and genotype might not only have an influence on the developing phenotype of that individual. But by means of a feedback loop, perhaps it might have an influence on heritable characteristics as well. Can it be certain no such feedback mechanism exists in a complex organism possessed of interacting endocrine and nervous systems?

Thus the peculiar coloring of each individual will, or a selective mix of such wills in various members of a species, may be of primary importance in the mix of circumstances which contributes to the evolutionary development of a species genotype. In fact, it may be found to be true of even the most rudimentarily organized of sentient creatures. Perhaps an individual ant, or even an individual ameba, contributes slightly to genotypic differentiation in this way, undetected by human observation.

MODERN evolutionary theory appears to adhere faithfully to Charles Darwin's notion of natural selection. But it strays considerably from his views concerning variation. Such physically reductionist processes as random mutation and genetic drift seem to be a principal concern of the Neo-Darwinist consensus. They are based on Mendelian genetics. But Darwin seemed to show a marked predilection in some cases towards the notion of acquired characteristics. And it may not have had anything to do with his ignorance of Mendel's work.

This view is evident in the early chapters of *The Descent of Man* and in *The Expression of the Emotions in Man and Animals*. In the latter, particularly, he demonstrates a strong preference for the idea that a habit can be acquired and passed on individually as an instinct. Of course, in such a circumstance, natural selection would remain the controlling factor in the radiation of the acquired trait through a population. Nevertheless, as one of the means of accounting for variation, it is a view which seems incompatible with the strict interpretation of the reductionist program.

Nor does this program account for a simple fact, which is the origin of the evolutionary process. If the first organisms were to pass on their traits, if they were to achieve success in preference to whatever was their nearest kindred, they would need to have a will to do so. They would need an inner impulse to forge ahead, to make use of whatever new advantage they had, and survive. But from what source would this characteristic have arisen in the very earliest appearance of a living organism?

Only if mind, already potentially inherent in all things, even a stone, were to be given open expression in a living form, could this be possible. If this mind was unity and sought unity in itself, it would seek to preserve itself, its unified expression as an organism. Such a mind in its simplest form is spirit, or consciousness. For consciousness is a unity.

IS life evolutionarily progressive toward perfection? In the material sense, it is not. Nevertheless, over time, the sum of increasingly complex types of organisms has grown. And life forms at each more complex level of development can be defined as expressing a greater degree of internalization of their environment.

So it can be said that every higher life form incorporates within itself a more encompassing schema of its world. And in general, whatever portion of this schema may be fixed from the inception of an individual organism or may develop over the duration of its existence through learning, is the means by which the organism interacts with its environment.

However, as already stated, the growth in complexity of an organism cannot be described as a progression toward the material perfection of that organism. For this development is of a purely mechanistic character. A more efficient machine is not more perfect. It is simply more efficient in some particular way, often at the cost of other applications.

This is why organisms are known to devolve in complexity, as well as being known to increase in it. For perfection is not a material concept. It is an integrated unity which is beyond that of the material. Thus it is a spiritual concept. It represents a movement toward the unity of spirit.

Because all forms of life—indeed, all things—are grounded in spirit, they are an expression of spirit. And since there is but one spirit, there is but one standard of perfection. That standard is a more complete expression of spirit. Thus their perfection is their movement toward a more complete expression of spirit.

So how does a human being fit into this? Materially, she is no better than any other form of life. But she appears to be more organized, more complex and efficient in terms of awareness, not only environmentally, but personally. This complexity and efficiency of personal awareness is directed toward a greater awareness of her conscious self: her self as spirit. Throughout her material existence, she continues to grow in this way by means of learning. So, in exercising this awareness, she incorporates more within herself than the material.

Hence her expectation that the process should continue, her fear that it might not. Her hope for a continued spiritual existence lies in the fact that all forms of life, including herself, are an expression of spirit. What they are, what they strive for, perhaps unbeknownst to many lesser forms, is that expression. The highest form of that expression is self-awareness as spirit.

This is not an intellectual condition, except in the sense that an expanded self-awareness penetrates into spiritual awareness. In doing so, it is aided and abetted by conceptualization. For it must be thought about. But it is not conceptual in its final expression. For conceptual schemes are forever subject to amendment. Rather, it is a direct awareness of one's grounding in spirit, an awareness which allows one to act upon that grounding in the same manner as the internalization of the material environment enables one to act within the material.

JANE Goodall either invented a new or rediscovered an old and forgotten scientific method. It can be called empathetic reasoning. This is somewhat different from what had been up to her time the usual practice of empirical investigation in field biology. The prior practice was reductionist, based on the idea that physical science lies at the basis of all reality. In physical science, where a strictly objective, or material, empirical investigation works best, a few isolated phenomena are singled out and controlled for observation. In this way, laws of the physical universe can be codified.

But a question arises: what if it is not possible to isolate individual phenomena in some things which are placed under study? This is what happens in certain aspects of life sciences like biology and physiology. Sometimes precisely what causes what cannot be determined. For a direct cause-and-effect relationship cannot be singled out.

Thus, when an investigator progresses to a study of behavior, particularly the behavior of the more complex organisms, like chimpanzees, it is hard to say with the degree of certainty which is expected in a physical science why it is that they do what they do. For a carefully isolated experiment is difficult to set up in which behavioral patterns can be observed with any degree of clarity as to their causes and effects. In special cases, it can be done. And this may create an illusion of progress in the research. But such a method of study inevitably fails to build up a comprehensive, integrated view of the internal character of an animal.

Man is the most complex of all animals presently known and understood. And he is also the investigator. So it might be asked: how well has he come to know himself? How precise in an understanding of human motivation are sciences like psychology and sociology? Statistics are often used in studies related to these fields. But statistics are a way of adding rigor to an investigation which is not exact. For the best statistical analysis cannot isolate cause and effect.

So is there any better way to understand a complex phenomenon like the human spirit? In her method of studying chimpanzees, Jane Goodall demonstrated that there is. She allowed herself to indulge in empathetic responses to the chimpanzee behavior she observed. For example, if a certain animal were rejected by its group, it would be observed to sulk and refuse to eat. Imagining such behavior in a human being, Goodall was able to assume that the animal was feeling lonely and depressed.

This led to further such observations which eventually built up a reliable and integrated model of chimpanzee behavior. Predictions could be made on the basis of this model. This is to say that known behavioral patterns could hone future observations in such a manner as to lead to new and surprising discoveries.

And it is prediction which is any scientific method's most important justification. This supports Goodall's practice. The method she used is reasoning by analogy. She made it clear that it can work where direct analysis is demonstrably impractical. However, it does require a good deal of imagination, which some observers may not possess.

The Mind's Mathematics

IN mathematical formulations, the number four is a symbol which stands for one plus one plus one plus one. All numbers, however large or small, symbolize such an operation. That is why the only substantial entity in this language is simple unity.

MATHEMATICS is a science of unity and division. With the exception of projective geometry, this defines it as a quantitative science. In arithmetic, unity is expressed in the unit one. The unit one is a unity. Division is expressed by means of one, zero, and all the integers, either standing alone or in the form of fractions and decimals. For, other than the unit one and zero, the integers are positive or negative multiples of the unit one.

Digits are the positive integers zero through nine. These ten integers are used as symbols in the expression of all numbers, including decimals and fractions. Thus they impart their character to them. They are even used in the expression of irrational numbers, insofar as irrational numbers can be expressed.

If the unit one is considered in terms of its being one of the integers, then zero is the only anomaly among them. For it is neither a unit nor a multiple of units. It serves as a place holder among the various expressions of numbers. It can represent the absence of a number. Or because the number system is set up in accordance with the ten digits (a base-10 number system), zero can also serve to represent a multiple of ten.

In geometry, unity and division are expressed in terms of spatial extensions. Thus both a continuous straight line and a uniformly curved line are expressions of unity. If a second line is joined to a first in such a manner that it becomes a further extension of the first in its manner of expression, straight or curved, then their joining may be considered a further expression of unity. For the distinction between the two joined lines disappears at the point of juncture.

But it may be the case that two lines do not meet. Or it may be that two straight lines meet at an angle, or that there is a change in the curve of a line. The change in the curve of a line is, in essence, a progressive series of indeterminately small angles. If either of these circumstances occur—the sharp angle or the change in a curve—there is, in effect, more than one line. And multiple lines are a geometric expression of division. For they denote a distinction of parts.

Thus all of enumeration and proportion is implied in the two concepts of unity and division. These concepts accord with the two fundamental intuitions of the mind, which are unity and plurality. This is why mathematics can be said to be a science of unity and division. For in its conceptual buildup, it is a direct expression of these intuitions.

THE Euclidean system is not an exact representation of physical space. Nor is any other geometrical system. They are ideal rather than real. Geometry is a simplification of reality. It is a template, a map, placed over the terrain of reality for the purpose of allowing a negotiation of reality to take place.

A LINE without breadth, as in Euclid's quadrilateral and his triangle, does not exist in nature. It is an idealization. Consider this line of Euclid's which exhibits no breadth. Has one ever been seen? Can it be drawn? No. When it is found in nature, such a line is in fact a quadrilateral having four sides, however narrow its width. So the ends of a line found in nature always express width, just as the narrower sides of a quadrilateral do.

Now, given that a line found in nature is a quadrilateral, let us ask what would happen if a person were to try tapering it to three sides, instead of four. Presumably this would give the line a point on one end which would express no width at its tip. Not so. For in nature this cannot be done.

In nature the tapered line becomes a triangle. And each vertex of the triangle, just like each vertex of a quadrilateral, must have some width at its point, however minute. Otherwise the very tip of the vertex could neither be seen nor drawn nor detected with a microscope. It would not enter into human sensory experience. It could be nothing more than a concept.

Thus, where two lines come together in nature, or where one line narrows to a point, even in a drawing, there must be at least some width at the tip of the vertex. That is one of the reasons why in nature there are not any true triangles. Another reason is that there is no such thing in nature as a straight line. Nor is there a uniformly curved line, for that matter. So triangles are mental idealizations, albeit very useful ones, as ancient Egyptian farmers well knew.

THE basic implication at the heart of the twenty-third definition of Book One of Euclid's *Elements* is that two parallel straight lines are two completely independent lines, understood as such by means of their different spatial locations. So, reasoning from the fifth postulate of that same book, a person may assume the following.

Two interior angles forming an equivalent to two right angles on one side of a straight line intersecting two parallel straight lines can be said to imply a 180° relationship between the parallel lines. This represents an equivalent to a 180° shift in a Cartesian plane. It is as if a point on the x-axis had moved to a position on the same axis which was on the opposite side of the origin.

For the parallel lines, this indicates a condition of sameness, in which the only characteristic distinguishing them is that they are spatially separate. For just as the x-axis on either side of the origin in a Cartesian plane is one line distinguished as two lines by means of the origin, so two parallel lines are distinguished by a separation in Euclidean space.

On the other hand, less than 180° in the interior angles on one side of a straight line intersecting two other straight lines represents a difference in orientation between the two intersected lines. So the two intersected lines are not parallel. For they are differentiated by their individual angles of orientation. Since they meet at some point in space, they are not distinguished by a complete separation in that space.

Another way of stating this is to say that, if two straight lines are joined at an angle of less than 180°, they are two straight lines joined, but not the same.

For if the two lines were joined at 180 degrees, they would be one line.

However, if one nevertheless wishes to distinguish between the two lines joined at 180 degrees, one must either separate them by means of a point of origin, as in a Cartesian plane, or separately locate them in the Euclidean plane in which they are supposed to exist.

By these means, the mind is able to visualize their individual character. Thus it can be seen that the fundamental problem with the twenty-third definition and the fifth postulate is a concern about the character of Euclidean space. For it is a Euclidean conceptualization of space which makes these relations pertinent.

INFINITE means "not finite." When a line is spoken of mistakenly as infinite, what is being referred to is an indeterminate line. Its extent is not known. But because a line is a finite entity composed of finite parts, however minute, the line is finite. The same would be true if an unlimited progression of natural numbers were mistakenly spoken of as infinite. It would be indeterminate rather than infinite because its numerical elements would be finite entities.

The "in-"finite, or "not" finite, is another matter altogether. Can an indeterminate extension of finite segments of a line or of natural numbers be spoken of? Yes it can. Can it truly be said that it is infinite, or not finite? Not in the same frame of reference. Finite and infinite are mutually exclusive terms. This applies to the indeterminately small as well.

THIS discussion is based on the Euclidean conception of space, as that space is understood today. It includes a consideration of angles in terms of degrees. A mention of degrees is to be found nowhere in Euclid's *Elements*. For this reason, the present discussion is philosophical and does not closely follow the reasoning of Euclid insofar as it concerns the manner in which his mathematical proofs are set forth—i.e. propositions derived from one another in a logical sequence.

Though the discussion centers around the issue of parallel lines, and thus the 23rd definition and 5th postulate of Book One of the *Elements*, what is of particular concern here is the Euclidean plane. For it is the Euclidean plane which is the fundamental imaginative ground of Book One (in fact, the first ten books) of the *Elements*.

So it is imperative that a person should keep this plane in mind, when considering Euclid's proofs, the purpose being to investigate the role that the plane played in Euclid's efforts to logically organize his material. That role is of particular interest when, in the 29th proposition of Book One, the issue of the 5th postulate arises in support of the 23rd definition concerning parallel lines.

In regard to the definitions and postulates which introduce Book One of the *Elements*, Euclid employs what are meant to appear as determinate ideas. That is, he uses ideas which can be specifically described, or drawn, with rule and compass. But these ideas only appear to be determinate. For concealed within them are indeterminate elements, elements of speculative thought which cannot be concretely represented.

For example, the definition of a perfect circle appears to be determinate, since a circumference can be described, or drawn, at a specific radius from an initial point. But in computation this idea is found to yield the transcendental number pi, which is an indeterminate quantity. Thus the relationship between the radius and the circumference is indeterminate. And that relationship is the essence of the perfect circle.

A similar sense of indeterminacy holds for the 23rd definition, setting forth the character of parallel straight lines. So, in an indirect support of this definition, straight lines are held to eventually intersect in the 5th postulate, thus establishing what the definition purports not to do and opening a means toward a logical transition to the 23rd definition.

Importantly, the 5th postulate appears to be determinate precisely because its lines are assumed to meet. For these lines describe the two sides of an enclosed angle, however acute or obtuse that angle may be and however long the two sides. The meeting of the two straight lines is established on the basis of another straight line intersecting them. This establishes a relationship of angles.

The interior angles which are formed by this intersection, and which are both on a specified side of the intersecting line, are together less than two right angles. Since in a Euclidean plane the three angles of a triangle together equal two right angles, it may reasonably be assumed that the lines meet on the side which requires a third angle to make that total.

In contrast to this, and according to Euclid's 29th proposition, parallel lines are not supposed to meet because the interior angles on one side of an intersecting straight line together form the equivalent of two right angles. Thus an additional angle would exceed the requirement for a triangle formed in a Euclidean plane. And since the alternate interior angles of the intersecting line are equal, no triangles can be formed on either side of the intersecting line. Therefore, the lines do not meet in either direction of their extension and behave in accordance with the 23rd definition. They are parallel.

Moreover, the exterior angle is equal to the interior and opposite angle on the same side of the intersecting line. This also is true on both sides of the intersecting line. So, in addition to the two intersected lines not forming triangles on either side of the line of intersection, all these conditions indicate something further.

They express a relationship of mutual uniformity of placement between the intersected lines—i.e. a parallel relationship—if it is assumed that they are straight lines and are located in a flat Euclidean plane. For the situation is equivalent to the intersecting line being perpendicular to both the parallel lines and that intersecting line being surrounded by four right angles at each of the points of intersection, making the two parallel lines, in turn, perpendicular to the intersecting line at different points on that line.

Thus the intersected lines produce angles with the intersecting line which total 180° between them. Since this is the full angular complement for a triangle, no third angle can be added to join them together. So, as already mentioned above, they cannot intersect. And it is this which again results in the logical implication which is that of the parallel hypothesis indicated in Euclid's definition of parallel lines:

> Parallel straight lines are straight lines which, being in the same plane and being produced indefinitely in both directions, do not meet one another in either direction.

But it is only a logical implication. For it is lacking in a figurative demonstration.

A person cannot draw two parallel lines out indefinitely. That is why the definition of parallel lines should be called a hypothesis. For, if this definition should only be considered a hypothesis, then it is evident that, unlike the statement of the 5th postulate concerning lines which are not parallel, the two parallel lines of the 29th proposition do not *figuratively* support definition 23. For neither are they drawn out indefinitely.

In other words, they add nothing to it by way of figurative demonstration. In either case, the proposed concept cannot be completed in the imagination. And a concept without an imaginative ground is ultimately meaningless. For by "figurative" is meant that these concepts do not define any kind of determinate linear figure. Which is no more than to say that the "parallel" lines cannot be followed out indefinitely in either direction.

Rather, the parallel lines are simply two separate and indeterminate figures—i.e. two straight lines, which are, as it were, adrift in space but connected in the 29th proposition by the intersecting line length between the points of intersection and by the angles described above. The latter are presumed to position them relative to one another in a flat Euclidean plane in such a manner as to make them parallel, or unable to form a triangle.

So this puts their relationship in space—i.e. in the flat Euclidean plane—in question. For their parallel relationship is presumed, or logically inferred. It cannot be physically demonstrated. Consequently, no imaginative image of it can be formed. And the concept inferred is not grounded on an image.

For example, in the 27th and 28th propositions of Book One, the parallel character of two straight lines is entirely deduced from the parallel definition, the character of a straight line, the definition of a right angle, and the fact that an acute angle is defined as being less than a right angle.

But unmentioned in the background of these two propositions lies the 5th postulate with its reliance upon the relationship of angles between straight lines. That is to say, the behavior of the acute angles described in the 5th postulate is determined by the definition of a right angle and the character of a Euclidean plane. For the definition of a right angle is dependent upon the flat plane. And the right angle is the condition which governs the reasoning concerning all angles—right, acute, and obtuse—and therefore the angles in the 27th and 28th propositions.

In other words, it is assumed that, due to the accepted logic of angles in a flat plane, the supposed parallel lines do not meet as they would in the 5th postulate. But for this reason their relationship remains physically indeterminate, much as the relationship between the radius and the circumference of a perfect circle is physically indeterminate, in spite of a symbolic representation with rule and compass in both cases.

Though in both cases—parallel straight lines and the perfect circle—the indeterminate relationships inherent in each may be logically inferred, they cannot be directly expressed in a physically determinate manner, such as a rational number in the place of pi would make possible in the first instance and a joining of lines in a single figure would make possible in the second.

In the first instance, the irrational, or indeterminate, character of pi is due to the fact that an indeterminate number of radii would be required to establish the uniform curvature of the circumference of a perfect circle. For any distance whatsoever between any two radii would leave the uniformity of the curvature in doubt.

In the second instance, the formation of an angle by the joining of two straight lines establishes the position of the two lines vis-à-vis one another. But if they are not joined, a uniformity of spatial distance between them along the entirety of both their lengths cannot be established because the lengths of the lines cannot be determined.

This is why Euclid's 5th postulate is stated in such a manner as to describe lines which will meet. The character of this description allows for the logical transference of an assumption of determinacy from the 5th postulate to the 29th proposition, where the 5th postulate is introduced, contributing to a logical justification of the parallel lines in the 29th proposition. This in turn provides a justification for the 23rd definition, which sets forth the definition of parallel lines. For it is this definition, like that of the perfect circle, which is in doubt.

In other words, because of the consistent reasoning concerning angles, parallelism should follow from the character of straight lines, of right angles, and the original determinate meeting of lines in the 5th postulate, which stands in opposition to parallel lines. But is this justification of parallelism anything more than an inference? Is it a determinate relationship like the angle, which is a meeting of two lines? Or is there a speculative leap from what is determinate to what is not—i.e. from the meeting of two lines to a parallel relationship between them?

What lies in doubt is the attempt to justify a parallel relationship between straight lines, based upon a definition of right angles and the 5th postulate's circumstances involving angles of intersection. The presumed spatial implications are uncertain. For it is by no means clear as to what a flat plane is without reference to assumptions about such things as right angles and the 5th postulate. Yet a flat plane must be assumed in order to make these assumptions.

So it is in this way that the possibility of parallel lines is suggested. By means of a series of logical inferences from the definition of a right angle and the stated conditions of the intersecting angles of the 5th postulate, a parallel condition of two lines is deduced in proposition 29. However, the parallelism of these lines cannot be physically demonstrated. And if it cannot be physically demonstrated, no concrete imaginative image of it can be formed.

Thus a logically deduced conception of parallel lines is established in support of an ideal definition of the same. It is not unlike the reasoning which takes place in the case of the perfect circle. For neither is the concept of a perfect circle drawn from physical experience. It only appears to be so.

Rather, it also is ideal, as is generally the case with all the definitions and postulates listed in the first book of Euclid's *Elements*. Albeit many of them are simpler idealizations, such as "a point is that which has no part," "a line is a breadthless length," or "to draw a straight line from any point to any point."

In a more complex way, the ideal properties of both the concepts of the perfect circle and parallel lines—such as the relationship between a radius and a circumference, or the opposition of circumstances between lines which meet and lines which do not meet—are brought together under the simple device of conceiving a reciprocality between determinate and indeterminate circumstances.

In the example of the perfect circle, this would involve a determinate radius and an indeterminate circumference or a determinate circumference and an indeterminate radius. This is why the circle must be introduced as a definition. It resembles the definition of the point which has no parts and the definition of the line which has no breadth.

And it is also why the existence of parallel lines is initially introduced as a definition and, even with the aid of the 5th postulate, cannot be given a satisfactory exposition as a theorem. Neither of these—the perfect circle or parallel lines—can be physically demonstrated beyond a credulous acceptance of drawing by rule and compass.

Moreover, insofar as the idealization of concepts in general is concerned, however simple those concepts may appear to be, it is true of all the definitions and postulates of Book One of the *Elements,* and therefore of their derived theorems, that they cannot be made entirely compatible with a human experience of physical reality. For Book One of the *Elements* is a book composed entirely of intellectually rarefied and ideal concepts.

MATHEMATICS provides one of the purest fields for an investigation of the workings of the human mind. So, as one more of many examples which might be presented in illustration of this fact, there is the peculiar character of the imaginary unit *i*, or $\sqrt{-1}$. To understand the function of this imaginary unit, it may be convenient to investigate the role of arithmetical signs in general. For these signs, plus and minus, exhibit vector properties. The vectors which they exhibit express direction. They also reflect magnitude. But they do not determine magnitude, as they do direction.

Now it is multiplication operations in particular which clearly demonstrate this vector property in mathematical computations. A plus sign may represent a direction of increase, as in a statement of the number +5, which indicates an increase of five from zero. This can also be stated as 5, where the plus sign is assumed without representation. But a plus sign can do more than indicate an increase. It may maintain a stability of increase or decrease. For example, in $5 \cdot 5 = 25$ the fives are both positive increases. So, since all signs in the operation are positive, the product, twenty-five, is also a positive increase.

On the other hand, the presence of a minus sign does something different. It may simply indicate a direction of decrease, as in the case of a simple statement of the number –5, which indicates a decrease of five from zero. But it can also function to reverse the direction of a numerical progression from a decrease to an increase or from an increase to a decrease. This directional alteration takes place with the numerical value of the operation being reflected in a change of direction, but without it being quantitatively affected in any way by the sign. The quantitative outcome is effected only by the quantitative elements involved.

For example, in the equation $5 \cdot -5 = -25$, the presence of a minus sign reverses the operation from positive to negative to indicate a numerical decrease. A positive integer (the first five) multiplied by a negative integer (the second five) produces a negative result: a negative integer which is minus twenty-five. Thus the direction of increase in the first number, which is plus five, is reversed in the final result to a direction of decrease, which is minus twenty-five.

Again, in the equation $-5 \cdot -5 = 25$, the presence of a second minus sign reverses the influence of the first, restoring the operation to a numerical increase. In other words, the first negative integer, minus five, is reversed from a direction of decrease to one of increase by the second negative integer, minus five. Thus the result is the positive integer, twenty-five.

But to revert once again to the first example involving a plus sign, it would be appropriate to demonstrate what is meant by a plus sign *not* changing the direction of an operation, when the initial direction of that operation involves a decrease. Let the first example given above in illustration of the character of minus signs, which is $5 \cdot -5 = -25$, be rewritten as $-5 \cdot 5 = -25$. Now the multiplication operation and product remain the same. But the order of signs is not what it was.

Consequently, following the progress of the operation from left to right, as one must do, it can be seen that the first integer is negative: a minus five. Thus the operation begins with a vector of decrease. But it is the second integer which determines the directional outcome of the operation. That second integer is a plus five. So, being positive, it maintains a stability of direction. It leaves the quantitative progression in a condition of decrease. This is indicated in the final result, which is a negative integer: minus twenty-five.

Thus it can be seen that in multiplication operations, the direction of numerical progression toward increase or decrease changes where affected by a minus sign and does not when affected by a plus sign. Moreover, with each additional minus sign brought into an operation, the vector of direction changes repeatedly. But with neither the plus nor the minus does the numerical outcome change. For the outcome is not affected quantitatively by signs. Only the direction of increase or decrease is reflected in any changes.

In other words, the final product is presented in either a condition of increase or decrease. And in each case, it is a simple product of the numbers involved, the outcome remaining quantitatively the same. For, when the signs are ignored, five times five is always twenty-five. It does not matter whether it is a positive or negative quantity. It does not matter whether the product represents a numerical increase or a numerical decrease. The quantitative outcome is the same. The final vector merely points the direction of an overall increase or decrease in quantity.

In addition, it reflects that quantity. So a magnitude is registered by the vector. But it is not determined by these signs. Thus, as this discussion of multiplication by signs demonstrates, a use of plus and minus signs in multiplication is not a matter concerning the quantitative character of numbers, other than to determine their direction of increase or decrease from zero.

Now arithmetical signs work in this way in regard to multiplication, squaring, and their reciprocal operations: division and square roots. So this discussion lends weight to an understanding of the imaginary unit *i*. For the imaginary unit results from one of these operations, namely the taking of a square root.

Consequently, the derivation of an imaginary number can also be understood to demonstrate the independent vector role of plus and minus signs. Note that in making this statement, an emphasis is again being placed upon the independence of these signs, just as it was in the multiplication problems above. For in each of the cases of multiplication, square, division, and square root—the latter of which includes the derivation of the imaginary unit *i*—the functions of the signs are independent of number and thus of whatever may be the quantitative outcome of an interaction of numbers.

So if a mathematical computation requires a derivation of the square root of a negative number, the minus sign must be separated from the integer in order to free the number from the radical. For, when considered strictly as a quantity, the number can be understood to be independent of its accompanying sign. Since quantities constitute the fundamental computational elements of mathematical operations, the minus sign is separated from the number *within* the square root radical. And the interested quantity is set free.

The minus sign is transferred to an imaginary entity, which is composed of a single unit and itself. This imaginary entity retains its position within the square root radical, while the original number is enabled to be released from the radical: as in $\sqrt{-25} = \sqrt{-1} . \sqrt{25} = 5 . \sqrt{-1}$, which is written symbolically as 5 *i*.

So the imaginary entity is the imaginary unit *i*, which is $\sqrt{-1}$: the square root of a one and its associated minus sign. In the phrase "imaginary unit," the one is the unit. And the minus vector, when considered in distinction from any number, is imaginary. (This will be further explained.) For in arithmetical operations, a minus or plus sign is always presented (or sometimes implied in the latter case) in association with a number. This is because a vector must have magnitude.

The number one is the foundational building block of all numbers, except zero. For it is the foundational building block of all natural numbers. And these natural numbers, with or without the assistance of a zero, make up the expression of all numbers insofar as they can be expressed, even fractions, decimals, irrational numbers, and imaginary numbers.

The number one is treated as imaginary in the case of an imaginary unit because, due to the negative vector being associated with it, it cannot be removed from the radical. For the rules for taking a square root would otherwise be violated. This restriction arises from the fact that both multiplicands of a square root must be identical.

Therefore, they must both be either positive or negative. Since in multiplication, *a positive vector working upon a positive vector* and *a negative vector working upon a negative vector* both produce a positive result, the product cannot be negative. Thus $-5 \cdot -5 = 25$ and $5 \cdot 5 = 25$. But they cannot equal -25. So a reversal of this process in attempting to obtain a square root of -25 creates a problem.

But there is a temporary way out, if certain imaginative liberties are taken. Because it is the foundational unit of all integers, a one acting as a multiplier or a divisor does nothing to change a quantity, as in $25 \cdot 1 = 25$ or $25 \div 1 = 25$. It simply states that the number is itself an arithmetical unit—a compound of unit ones—or it asserts that the arithmetical unit is composed of foundational unit ones. So one twenty-five is a twenty-five. And the number of ones in a twenty-five is twenty-five.

Thus, since a square is a form of multiplication and its reciprocal, a square root, is a form of division, 1^2 {i.e. $1 \cdot 1$} = 1, and $\sqrt{1}$ {i.e. $1 \div 1$} = 1. So the one changes nothing quantitatively. This demonstrates the fact that, *for computational purposes, an isolation of the minus sign with a one under a radical is nothing more than the isolation of the minus sign under the radical alone.* The minus sign is simply being attached to a one because a vector must register magnitude and because magnitudes must be employed for arithmetical operations to take place.

In other words, $\sqrt{-1}$ is simply $\sqrt{(-)}$. It might be expressed in this manner were it not for the fact that the negative vector is being held in abeyance from a series of mathematical operations into which it must at some point reenter. To reenter such operations, it must be accompanied by a quantity. So it is accompanied by a one for the purpose of any future computation.

Numbers are what are employed in mathematical operations. The minus sign is simply a directional entity. It signifies a decrease or a reversal of an increase or a decrease. But it is a decrease or a reversal of an increase or a decrease of something. That something is a quantity. So the vector registers a magnitude as well.

As a result of its possessing both a negative and a quantitative value, a minus one is held under the radical because it cannot be brought out from under it, due to the type of operation indicated, as explained above. But since in truth the $\sqrt{-1}$ is simply a (–) held in abeyance, the imaginary unit, symbolized by an *i*, provides a convenient notation for this isolation of a minus sign. The isolated sign, reflecting a minus vector held in abeyance, clearly exhibits the directional role of signs. It is in this directional manner that signs act as vectors in multiplication, squaring, division, and square root operations.

The Thinking Arts: Painting, Sculpture, Literature, and Music

THE word "art" means the raising of a particular craft to a level of philosophical insight. Most of those who are called artists are not artists. They are merely performers.

MODERN commercial society rejects what is truly meaningful in art. This is because a commodity, to be readily marketable, must shine like a waxed apple. Good art does not shine. It glows.

THERE is a problem with much of modern visual art, literature, music, etc. It is that so much of it represents an abandonment of the humanistic tradition. It emphasizes non-human-based qualities and relations. No doubt, this is owing to the terrible events of the twentieth century: World Wars I and II, the Holocaust, the Stalinist Purges, etc.

But a belief in Humanism is still valid. It is the idea that a better world can be discovered through a deeper understanding of human nature and experience. So, rather than that this idea should be abandoned, it should be clung to. It lies at the heart of Christianity. And it has been dominant in Western Civilization since Giotto painted his dramatic frescos in the fourteenth century.

WHAT makes art endure is its underlying foundation of deep thought: its philosophy. When deep thought dies in a culture, art becomes fashion oriented and excessively self-referential. It then fails to endure, to survive into subsequent eras. This is because it cannot hold meaning for them, other than to satisfy some vague and ephemeral curiosity. Such art loses insightful reference to the fundamental obstacles and triumphs of life.

THE core philosophical element in all great works of art is an integrated view of the world that involves a fresh way of seeing life, expressed as an attitude.

GREAT art is a product of great intellect. Because art involves indirect expression though emotion, its intellectual insights may initially escape notice. But they will surface in the minds of attentive readers, viewers, or listeners over time. For they cannot be permanently overlooked. Moreover, what they clearly are not are verbal, visual, or musical tricks and high jinks of style. They are genuine insights.

ART is precise in being imprecise. This peculiar balance is what makes it art. In fact, its craftsmanship, which is important, lies in a precise delicacy of imprecision. So does its philosophy, its deep seeing, which is equally important. The philosophy is understood without overt articulation.

Take a literary work, such as a story. What this precise delicacy of imprecision does is allow an image, character, situation, or combination of these, to play loosely in the mind. It permits, indeed insists upon, a multiplicity of interpretation, yet within a specific framework. Thus the mental play is subtly directed in such a way that each suggestion in the mind leads to another suggestion, causing a forward movement of the action.

IF at one moment the enduring heart of human nature is referred to, and at another moment the eternal struggles of life are spoken of (those which are often repeated under many guises and settings), if these two things are spoken of, they are the same thing. This is of course stated in reference to visual art, literature, music, etc.

What is being said is that human personality is a compound of universal inner traits shared by all. These are the capacity for love, hate, etc. But they are invariably intertwined with environmental and social obstacles which result from the simple fact that human beings are limited in capacity. Put these inner and outer factors together, look at them with honesty and penetration, and what is found is what sincere art thrives on.

THERE is a gulf between talent and genius. To effectively put strong feeling onto a canvas is something common. So what is it that keeps most people from making the leap from sometimes strongly moving works into works of originality and uniqueness of vision? It is the conceptual element that is lacking. By conceptual, philosophical is meant.

Unless a person is willing to think long and deep upon some topic of life, unless that person is willing to risk ridicule or the terrible loneliness of simply being misunderstood and ignored, unless there is some truth about the human condition which has been discovered in these long hours of patient thought and exploration, there can be no breakthrough into a new level of awareness. That breakthrough is what is called genius.

An illustration of this can be taken from a local New Mexican poet who has an impressive lyrical command of language. Upon first acquaintance with his work, a reader is readily transported by the beauty of his verse. But on closer examination, if the reader should momentarily set aside his musical flow of words and look for the meaning of the poem, she is disappointed at discovering the pedestrian nature of its underlying thought.

There is no truth to be discovered, no unexpected enlightenment to assist and delight in the weary but often intriguing sojourn of life. In short, works held together only by talent may be pleasing in expression. But they leave nothing to a deeper contemplation. It is that element of contemplation, especially within an illumination of fresh insight, which lies at the core of every great work of art, every work of genius.

A FUNDAMENTAL problem with any examination of details in a close and minute analysis is that the mind is susceptible of becoming lost in those details and their proximate relationship to one another. In doing this, the mind commits the common fallacy of assuming that the whole is no more than the sum of its parts.

Thus it loses sight of the meaning of the whole. This fallacy is particularly harmful in a study of the arts, since it withdraws attention from the general outlook being presented. No reasonable person would argue that a Rembrandt painting is no more than so many pigments arranged in a pleasing relation to one another.

IN a painting, what is seen is not as important as how it is seen.

IN painting, focusing upon the act of seeing can become too self-conscious. But this focus, properly regulated, is present in all great paintings.

IN painting, the act of seeing is a moral seeing. Its concern is with the human centeredness of experience. A calmly measured attitude of human centeredness in relation to experience is the essence of wisdom, as opposed to knowledge.

SOMETIMES it would seem that the standards of art are defunct in the modern world. Hardly anyone seems to care about the foundation of enduring art. It is certainly not technical expertise and innovation alone. These are only means to an end. The end is a deep and penetrating awareness of the human condition which allows people to see in a fresh way. The true vision of great art retains its freshness because it derives its power, not from momentary fashions in means of expression, but from an eternal rootedness in what is most fundamental in human nature.

Human experience can only be understood from the perspective of human nature. So it is when this human nature is brought into harmony with something new in experience that the experience becomes attached to something enduring: the unchanging character of men and women. Enduring art is created from this blending of the experience of a particular time with the unchanging core of human nature.

Evolution is not at issue when an unchanging human nature is spoken of. The history of art is young, even if Cro-Magnon cave paintings are considered. So the parameters of any discussion of art need not be unfocused by great stretches of time. Art being relative to its creator, it is unnecessary to relate it to the perceptions or awareness of a creature altogether different, such as would be found in a seriously altered human nature.

THE nineteenth century was one of the greatest periods in the history of Western Civilization. Though it did not achieve the high philosophical tone exhibited by Dante, Shakespeare, and Cervantes in the Renaissance, it assumed a profound earnestness in the close observation of individual experience. This is realism in the broadest sense.

Nineteenth century realism is an extension of Renaissance humanism. For a realistic approach can be traced to the fourteenth century, where a humanist outlook was first expressed. It is here that the sins explored in Dante's *Divine Comedy* became living, passionate expressions of an easily recognizable human will. And it is also here that the painted figures of Giotto took on individualized and emotionally accurate gestures.

WHY is it that the concept of beauty would appear to be so nebulous? Everyone knows what it is. But when examples are sought, they begin to disagree. Yet certain works in literature, visual art, music, etc., though having fallen into temporarily decline, will reemerge to be recognized as masterpieces.

This would imply two things. One of them is that beauty encompasses a family of resemblances, a body of characteristics which can be found in all works considered art. But not all these characteristics will be found together. For example, Michelangelo might be admired chiefly for his powerfully expressive draftsmanship and sense of form, while Titian is equally praised for his evocative use of color. To judge either of these artists by the other's principal strength would be to judge unfairly.

Family resemblances are therefore likely to confound critical judgment. Thus they are the principal cause of so much uncertainty and confusion in aesthetic matters. So a second point follows, one which is deeper than these more salient features which are customarily recognized and confused.

Though this second point may not be readily understood and is often obscured in contemporary practice, it is characteristic of all enduring masterpieces of art. Its tendency to be ignored is what accounts for the checkered history in public acceptance which some great works have suffered.

To complicate matters further, the second point must be divided into two principles. One of these principles concerns the way a work of art is enabled to elicit a public response. For the method is not the same between literature and the plastic arts. Nor is it the same in other forms. But this much can be said of it: however the components of a work of art may be found to function so as to elicit a strong response, they must certainly do so. For eliciting a strong response is one characteristic of great art.

But that in itself is insufficient. For works of only ephemeral appeal may momentarily draw crowds of fervent admirers. A great work of art must elicit an enduringly strong response. So there must be something permanent in the powerful effect a work has on its appreciative readership, viewership, or audience. It must be able to create the same, or nearly the same, effect in different times and places, where the customs and tastes of people will differ.

Anyone in the twenty-first century who wrote plays like Shakespeare would fail. But the universal power of the plays is undeniable. That power can only result from one thing: fidelity to human nature. It must not only present human nature truthfully. It must represent human nature in its deep, unvarying character.

A work of art which can achieve this power, and do so with its available resources, will have continuing appeal, once the mind- and emotion-obscuring prejudices of contemporary fashion are put aside. The anger of Achilles still affects. The tragic weakness of Othello still shocks and elicits pity.

The self-portraits of Rembrandt reach in to an enduring core of emotion. The powerful sea vistas executed at Prouts Neck, Maine, by Winslow Homer bring the awesome force of nature into the human interior. They each do this because they are as true to the human condition today as they were when they were created.

Fashions change. Modern poetry enthusiasts do not gather in drafty halls to listen while wandering minstrels sing of heroic deeds. Today's pedestrian sensibilities may not believe in such complex heroes. But people know that if they were wronged as Achilles was, they might well feel the same wounded pride and anger. Even though people do not value and honor pride today in the same manner that the ancient Greeks did, they know a human being from the inside. For they are human beings.

This is what endures in great art. Humanity in its essential humanness endures. So, in addition to this, there is the individual artist's ability to reach and powerfully affect the eternal emotional core in his appreciative reader, viewer, or auditor. For, when people see themselves—their tender, terrible, frightened, loving, angry moments—mirrored or suggested with unforgettable power, the experience enters into them and resides there permanently.

THE difference between a philosopher and an artist: a philosopher attempts to extract meaning from a set of circumstances; an artist attempts to inject meaning into a set of circumstances. Thus the philosopher moves toward abstraction, while the artist moves toward the particular. However, there is a good deal of intermingling between these two functions.

An interesting note: nineteenth and early twentieth century novels and short stories, though projecting meaning into circumstances, also made it their unique effort to deliberately extract meaning from their created circumstances. Such a novel or short story was always an investigative research. This tentative quality is one of its strengths, perhaps the chief one.

ETHICS based on principle alone is always starved for specific examples. It knows what ought to be done in general, but not what is applicable to the specific case. For this fleshing out, only experience will do. A person learns by what he feels and observes. The arts are helpful in this matter, because they can refine a person's capacities.

Music elevates and articulates emotional feeling, purging it of the dross and the confused. Painting helps a person to see clearly with both mind and emotion. It forms a refined attitude. Literature, revolving about human actions and emotions, develops subtlety of moral imagination. It instructs one person in the character of another person's interior circumstances.

Regarding each of these forms, one can only speak in terms of the most developed expression of that art: great art because it is original and honest. Great art is sincere. It cleanses the heart and mind of any subtle or deliberate self-deception. It can develop in a person a sincere and empathetic nature, which is the essence of morality.

NOTWITHSTANDING the emotional power which can be attributed to music, the arts of painting and sculpture are the most immediate of the arts. This results from the fact that most human beings are strongly visual creatures. For this reason, the visual arts are also the most universal. For example, it is easier for a Westerner to understand an Indian or Japanese paining than it is for her to understand their music.

However, music is felt to be the purest art form because it impacts directly upon the emotions, thought arising from this impact as an effect. Thought arises from the visual arts in a similar way, albeit with the important qualification that its origin is in sensory perception. Thus, since it is prior to the generation of an emotional response, it is earlier in its mental delineation.

But in literature, thought is the predominant element. It is never far below the surface of a person's awareness. This is due to the role of language in both literature and thought. Language is the most recognizable form of thought qua thinking, though there can be other forms of thinking. So, even when it does not assert its views discursively, language's usual instrumentality as a recognizable vehicle of thought continually suggests the ever-present role of thought, giving it dominance.

SERIOUS literature is moral philosophy. If it is not that, it is nothing.

WORD for word, no literary work ought to take longer to read than a philosophical work.

A GREAT literary work should be appreciated for what it is, not for what can be superficially imposed upon it by a scholar desperate for a reputation within her scholarly circle.

HUMAN civilization has transcended time through the works of the mind. It has done this chiefly by means of written language. The invention of writing was not simply another technical innovation. It was the creation of an environment of precisely, and often directly, articulated truth, where thought and emotion could be refined to their essence. By this means, people have forged relationships with one another, with past lives, and with enduring principles which they could not otherwise have experienced.

There are other expressions of serious culture, such as painting, music, and mathematics, each of which preserves and passes on its own vision of truth. But there is nothing quite so rich, self-contradictory, and sterling as tempered language. It carries within it both the complexity and the simplicity of thought and emotion, registering the conflict of human beings and ideas, while exhibiting a fundamental underlying unity of human experience.

UNIVERSAL perspective is one of the most important assets of a writer, if he wishes to achieve a literary work of lasting importance. It does not matter what the topic is. He can portray a world as narrow as Jane Austen's, focus upon a point of view as specific as that of Langston Hughes, or convey a range and expression of thought as peculiar as Thomas Carlyle's.

The universal perspective will be found in the tone of the work. But how does any work get such a tone? It must come from the mind of the writer, who is, in one form or another, a thinker. He should see himself as addressing the world in both time and place, not a portion of the world. He should look out upon history and all cultures as being one, populated as they are by human beings.

But he should not lose his sense of rootedness in his origins. If his perspective is broad enough, it will find a ready response, regardless of his roots. His range can be as narrow as he pleases. He will find a place in the company of the great. This is because literary greatness is based upon largeness of sympathy, accompanied by depth of insight. It is greatness both of mind and of appeal.

Once having become a member of such a fraternity, a writer's stature among the great will also be determined by the range and penetration of his treatment of his topic. If he would go so far as to become a Shakespeare or an Aristotle, then he must have an extraordinary abundance of this breadth of perspective, accompanied by an unmatched depth of thought and feeling. (Yes, there is feeling even in Aristotle.)

THE two branches of ethics are descriptive and normative (or prescriptive). Descriptive ethics seeks to examine how people behave and why. Normative ethics attempts to determine how people should live. So how might serious literature fit into this? How might it be thought of as ethical without its falling into a didactic role?

Serious literature has two fundamental characteristics in this regard: insight and vision. It expresses insight insofar as it shows how people really do act, interact, think, or feel. That is the descriptive side of ethics. The normative side is expressed in terms of the writer's overall attitude toward the human condition. This is her general vision.

If these two functions of a poem, novel, play, or an essay concerned with human experience were understood, then it could be seen that serious literature is inherently moral. It deals with both aspects of ethics, prescriptive and descriptive. And its fundamental purpose is to do so in such a way as to insure that a reader or audience is caught up into its maelstrom of thought, emotion, and feeling, experiencing moral problems from the inside, rather than finding herself standing on the outside indifferently contemplating principles.

ETHICS is prescriptive. Moral philosophy is descriptive. The first seeks to determine how people should behave. The second tries to understand why they form the rules they do and how they act in relation to them. The first, however practical, is grounded in the ideal. The second is founded upon an observation of what is.

The creator of a literary work will have come from a particular ethical milieu. He will have inherited certain principles as norms of behavior. These will inform his general view. But if he is insightful, and not a purveyor of platitudes, he will press against the ethical standards of his day, both good and bad, in an effort to discover the springs of human nature and separate them from the norms. Thus a philosophy of literature should be based on moral philosophy and not upon ethics.

For this practice on the part of a creator of a literary work, of seeking to discover the springs of human nature and separate them from the norms, is what allows the philosopher of literature to investigate the moral insights of a literary work. From this, the philosopher affirms his general view that all literature, especially literature of action (plays, novels, and stories), is principally moral in the descriptive sense. If it is not, it is not literature in an enduring sense of the word. This is because fidelity toward a descriptive truth concerning human nature is what preserves such a work.

The philosopher of literature should begin his analysis of the moral structure of a particular work in light of a general recognition that the work in question is truly an enduring work. Otherwise, there would be no reason to continue further in his investigations. If he discovers that the work is of an enduring character and sees that he should continue with his study of it, he may learn from it and develop his own philosophical insights into the human condition, much as he does from a direct study of life.

Among the enduring thinking arts, all are moral in both mood and insight. This includes painting, sculpture, and music, as well as literature. Thus great literature is moral because it is an enduring art. Its overall mood expresses an attitude, or relationship to life. This mood is prescriptive. But it must be prescriptive in an honest and insightful manner, which renders the moral detail of the work descriptive, or true to moral experience.

For the mood of the literary work suggests an attitude which might be taken. Any other great work of art does the same. By means of its mood, it suggests an attitude of mind which may result in a course of action. For this reason, poetry or a literary essay, or a painting for that matter, are as much an expression of moral imagination as is a novel, story, or play.

So like all great art, great literature enlarges moral imagination. That is its power, which is derived from its insight into the human condition. And it is also the means by which it gives pleasure. It is pleasurable because it empowers the understanding of the person who comes into contact with it.

If that person is reflective, he will grow personally with the experience of it. If he is philosophical, he will organize that reflection into an instrument of increased moral and conceptual awareness. For it is the role of philosophy to enlarge conceptual imagination, as it is the role of the arts to enlarge moral imagination. It is in this way that philosophy and the arts build the man or woman of complete understanding.

GREAT literature deepens a person's engagement with life by increasing her understanding of it. So it must probe deeply into human experience. What makes literature deep? How does it broaden understanding? This is achieved through a writer's recognition of the simple truth that human beings change culturally but not in their basic humanness. Human nature has been consistent across the ages of recorded history. So honing in on that basic humanness is a thinker's and a writer's strength, her weapon against time. A great painter would call this same outlook a "return to nature."

This is why the ancient Greek play, *Oedipus Rex,* still appeals to those who read it and see it performed. It is much more than an identification with a representative character. It is more than a purgation of emotion within a reader or viewer. It may be these things. But more importantly, what matters in literature is the occasion it provides for an honest immersion in life. This immersion, if it accords well with the most elemental emotional responses and perceptions, enriches a person's understanding of life through an enlargement of her awareness of the fundamental, unchanging intellectual and emotional conditions of her own experience.

So what a writer should be concerned with is human experience. That is to say, she should be asking, how would I have felt in that situation? Or how do I feel about that situation? How deeply must I look into myself to get at the true feelings or perceptions appropriate to the imagined situation? How honest am I being? Beyond that, specific cultural references are no more than the sea a writer's ship is set afloat upon.

T. S. ELIOT declared that poetry warps language into meaning. This is true. Poetry brings images into a close and unusual proximity with one another. These are visual images or images of the other senses. In the close and unexpected proximity of a poem, they incandesce. That is, they escape the logical and syntactical constraints of language and float freely in the mind. This process permits a broad range of free association.

GEORGE Orwell's *1984* is one of the most important novels of the twentieth century. This judgment is not based on the usual criteria for judging a novel. Admittedly the novel's individual characterizations are not memorable. Its incidents appear fantastic. Thus its reference to life does not at first seem compelling. But this latter judgment arises from a mistaken criterion, which is that the novel is a portrayal of a negative utopia.

Certainly, the novel is, in a superficial sense, the story of an oppressive future society. But that is the illusion. The novel is an allegory. In truth, it is about the modern world. The book was written in 1948 and published in 1949. It is no accident that its title, *1984*, contains the number 84 as an inversion of the number 48. That inversion, like the book itself, is a distorted mirror image of an existing reality.

The present world is the one with lotteries in one form or another. It is where little wars are fought for no good reason other than some vague political platitude which is never sure of its purpose. The present world has a memory hole: a marketplace for ideas in which truly productive insights are simply overlooked and forgotten.

There is "doublespeak" in politics, advertising, job hunting, sales, news presentation, political correctness. In fact, in every aspect of life, the present reality in these things is worse than the book's portrayal. There are thought police too. The Romans consigned what they saw as problem people to the arena. The present world ostracizes them, a far more effective form of annihilation and control.

In short, *1984* is a distorted mirror image of the present world. It was Orwell's world. And it has not changed. The distortions merely serve to point up existing lineaments, like a hall of mirrors. And the major protagonist of the novel is not Winston Smith. It is society itself. Winston makes it to the top of the social order and cannot find Big Brother because the entire social system is Big Brother. So it is now. No one person is really in control. For this reason, the world does not attack the few remaining honest individuals as a shark does. It surrounds and eats away at them like a school of piranha.

WHAT is the precise purpose of literature? That is a question which has been debated for millennia. Why should people read literature? To begin this discussion with a consideration of the novel makes the answer simpler, since it can be maintained that people should read great novels because they help them to see into themselves and refine their emotional responses to the complex moral situations of life.

This can be said of poetry too. The novel gives readers character, even multiple characters, as an emotional compound leading to the overall emotional attitude of a story. Poetry is more direct in its approach to emotional attitudes. So, together, novels and poetry constitute a refined exposure to life's many possible situations.

Can the same be said about dramatic works? What of Aristotle's contention that Greek tragedy provides a catharsis of the emotions? The viewer vicariously experiences the crises of the protagonist's dilemma. And he is emotionally cleansed—wrung out, as it were. This, it would seem, is a different view of the function of literature.

But when the situation is looked at closely, it can be observed that the catharsis is a type of emotional involvement. That involvement provides an exposure to the subtle twists and turns of a human emotional response to a situation. Much of the experience of catharsis is that of having "come through." But is not this sense of coming through an expression of the fact that one has been involved in and grasped the significance of a situation?

So it would seem that a person has, as a result of such exposure, been formed in his character for some type of human situation. And it follows that many such formations would enlarge an individual's emotional and moral awareness. Just as in life, so in great literature, a person learns by doing (or at least by experiencing).

It is true that reading a book or watching a play involves an individual in a secondhand, or vicarious, experience rather than in a direct, firsthand experience. But it illuminates the mind and emotions nevertheless. And its advantage is that in a vicarious experience a person is free to think. He is not busy involving himself in or extricating himself from troubles.

So in this way—that is, through exposure to great literature—a greater subtlety in dealing with the myriad complexities of life is obtained. For no matter how many rationally developed principles there may be in a particular ethical code, that code can never be anything more than a modifiable template for possible action. The subtlety and variety of emotional awareness, on the other hand, will determine the moral effectiveness of any act which is chosen in a specific situation.

The more alternative interpretations of another person's motives that can be clearly seen, the more a personal range of responses both to people and events is enlarged, the greater the power of choice among those avenues of response, and the better an individual is able to select a safe path through moral problems. It is this refinement that literature supplies to moral understanding. And it is for this reason that great literature is ultimately moral, as opposed to its being merely didactic or simply amoral.

HISTORY and art pass into human awareness in different ways. As Aristotle pointed out in his *Poetics*, history exhibits individual actions in a particular situation, the historian providing an intellectual interpretation of the motives she thinks caused the person to act the way he did. Since a reader is left in some doubt concerning these motives, the history is held in her mind as a form of knowledge, to be continually brought under critical examination when in the proximity of other such knowledge.

On the other hand, a protagonist in a work of fiction or drama is given motives which develop within and inseparably from the action. These are "probable" motives, as Aristotle indicated. They are consistent with the action of the story. But the specific action is not presented as something which has actually occurred.

However, if this action is forceful and made to seem probable, it enters into the mind of the reader, not as knowledge, but as experience. This experience is then held in the mind with other experience, both fictional and actual. And the full range of both kinds of experience becomes available as material for making ethical judgments.

It should be noted that the author of a particular fictional or dramatic work has an attitude toward life which she conveys in conjunction with the action and character revelation. This authorial attitude is akin to the manner in which ordinary experience is undergone. Ordinary experience is accompanied by the attitude of a person's response to a situation. So both attitudes, fictional and actual, provide material for forming an ethical perspective.

History also enlarges a person's ethical capacity. But it provides less of a direct emotional experience. It is much more rational in the way it becomes conscious, raising questions in the form of an intellectual debate. An historical work is something thought, rather than felt. For it is intellectually grasped within an independent analysis of the mind. It is not felt in the complex emotional and intellectual unity of a work of fiction or drama.

IN this practical era of careful and precise observation of the world, some say a thoroughly objective and "scientific" kind of history is needed. There should be none of the imaginative dressing which has made history so readable in the past. But where is there a thoroughly objective history?

And who would read it or derive any benefit from it, if it were to be rendered so dry as to avoid an interpretive viewpoint altogether? Is interpretation not always the invention of the writer? If historical narrative were utterly grounded in facts, it would not be an interpretation at all.

Take the Roman historian, P. Cornelius Tacitus. It is presently maintained, in a high scientific tone of disapproval, that he was rather unfair to the Emperor Tiberius. Probably so. But most of his facts are good. And where he has spilled out a certain amount of personal invective, has he not delivered a portrait of his own temperament and character in exchange for judiciously pared down facts about the original subject?

He was a Roman senator living a generation and some years after the events he was dealing with. At the present great distance in time, such a small gap in the sequence of events seems unimportant, nearly invisible. So the world today has before it a portrait of a Roman aristocrat of that general era: Tacitus himself. It is illuminating history because his clearly rendered personality puts modern readers in direct contact with a living Roman!

BEAUTY is essentially balance and harmony. But inventiveness is also important. For it refreshes the mind, leading to a new, and perhaps more elevated, sense of balance and harmony. Nevertheless, balance and harmony remain the principal ingredients of beauty. For it is these which the order-loving mind continually craves and reacts to with satisfaction.

WHAT is beautiful differs from what is pretty. That which is considered pretty exhibits a perfection of form, a pleasing uniformity of features. But beauty expresses an anomalous appearance in conjunction with that uniformity. For example, a sense that something is beautiful may arise from an encounter with an unusual, even an extreme, degree of refinement in a uniformity of features.

Or it may arise from the recognition of a disruptive feature in the midst of such a uniformity. An example of this would be a beauty spot. However, the disruptive element must never call attention solely to itself or disturb the general uniformity. It must simply raise the uniformity to a position of rarity.

THE impact of line and color alone will never constitute an enduring work of art. What *will* do so is an effective arrangement of line and color expressing some deep, insightful understanding of human experience, even if it is only emotional experience. Why is this? It proceeds from the fact that a work of art endures when it continues to resonate meaningfully in human awareness. What are human beings aware of, if not the experience of living?

PISSARRO often puts one in mind of Rembrandt. In his painting, he expresses a similar largeness of heart and complexity of mind. There is also a like humility which is assumed in the face of reality. For Rembrandt the humbling mystery is largely human. For Pissarro it is nature.

THERE are two fundamental elements in great art. Skill in a particular artistic medium is one. Philosophy is the other. For philosophy is essential to all great art. What is meant by philosophy is deep thought, or penetrating intellectual insight, which is not necessarily of a logical or verbal character.

When Cézanne declared that Monet was "just an eye, but Lord, what an eye!" he was referring to Monet's philosophy, his deep thought, or penetrating vision, in terms of nature, human responsiveness, color, and line (however unobtrusive the line). Of course, Monet's technical skill with palette and brush was the means for expressing that deep thought. It was even the means of his thinking it. This is to say that it was not reasoned discourse. But it was profound thought nevertheless.

VISION is broad. Or it may be narrowed within its course. Thus an abstract artist like Kandinsky, Pollock, or Rothko has the problem of having deliberately restricted his vocabulary. For with these men, the vocabulary of general experience is largely reduced to a vocabulary of color and line. Consequently, each of them has a powerful but limited vision. His language is at once focused and at a loss for an adequate vocabulary to express a more enlarged range of vision.

Picasso is a example of this limited vision in a different way. In his case, it was not a lack of means to articulate his vision. For his creative resources were immense. Rather, it was lack of will. He had great flexibility and variety of expression but little depth of penetration into the human condition.

"Guernica," the most iconic painting of the twentieth century, is the great exception. Here all the variety of expressive tools Picasso had been half-heartedly playing with—as though the art of painting were a mere intellectual game—was suddenly, and no doubt quite unexpectedly, focused upon a genuine and deeply felt complex of emotions, a vision of his anger and shock at the German bombing of the Spanish town of Guernica.

That painting has come to represent the brutality of war and genocide in the twentieth century. In this way, Picasso's tools were sincerely brought to bear upon a universal human problem: man's inhumanity to man. The result was an extraordinary depth of honest feeling gathered forcefully under intellectual control.

HOW does a Cézanne painting achieve its extraordinary effect upon the viewer? For a comparison, let his younger contemporary, Vincent Van Gogh, be brought under observation. When a person looks at a Van Gogh painting, he feels the passionate intensity and the spiritual philosophy of its creator. The work fairly crawls with spiritual energy, executed in the form of an emotional application of color, line, and expressive brushwork.

But the emotion is not raw. Emotion and thought unite together to create an attitude. And that attitude is a filter for imaginative ideas. This is what is meant by spirit. It may be said that someone is of such and such a spirit or that the spirit of a situation, country, or historical moment is such and such. What is being referred to is a combined intellectual and emotional attitude.

Van Gogh saw the universe as spirit, which is to say he saw it as full of living energy, morally expressed. Thus his work took on a dynamic attitude. It filled the world with a passionate sense that all things come together with purpose and meaning. However, individual things may appear at times to be at cross purposes. Hence the tragic sense in some of his works.

Paul Cézanne differed from Van Gogh in that he created a stillness rather than a dynamism. But this was not due to a lack of complexity. All great artists are multilayered and of seemingly inexhaustible interpretation. Nevertheless, Cézanne's complexity was different from

Van Gogh's. His still life paintings provide a good example of how he attempted to accomplish his purpose.

His broken planes appear to reveal two levels of one table top. And his fractured volumes enable a viewer to look down into a vertically standing vase while viewing it from a horizontal perspective. These effects are combined with a lack of defined linear perspective. Such an abbreviated view foreshortens the picture plane. Thus, when taken altogether, these effects pull a viewer into one of his paintings and surround him with its internal artifacts and their interrelationships.

Cézanne's landscapes, bathers, portraits, and human profiles seek a similar effect. That effect is to bring the viewer into an intimate relationship with the painting. The viewer finds himself penetrating volumes and slipping between planes. The result is an ineffable stillness, a sense of monumentality, of time standing still.

This is because all activity, all movement within the picture, culminates in the viewer himself. He is not viewing the scene. He is at the center of it. Planes and volumes emanate from the viewer and thus have their life in him, not apart from him. Since the viewer is the center of all the movement and variation of the painting, it achieves a harmonious unity in his contemplative moment.

In this much, at least, Cézanne resembles the late seventeenth century French painter, Nicolas Poussin. But Poussin does not locate the viewer within the painting. Poussin is cool and objective. His aesthetic experience is an artifact of the mind. Emotions are drawn into intellectual contemplation for the sake of intellectual harmony. The effect is that of conceptual balance, which is what confers the sense of emotional peace, even in a picture whose motif is one of physical tumult.

Cézanne, on the other hand, is an Impressionist. He wants the viewer to *feel* the landscape, still life, or portrait. But not without the full engagement of the mind. So he simplifies and recomposes the volumes and textures of nature to admit the mind, as well as the emotions, into nature's infinite complexity.

Yet people as viewers are at the center of this complexity, responding to it both intellectually and emotionally. They are engaged on all sides, though still and silent in the contemplative moment. It is like taking a walk in the country. If a person individually notes the murmur of a stream, a rustle of leaves, the slant of light and tilt of the wind, he experiences only particulars.

But if he lets go of these specifics and thinks about something else, suddenly and quite unexpectedly he realizes that all these rhythms acting upon him simultaneously create an inexplicable, complex experience of harmony which silences both mind and heart in rapturous and spontaneous awareness. This is Cézanne.

THERE is a way in which the philosophical concept of wisdom might be applied to the arts. In philosophy, the pursuit of wisdom differs from the practical business of accumulating knowledge in that the primary concern of the philosopher lies neither in any set of facts nor their relationship to one another, but in the general relationship of human beings to the facts of their existence.

This is, of course, the precise nature of art—great art, as opposed to ordinary talent and individual emotional expression. The predominant role of truth should not be overlooked, either in great art or in philosophy. It is a truth relating a person to the facts of her existence. So what should be of principle concern to any person is what this truth is which philosophers and serious artists concern themselves with.

Under the term "philosophy," any degree of practice below that of serious work is not admitted. It is simply not philosophy. Unfortunately, this distinction cannot be applied to art, since art is a term which applies to craft alone as well as to serious work. Consequently, there is much mediocre art. But there are no mediocre philosophers because mediocre thinking is not philosophy. Anything short of rigorous thinking and sincere insight either does or should come under some other label.

But art (especially as it is understood in the public imagination) is a purse carrying items serving purposes both necessary and vain. Much of what the public calls art is nothing more than craft. And a good deal of the rest of it is a rather uninspiring salad raising pleasant emotions at best. So what is the philosophical element in art? What is it that makes art a type of philosophy? For there is a philosophical element in great art.

It is precisely that which elevates a work of art to a position of indisputable greatness. Of course, the greatness of any particular work of art would appear to be in daily dispute. This is because a hoped for elevation of the human mind is so rare and unreliable. Without an elevation of mind, there can be no refinement of taste, no recognition of great art. People in general do not always know what is insightful, whereas profound insight is the wisdom contained in a work of art which constitutes its greatness.

In other words, art is great precisely when it is philosophy. So what is philosophy, or the pursuit of wisdom? Its principal concern lies in the relationship of a human being to the facts of her existence. When this relationship is expressed with power and fresh insight, whether in reasoned discourse or the persuasion of art, it produces greatness.

Permeating any work of art is the artist's attitude toward her subject, or motif. This motif is made up of some portion of the observed facts of life. If the attitude attached to it turns out to be complacent and common—that is, devoid of fresh insight and any extraordinary power of conviction which can be felt in the execution of the work—if it is merely ordinary in its grip and transforming power over the viewer—if, in other words, the artwork is insipid, then the artist will possibly have a following at first, which will fall off over time.

This is because the average person, who accepts platitudes rather than insight, is not thoughtful. Genuinely reflective habits of mind are rare. In time, however, serious people do wander into contact with and properly experience serious artwork. When this happens, the philosophical strength, or wisdom, of the artwork is finally recognized, propagated, and preserved.

So what is the ethical value of art? Why should anyone care about what has just been said? Clearly, art's moral service to humanity lies in its capacity to put human beings into an honest relationship with themselves and their experience—that is, with the so-called facts of their existence.

Facts, of course, are always changing, whether in systematic science or the everyday practical business of living. So in an ever-changing universe there must always be philosophers and artists because people are continually in the process of refitting themselves into the world they are born into.

Of course, the changes in vision required to make art both great and serviceable to any particular period in human history are relatively minute in comparison to the general popular taste, which swings wide in its histrionic sweep of momentary passion. For great art is always grounded in the same essential human nature.

For this reason, the philosophy and art of the past, its cumulative wisdom, continues to enrich and morally improve humanity in a meaningful way. And if any person would have wisdom in herself, she must, as has been the case at any other time in history, and as others before her have done, pursue the refinement of her mind and heart in a vigorous and serious manner.

Continual exposure to philosophy and art makes the mind and the heart into supple and highly adaptive instruments capable of effectively and wisely responding to the subtle complexities of interpersonal relations and to the always limiting demands of the physical world. Anything short of that effort is a waste of a human existence and a probable injury to those others who may come into contact with such a diminished person.

ART is a science of emotions. It should be taken seriously as such. It exists on two levels. The first is the relationship of the content of an artwork to human experience. This is art's objective reference. The second level, its subjective reference, lies in the relationship of the artwork to a human being experiencing it either in the act of creating it or in the act of appreciating it. So, on one side, the artwork references experience common to all people. On the other, the concern is with how the artwork is experienced by someone.

Let the first level be brought under consideration. This is the level in which common experience is reflected in the content of a work of art. In literature that content can exhibit both a direct and an indirect display of human emotions: emotions as they are encountered in life, and emotions as they relate to life.

For these usually come together. But they need not do so. Thus a short story, novel, or play will transcribe and record how and why a character acts or reacts to a situation. And there will also be the writer's personal envelope of emotions within which he composes the story. This is his attitude.

On the other hand, a poem or essay, unless it is itself narrative in character, will more likely be a direct expression of thought and feeling on the part of a poet or essayist, again expressing an attitude, but neglecting direct action. In any case, whatever the mode of representation may be, it ought to ring true to human nature, if it is to be a work which will endure.

This emphasis on emotion is also true of music, which represents emotions directly, though within a structured form. This structure is its intellectual architecture. But however complex the music, the feeling is always paramount. In this direct emphasis on feeling, it is close to poetry, though poetry directly encompasses a broad range of ideas as well. For literature is the most broadly intellectual of the arts. It broaches ideas about general experience. These are its reason for being. They not only structure the emotions of the work. Directly or indirectly, they explain them.

Structure—in this case, prosody—is important in poetry. But it is subordinate to feeling and ideas. In contrast, the structure in music is more prominent in the mind of a listener than it is in poetry. For it not only regulates, but interprets, the emotion. Thus, in its initial thrust toward the listener, music puts aside all considerations other than those of emotions themselves and their structural representation.

Other elements, such as those of pastoral feeling, national sentiment, or personal appeal, are greatly subordinated to the musical structure. They are not sequestered out of hearing. They are just subordinate. For this or that particular structured representation of feeling is what must be capable of continuing to resonate with a broad range of tastes and with future generations. At least, it must do so if it is to endure among so many different people.

In its organization, a painting is the inverse of music. Initially, it sets feeling at a subordinate level and concentrates on form. Consciously or unconsciously, when a viewer first encounters a particular painting, his interest is commanded by form. The form directs him to a set of emotions governed by an idea. This is the attitude of the painting, as it is of the artist who produced it. So it is the overall form of the work, expressing an attitude which must achieve a correspondence to an emotional experience of the world.

This is so even when the form is reduced to an experience of colors and lines. For these are emotional colors and lines, emotions brought together in form. There is no such thing as a painting which is without reference to human emotional experience, however abstract the representational form may be. In fact, no art form can be fully nonrepresentational and remain an art form. It must make a reference to emotional experience in life, however vague and not immediately apparent the representation may be.

Take, for example, the later works of the twentieth century painter Wassily Kandinsky. Both in emotional directness and precision of form, they come close to music and affect a person almost in the way music does, but not quite. For there is an inversion. There is a stillness of contemplative thought wrought by form in the painting, which is unlike music.

Both music and Kandinsky's paintings do evoke feeling. And they both invoke thought. But thought accompanies form, not feeling. So, since, unlike music, the initial emphasis in Kandinsky is on form, there is an immediacy of thought in response to his paintings. As the viewer's awareness extends by means of the form (the relationships of color and line) to the expressed emotion (the color and line itself), thought emerges in relation to the form. Thus the thought is fully wrought within a moment of viewing. For the painting is immediately present in space and does not unfold over time.

In music, the initial emphasis is on feeling. Thus thought emerges in the listener's mind only as the form of the music is revealed over a passage of time. Nevertheless, in both cases form and emotion are thoroughly integrated. Though in a painting the emotional effect is offset in precedence by the form in which it is expressed. And in music the form is offset in precedence by the immediacy of felt emotion.

However, the close integration of form and feeling is most keenly felt in music as an unfolding integration. In other words, it is experienced as an ongoing interplay between emotion and form. Though thought is delayed, it is delayed because the form must be revealed. As the form progressively organizes the emotion, new feeling is being added. So a search, conscious or unconscious, in the listener's mind for this form emphasizes its necessary connection to the emotion. They seem to unfold as one.

Yet the close integration of form and feeling is experienced almost as intensely in a painting. But the suddenness of its full apprehension causes the form of the painting to dominate the consciousness of the viewer, almost as if the emotion were being pushed into the background. Nevertheless, the emotion is absolutely pertinent to an understanding of the form.

In any case, this inversion always persists between the plastic arts and music. It results from the fact that a painting is constructed in timeless space, where static form takes precedence. And music is constructed in spaceless time, involving ongoing change, where emotional development takes the lead.

Now let a review of the second level of art as a science of emotions be undertaken. It is here, where the subjective reference of the artwork is emphasized, that the artwork must be considered as a whole and not as a reference of its individual elements to whatever corresponding elements may exist in experience.

For the question to be examined concerns its internally integrated approach to experience. How do all parts of the work, taken together as a single phenomenon, reflect and interpret experience? In other words, how does the artwork make an impression of its overall reference to experience on both its creator and a prospective viewer?

There is a reciprocal relationship between creator and viewer. For in a sense, both are creators and both are viewers, but in a manner in which one is the inverse of the other. The creator is a viewer of both experience and the developing artwork as he creates. And the viewer is a creator as he views, comprehends, and interprets the artwork. For the viewer must recreate the artwork in his mind.

Accordingly, a certain question arises in connection with the creative act. It expresses the reason for the creative act's occurring. And this question, being passed on through the artwork from creator to viewer, directly affects the viewer in a manner which is the same, or at least similar, to the manner in which it affects the creator.

It is: what is the attitude of the artist toward life in creating the work? It is this attitude which the creator will want the viewer to experience in the work he is creating. He is concerned with how the work will orient the viewer's emotions toward aspects of life which are pertinent to the artwork and his (the creator's) own creative outlook.

In literature, or at least in great literature, the attitude is moral in the broadest sense. It suggests a way of being, or of relating to the world. It incorporates an idea about the expression of emotion in a situation or set of circumstances. The idea determines that emotional responses to those circumstances should occur in such and such a way. Thus given an enlarged insight in the capacity of the artist, they should reflect a broad and flexible approach to the general circumstances of life.

For example, should the Greek protagonist Antigone have behaved as honorably as she did, sacrificing her life to her principles? What does her attitude convey, in a broadened interpretation, about an individual who is set in opposition to the will of a community? Again, should Shakespeare's Othello have let his fevered imagination run riot under the influence of an ungoverned passion? And should this have been allowed to happen as a result of Iago's sinister influence?

Should not Othello have been more aware of his own emotions and of the insinuating malice of his confidant? What exactly are the insinuating effects of such evil: imaginative images translated into emotions drenched in pride and fear? And how should they be detected and resisted in oneself, as well as in another from whom they may be unwittingly absorbed?

And once again, does Dante's vision of hell, purgatory, and paradise represent a profoundly integrated ethical understanding of human nature? Are the human failings and strengths appropriately matched with their eternal consequences? In other words, can a moral life be maintained in accordance with the hierarchy of punishments and rewards suggested by this poet's intensely vivid verbal picture?

In music, prominence is given to emotions shaped by form, largely without reference to anything other than the relationship of form to emotion-producing sounds. But here, where emotion is immediately experienced, and where form is intimately associated with that emotion, shaping its interrelations, there is also an attitude. It is an attitude about the emotions themselves and how it is that they should be shaped, or refined, into musical meaning.

Thus the attitude is not about how an individual might relate himself to the external world of experience. That is expected to come later, as the listener's understanding of his own emotional character increases in subtlety of refinement as a result of listening to great music. This subtlety of refinement in his emotions is what he will eventually carry as an attitude into the world. For he is educated by music almost unconsciously. Nevertheless, largely unconscious though this education may be, the listener's increased subtlety in discerning emotional nuance will serve him well in understanding not only his own, but others' emotions.

Finally, in a painting an attitudinal position on the part of both the artist and the viewer is again encountered. It exhibits how a person ought, at least for the moment of his viewing the artwork, to look at the world, how he ought to feel about what he sees. If he is serious in his viewing, it can shape his outlook on life. For in the painting, feeling follows form and, as it were, comments upon it.

The form is the emotional structure of lines and colors. These, along with whatever representations there may be, shape the viewer's vision, his emotional and ideational attitude toward life. So, minimally, emotion itself is the focus, as in Kandinsky. But vision, of course, has a broader range of reference than color and line. By means of color and line, a painting may comprehend the physical and even the psychological world. The Spanish artist, El Greco, for instance, uses elongated forms and dark colors to emotionally transcend the physical world and introduce spiritual states of mind.

A visual representation may be a matter of seeing into the psychology of a portrait or into the meaning of an historical or social event. It may comment upon values, as in the case of the French illustrator and painter, Honoré Daumier. Or both artist and viewer may simply focus upon seeing into the business of seeing. Such seeing into the act of seeing asks, how should one understand a painting as a painting? For paintings are themselves both objects and events in the realm of human experience. The Frenchman, Edouard Manet, was often concerned with this latter problem.

Attitude, then, constitutes the second level of art. It asks, how does a person relate himself to some aspect of life, or to life in general? How is this done through a work of art? So, to bring this legitimately about, the emotional content of the artwork must be true to human experience. This involves deep insight and cannot be feigned.

Thus the form, or structure, of what is experienced in an artwork as the conveyor of its expressed attitude, should be felt and recognized as valid in its internal integration and expressive power. In addition, what is seen in the work, and in the world upon a viewer's experiencing the work, must be honest and insightful in expression and representation. This is so, even if the representation is purely emotional without a further connection to experience. Whatever the case may be, the expression must not be sentimental.

It is in these ways that the viewer's role becomes important. For his response to the artwork concerning the attitude presented to him is at issue. Initially, he should seek to understand the work in its depth. He should linger as reader, viewer, or listener, not glance casually, as it were, then walk away, more interested in a public exhibition of his sophistication than in a careful study of the work. Moreover, once its insight has been absorbed by him, he should seek to apply it to himself and to his relationship with the world.

Perhaps the insight is a problem presented by the artwork which should be appreciated and understood, its application to life only gradually growing out of an increasing elevation and complexity of mind gained over many viewings of that one work, as in a Rembrandt painting, or through exposure to many similar works, as in the modern works of Paul Klee. Or perhaps the artwork simply conveys a sense that life should be accepted and more deeply understood as it is, as in the work of Toulouse Lautrec.

Or perhaps again the artwork suggests that an immediate and direct act or set of acts should be carried out concerning some particular circumstance in life. This latter response is rarely the case, as is appropriate. But sometimes it is the work's conveyed attitude nevertheless. Much of the work of the Spanish painter, Francisco de Goya, is an example of such an appeal to direct action. His work is an immediate and anguished cry for humane standards.

Whatever the case may be, insight through the development of an attitude is what art provides. For an artwork is a complex integration of varied but related emotions under a controlling conceptual framework. The whole of this emotion-fraught thinking, this philosophy delivered in terms of a direct emotional statement, is the work's attitude. And that attitude must ring true in relation to experience. It must faithfully reflect the content of the work, which in turn accords honestly in some way with life.

Finally, a repeated experience of deeply true works of art—which is an encounter with attitudes based on clear insight—is what builds up a strong and broadly responsive sensibility, which is the mark of a cultured man or woman. A cultured man or woman, possessed of this enlarged awareness of life, is thus equipped to deal with the subtle variations of moral circumstance. And that is the moral value of art.

Acquiring an understanding of art's contribution to this kind of emotion-based knowledge is what constitutes a science. It is a science of emotion, a science which should be carefully cultivated, and therefore understood, like any other body of knowledge. It will lead to a deepened moral understanding among people. For it is not a dilettante's idle play.

Such an exercise of the mind would, of course, be of no value if there were no basis of truth to it. And initially, it can be difficult to distinguish a cultured individual from a merely knowledgeable one. But the difference is certainly evident. For the superficially knowledgeable person only knows how to appear to possess what he does not.

So since his pose is an act of cunning, of false pretense, he may have some idea of how to substitute this cunning for genuine feeling, awareness, and moral and aesthetic sensibility. But when directly confronted with the depths of truth in both art and life, he will invariably fall into an easily recognizable confusion.

The Art of Philosophy

WHEREAS a work of art is a philosophy of life exhibited through the emotions, a philosophical system is a work of art expressed in terms of reason.

THE goal of an idealist empiricist philosophy, as opposed to a materialist empiricist philosophy, is to bring the spiritual underbelly of the universe to light. It is to demonstrate that the entire material edifice of science rests upon a foundation of consciousness and spirit.

HUMANKIND is eternally in search of truth. Yet it is never truly found. Nevertheless, the fact that approximations appear to approach nearer and nearer to the desired goal is sufficient evidence that there is such a thing as truth. A person could not get through the snowy Sierra Nevadas if he had a map that did not fit the terrain. But having a map that does fit the terrain well enough to get him through the mountains in winter does not mean that the map is a flawless representation of those mountains.

PHILOSOPHY is an imaginative enterprise. No one should stand in fear of that fact. While it is true that philosophy's principles ought to be laid out in a clear and logical fashion, philosophy is not mere argumentation. It is not logic-chopping. It is rather the setting forth of a consistent vision.

When the vision fades, what remain are the insights gathered up in that vision and expressed according to its parameters. These insights are what endure. They are what the next philosopher picks up and uses as the building blocks of his own unique vision. He does this by adding his own insights to them.

PHILOSOPHY is an art. It is part of literature. As a poem is made from images and structured by the rules of prosody, or versification, so a philosophical system is made from concepts and structured by the rules of logic. A poem seeks to enlarge moral imagination by expressing feeling in its accuracy and depth. An understanding of subtle feelings, which become the turning points for will, is a basis for moral awareness.

A philosophical system enlarges the imaginative power of conception. Though such systems are superseded by other systems in time, their conceptual insights remain. They are like those flashes of meaning that come from the images of a poem. In both cases, these are what are remembered. They help the mind to see.

TO be a philosopher is to be a poet. And to be a poet is to be a philosopher. A philosopher begins in thought and arrives at beauty. A poet begins in beauty and ends in thought. There is a spiritual sense in this: it is the recognition of a harmonious rectitude in all things, including the seeming divide between reason and emotional sensibility.

THE poet is closer to the philosopher than the scientist is. Yet many would treat philosophy as if it were a meta-science. In all their speculations about the universe, the limits of knowledge, etc., what people really want to know about is themselves. How do they relate as human beings to this or that phenomenon? Hence, what is the nature of the phenomenon? And how does it relate to themselves?

SCIENCE is knowledge. Philosophy is wisdom. Knowledge is communal. It is developed with other people and from a collective reasoning about common physical experience. Wisdom arises out of a dialogue within the individual self. People often confuse knowledge and wisdom. This is sometimes even true of philosophers. But when Socrates says, “Know thyself,” and “The unexamined life is not worth living,” he is not talking about knowledge. He is talking about wisdom.

REASON is sterile without imagination. But reason is important because it disciplines imagination. What was once associative and wildly free falls under the critical order of logical relations. Here associations may be examined for their consistency with one another. Here imaginative images are replaced by concepts, which are images set by definition. Order and mental truth are brought to bear on creative power.

A high respect for reason is the great innovation now associated with Western civilization. Too much faith in the rigors of definition and logic can lead to a stifling of the creative power which arises from a free association of flexible imaginative images. But too little of it impedes intellectual honesty and the structural development of human thought.

CONTRA the view of Bertrand Russell, philosophy is not a simple expression of curiosity. That is science. Though, of course, there is a great deal of curiosity in philosophy. But philosophy is principally motivated by a search for the good life. This is the definition which Socrates originally gave it. And it still holds.

It even applies to the pre-Socratic philosophers. Though some of them may not have considered it in this way, as their focus was on an understanding of the nature of things. But that understanding was sought for the sake of the good life. The same general view also applies to the Eastern thinkers of India, China, and Japan.

PHILOSOPHY does not compete with science. It is sometimes believed that modern science will eventually answer all questions about the universe. True, it will answer the questions it asks. But there are many questions it does not ask, such as: What is being? What is self? What is free will? and What is consciousness? It is the business of philosophy to ask and attempt to answer these questions.

For example, someone might ask: where did the universe come from? Science might answer: from the big bang. But that does not explain how the universe came into existence. It expresses how it came into its present form. This is process. Philosophy attempts to push the question beyond process. A Far Eastern sage once remarked, "Before there was nothing…" and left the remainder to be pondered. That is philosophy.

PHILOSOPHY is a science founded on qualities, not on quantification. That is why its truths cannot be uncovered by logic alone. But once imagined by other means, a philosophical argument may be set forth and validated according to the form of an argument. For it is argumentation, not the substance of the argument, which is subject to rule.

A CHARACTERISTIC of modern times is the need for a narrow specialization due to the limitations of a human lifespan, the complexity of approaches to different fields of knowledge, and the massive amount of information available in each field. But this specialization comes at a cost. And that cost is the narrowing of imagination and hypothesis into ever more constricting limits.

On the other hand, to ignore these limitations is to find oneself scattered amidst a plethora of uncertainties. It means taking ever greater risks of being wrong in the details for the sake of a more comprehensive vision. If the vision succeeds, it may change the nature and relation of the details. But if it fails, oblivion—or worse, a cult following—may result.

PHILOSOPHY must be personal as well as abstract. All philosophy is lived philosophy, even when the philosopher has become so involved in abstruse speculations, he has forgotten that this is the case. Human beings ponder the meaning of life because they live it. But it is also true that they live it in the manner in which they ponder it. To live with less than such a habit of reflection is to deny humanity to oneself.

TRUTH is simple. Convoluted explanations are a sign of untruth. Look anywhere. And it will become clear that this is so. Look at science. Was it not the simplicity of Copernicus' explanation of the movements of the heavenly bodies that revolutionized the world's view of them? Sometimes complex explanations for things have to be worked with because the simple ones have not been discovered. But they will appear in time, if a lookout for them is kept and their messengers are not ridiculed and destroyed. The same is true of religious doctrine. If it seems convoluted and incomprehensible, that is no doubt because it is. It is far from the truth.

ONE should not attempt to present a philosophical system as final. Systems come and systems go. Only their insights remain. However, there are systematic parameters in philosophical thought. A philosopher tries to point the mind in a particular direction. She says: take this perspective; here are my arguments for it; follow it on out in your own way to see where it leads you.

PHILOSOPHY works best when it is continually challenged, not when it becomes doctrine. No matter how impressive a philosophical system may seem, further discussion is the only means of teasing out its essential enduring insights.

PHILOSOPHICAL systems come and go. All of man's attempts at systemizing are mere templates placed upon the face of reality. In the end they must fail. But each such attempt creates new insights which are carried on into the next such attempt. It is in this way that human beings progress in conceptual understanding: by a rearranging of the elements of knowledge under new systems of insight.

A PHILOSOPHICAL system, inasmuch as it is a system, is of the greatest unimportance. What matters are the insights revealed by the structure of that system. These endure. These are picked up by later imaginative thinkers and woven into new systems of thought, which reveal their own insights in a new structure.

This is the dialectic and evolution of human thought: high points taken from old combinations and being brought together into new combinations with different high points. Thus thought, like nature, never creates something out of nothing. This is because thought is subordinate to nature, upon which it depends for material.

PHILOSOPHY is about seeing. It is not about argument. However, philosophy uses arguments to present its vision. Within that vision are specific insights concerning the relationship of human beings to all that pertains to them. These insights are what are passed on through the ages, to be taken up and reused by philosophers with new visions. The new visions are composed of both the old insights and some new ones. The vision itself inevitably fades into history.

The same is true in the arts. For example, a painter works with color and line, just as a philosopher works with arguments. But it is the vision of the artist which contains enduring insights. For art too is about seeing. And this aesthetic seeing also pertains to a human being's relationship to the conditions of her existence.

EVERY philosophical system that dies may be exhumed for its precious minerals. It is the individual insights which went into the building of the system that endure and are used over and over in later systems of thought. They are not reused once, but many times.

THE wisdom traditions of the world are preserved in many literary sources: principally religious texts (scriptures), works of creative imagination, and philosophical writings. But the essence of wisdom is that it is a search for the *way*—that is, the way to live life. If that search is overlooked, these sources can become distorted.

For example, religious institutions often propose simplified formulas based on scriptural sources, which formulas are designed for easy, convenient, communally and politically useful practice. They are a reinterpretation of the original sources, carried out for institutional purposes and often blinding the adherent to the original meanings of the sources.

Another example is to be found in high schools, colleges, and universities. For the sake of a conformity with social fashion, these institutions frequently teach literature as though it were a course in science or engineering. In such teaching, there are no longer suggestive images and events relating to life that may be interpreted as a way of understanding life. Rather, there are wooden, inflexible symbols memorized without the need for individual aesthetic interaction with the material at hand. And there are mechanical rules for creating and interpreting emotional effects, as if the effects alone were the purpose of great writing.

Philosophy has the saddest history of all. Since the time of Descartes, there has been an emphasis on intellectual truth without much reference to the overall human condition. The brain, which was once a soft, living thing in a sea of impulse and feeling, has become a hard, dry sponge designed to memorize logical approaches in an atmosphere of pure intellectualism. It has little relation to life.

But human beings must *live* life, not simply know about it. They are not disembodied brains. They are flesh and blood, emotion, desire, disappointment and joy. How to live in the midst of this flood of feeling is the most important issue. If knowing the character of the universe or exploring the nature of understanding can contribute to this, all is well and good. But if not, such erudition is wind in an empty tunnel.

THERE is a philosophy of common experience. This means that in such a philosophy there should be a continual reference to something in common human experience. This common experience anchors any of the abstract concepts formulated within the philosophy as an interpretation of life.

However, it does not mean every concept must be tied to something which can be verified by what is generally thought of as empirical investigation. Philosophy is not a science. It is a self-integrated vision.

So it can afford to range into areas of experience which science would, by convention, avoid as unverifiable.

For example, if consciousness and spirit were held to be the same thing. And if it were further asserted that all things have a spiritual core (something correlating to what consciousness is in a human being or a higher animal). This assertion is certainly not being referenced to experience in a way which is open to experimental verification in the scientific sense. For how can a plant or a rock be investigated to determine if it has a spiritual core?

Nevertheless, the idea is founded on common experience. All people do experience consciousness in themselves. Or at least, it is mutually agreed among them that they do. So to assert that there is something like this at the core of all things, as indigenous religions appear to do, is simply to chose not to grant a precedence to the rational pattern of mental content which a typically modern human mind may have trained itself to cultivate.

In making this choice, what is being acknowledged is that the rational content of the human mind is predicated upon a demonstrably fallible human reason. And this is not to mention the even less reliable information of the senses, without which the rational content could not be formulated.

Given such a view, the idea that empirical reasoning should be a law unto itself can be ignored. That is, there is no obligation to assume, as many Westerners are trained to do, that the physical universe is nothing more than a cause-and-effect mechanism, mathematically arranged. Because a materialist viewpoint is all that can be derived from the senses by a faculty of reason limiting itself to the evidence of those senses alone is no reason to accept such a straightjacket. There are alternatives.

One of those alternatives presents the suggestion of a priority of spirit over matter. It is founded upon the observation that consciousness is prior to its content. In other words, the presumed input of the senses is subordinate to the mind which perceives it. For that information could not be known without the perceiving mind, which is the conscious mind. Such information is a product of the conscious mind, not the origin of it.

The only matter a person can look into is herself. Penetrating beyond the surface of her own material appearance, such a person perceives spirit. She experiences consciousness in itself, irrespective of its content. So why should she assume that all other matter, whose appearance she cannot penetrate, lacks this spiritual core? Should she take the surface appearance to be more vital to her understanding than the depths of her own being?

Such an argument as this is based as much on common human experience as any other. The abstraction from appearances which it entails results in an extension of the idea of spirit or consciousness to the foundational core of all things. Thus it bears a reference to what any human being can understand as pertaining to her most essential knowledge of life. For it references that consciousness which is not only her own ground of awareness. It is also that of any other person to whom she may choose to communicate her insights in depth. Thus it is a philosophy of common experience.

THE philosophy of common experience avoids empty abstractions and vacuous discussions. There is a bone-weary waste and discomfort in arguments for argument's sake. They are no more than a distraction of petty ambition. For one senses a penetration of ego into the fabric of such a discussion. At such a time, it is best to turn away to concerns of greater immediacy and importance.

But this does not imply that the human mind should imprison itself in a practical, material realm. Nor does it indicate that a person should avoid speculative discourse. For there is nothing more practical than a desire to be in a right relationship to one's own being. The desire for this is the love of truth. Its practice is the pursuit of wisdom. But a longing for truth should never become a matter of ego. Ego is a subtle foe. Many an individual has been lost to the false individualism of ego. For this reason, it must be guarded against at all times.

PHILOSOPHY can and should embrace ideas which the precision of mathematics would reject. Philosophy is more inclusive in its principles and less precise; mathematics less inclusive and more precise. Completeness of thought demands inclusiveness. Rigor of thought demands precision.

MATHEMATICS is subtle. Philosophy is profound. Subtlety is the ability to clearly see specific relations within a complex situation. Profundity, on the contrary, is the capacity to extract from a complex situation its simple, underlying, and unifying truth.

THE goal: to find an explanation of consciousness which will provide a foundation for spirituality and will be grounded in material nature without becoming mechanistic.

PROVING or disproving anything in science is not a concern of philosophy. There can be no question concerning the effectiveness of science in the business of manipulating experience. But this practical use of the mind does not explain the mind's relationship to experience. So the province of philosophy is to demonstrate how the mind works, to explain how it idealizes experience in order to classify it and effectively organize it into thought, and to probe the depths which lie beyond the mind's material representations.

ANIMALS exhibit curiosity: a cat with a ball of yarn (this is sometimes called play), a hummingbird hovering inches from a person's face and staring into it, even an ant forced into hiding and acting as though wanting to know why it has been impeded in going about its business. Is curiosity a form of nonverbal philosophizing?

Are asking such questions and the pursuit of answers to them one and the same activity? Are there ways of thinking without words? Painters think without words. They do it with color and line. And what questions they raise, what philosophies they inform us of, what wonders they awaken in us!

Philosophy is the business of asking certain kinds of questions: those which often cannot be answered. Does this pushing of questions beyond solution, this entertaining of antinomies, imply that the question alone is the goal? Why, that is curiosity! So are philosophy and curiosity, or at least a certain kind of deep curiosity, one and the same? One might observe that philosophy is in earnest, seeking profound solutions to life's problems. Interesting. Is that not, at least in some sense, how biologists explain the behavior of animals—that their curiosity is a form of play designed to better fit them to the world?

REASON is not an infallible instrument. To recognize its limitations is not difficult. But what do human beings have, other than reason? A person may directly experience the things of spirit. But she can say nothing about that experience, unless she uses reason. Thus human consciousness, a work of art, or a mystical experience may be directly known by a man or woman. It may be known by a thousand or millions of men and women. But it cannot become an object of discourse or of shared values without reason. Reason is the mother of civilization, though much of that civilization's substance may lie elsewhere.

IN the pursuit of an intellectual awareness of the human condition, two things should be considered. Thought is not identical with consciousness. It takes place within consciousness. And philosophy is not the pursuit of knowledge. It is the love of wisdom, which seeks an understanding of the relationship between knowledge and human beings.

AN undisciplined skepticism is a refuge for small minds. All things can be brought into doubt. So, if a person has no ideas, she can doubt. And this will appear to be wisdom.

BOTH mathematics and logic are instruments of quantitative reason. That is, in this type of thinking, things are related in terms of units. "All dogs are mammals" relates the unit "dog" to the unit "mammal." Dogs and mammals are the quantified terms of this statement, or proposition. Dogs are quantified as "all dogs," which is the unit "dog." And mammals are quantified as "some mammals," which is a division of the unit "mammal." For all mammals are not dogs.

However, qualitative thinking may relate these phenomena in a different way. It may compare them by means of likeness or difference. No doubt this form of thinking has already abstracted the quality "dog" from an investigation of many dogs of different character. It has identified those qualities all dogs, or at least all dogs encountered, have in common. Having abstracted these qualities to the classification "dogs," it thus quantifies them as the unit "dog."

Now qualitative reason, in making further comparisons, may observe that cats, dogs, horses, etc. all nurse their young. It abstracts this quality of lactation and groups the animals possessing it into the unit "mammal," which thus once again becomes a quantified term. These two quantified terms, "dog" and "mammal," can be logically related in the quantifying proposition mentioned above: all dogs are mammals.

Modern physical science began by focusing on the quantifiable aspects of phenomena—i.e., extension in space, motion (or change of place in space), and change (or change of condition in time). Proceeding in this manner over four centuries, it is still quantifying the world. Today the quantifying perspective dominates Western culture.

However, this way of reasoning subordinates qualitative relationships. Qualitative thinking not only relates things to one another by likeness and difference. It relates them to humankind. To ask, what is the function of this? is to ask, what is its meaning? When the mind approaches this state of a quest for meaning, it enters the domain of wisdom and beauty. It can only enter this domain qualitatively. So ignoring qualities leaves ethics and aesthetics in neglect. It creates a civilization weighted too much to one side.

AMONG British thinkers, it is not only David Hume who had a major impact on the German philosopher, Immanuel Kant. There is also Bishop George Berkeley. Kant's first glance at the phenomenal viewpoint could well have been derived from a reading of the good bishop. For all that Berkeley removes from any conception of an external world is the idea of a thing-in-itself, which would later become the unverifiable basis of Kant's noumenal world.

Anything a person might wish to conceive concerning a world known through the senses can be thought acceptable to the good bishop, so long as no one insists on separating that world from the direct agency of spirit. This is because, according to Berkeley, the world is conveyed through mind, which is spirit.

So if in Berkeley's day it had been possible to put aside an insistence upon the separate existence of things-in-themselves, people could have gone on to do good science without that belief. For in such a case, all the relations of things would remain the same. And science is based upon the consistency of relations. This is, of course, what the scientific thinkers did, though they did also cling to the concept of the thing-in-itself. For they thought Berkeley was wrong.

The reason many thinking people, like Samuel Johnson, thought at the time that Berkeley was wrong is that they erroneously conceived of him as denying material reality. That is to say, when considering such a case, they mistook visions of solipsism for Berkeley's simple denial of the thing-in-itself. For this reason, Kant was necessary.

RENÉ Descartes provided the form of a modern argument with his mind / body split. Then John Locke set out to explain how it is that things which are body can be known by the mind. But in doing so, he failed to make secure the connection between sensory experience and the object of that experience. So to eliminate the gap, George Berkeley simply dismissed the material object, the thing-in-itself. For him experience was mind and mind only.

But David Hume would have none of it. He discarded the foundations of metaphysics, and science as well, and thus awoke Kant from his Promethean slumber. In an effort to save science, Kant closed the breach between Rationalism and Empiricism, between what might be innate in the mind and what was direct sense experience of the world. He developed the thing-as-perceived, grounded in both.

That is the story. But in truth it was a battle waged over centuries, expanding far beyond the lives of these five philosophers. It was humankind's confidence in its use of reason which was at stake. How many people realize what has happened: Prometheus up on his rock agonizing for all mankind?

How many know that the progress of science initially floated on a cloud of intellectual faith and uncertainty? How many realize that it still does? The final definitions are not gathered in. There is always a new understanding, always something left out of the former comprehensive view. Yet struggles such as this take place out of sight of most people. And there is nothing insignificant about them.

SOCRATES was a mystic, Plato a pure rationalist. Plato dogmatized Socrates' notion of the eternal ideas by equating them with the mind of an eternal being, rather than by simply associating them with it. In other words, reason, or some portion of it, may emanate from this being. But the mind of eternal being may be something far above reason.

Socrates would not have had a problem with this. But Plato would. The problem for the modern scholar has been the tremendous impact this has had on Western Philosophy. Too often reason has been seen as being above and beyond nature when, in fact, it is merely an integral part of it.

PLATO provides a definition of wisdom which expresses an outlook that concerns, but is not limited by, his concept of eternal ideas. This practical insight could be beneficial in contemplating ethical problems. For the definition indicates that wisdom is comprised of a relationship between correct ideas of things and the human being who has those ideas.

Plato's concept of knowledge is that it occurs in the realm of being, or intelligibility, which is the domain of the mind. This is opposed to the realm of becoming, which is the material world as perceived by the senses. The separation of the mind from the senses occurs because human beings are, in Plato's view, born with a stock of innate ideas which constitute an expression of the essence, or fundamental nature, of things. Since these essences are inborn and originate in transcendent being, each of them is a permanent, immutable idea.

It is only by means of these immutable ideas that the ever-changing material objects encountered intermittently through the senses can be made accessible to reason in a clear and intelligible form. This is because reason, drawing on these eternal ideas, gives the perfect, unchanging character of things, not their changeable and thus varied character.

Things remain unclearly perceived under the imperfect observation of the senses. Whereas the eternal ideas are innate and do not change. But the eternal ideas do correspond to the objects of physical experience. So reason, employing these immutable ideas in relation to physical experience, leads to a knowledge of that experience which could not otherwise be known.

But this straightforward and highly specific knowledge is not all that is available to an inward looking mind. There are aspects of experience which can be apprehended by a faculty higher than knowledge. This faculty may be called the understanding. Its interest is the universal. The universal encompasses such ideals as the Good, truth, beauty, and justice.

Unlike the more specific ideas which represent the individual essences of objects to reason, this faculty generates ideas which govern the relations of things, particularly the relationship between things and people. Like specific ideas of things in themselves, these ideas are unchanging and eternal. Because of this and its final, overarching character, bringing things together in a meaningful way, understanding leads to wisdom.

So how would a person relate the specific ideas apprehended as knowledge to the more abstract, relational ideas grasped by the understanding? The specific ideas provide knowledge about specific things, while abstract, relational ideas relate those things and, most importantly, relate the knower to those things. This higher understanding becomes wisdom because it provides human beings with a means of acting well. People discover how they should relate to other people and things.

Among the universals, the Good is held to be the highest truth. It is being itself, which, when understood, is truth. So it is all that is true in itself. Everything which is true in itself is clearly recognized not only in its own nature, but in its relationship to other things. For being is one. The beautiful, therefore, is anything understood to be harmonious within itself and, most importantly, in its relationship to humankind.

For beauty, constituting a unity between material experience and human awareness, provides an approach to the final unity which is recognized within the mind. Justice, on the other hand, is confined to a harmonious relationship between human beings. Justice is therefore a limited form of beauty. Thus, with these examples of harmonious, or integrated, relationship, it can be seen that the Good underpins knowledge in general, bringing it together in understanding.

If the ultimate, ontological nature of something is known, the knower must certainly have a solid and irrefutable grasp of what it is. So the Good, conceived in this way as the very ground of being, can be understood as the source of all things and therefore the cause of their interrelationships as well. To grasp this is to approach final truth. According to Plato, it is what is attained by means of the highest wisdom.

So, discarding the abstruse notion of eternal ideas, how might practical use be made of Plato's concept of wisdom? It can be employed in understanding how the mind thinks ethically. To do this, two things are required. First, there must be a clear grasp of what is being thought about. Secondly, there must be a sense of where things belong in the *general* scheme—especially inasmuch as they have a relation to humankind. For a clear grasp of what things are and what they mean for people is the eternal and highest preoccupation of human beings. Thus it is wisdom.

EMPATHY, kindness, enlargement of sensibility—these qualities are not apprehended by the intellect alone but by imagination and sympathy. A person's imagination must be enlarged to encompass other people. Then feelings of sympathy will follow. The mind must be willing to see others in ways which have not been anticipated before. As a result, sensibility will be enlarged.

But what is the role of philosophy? It is hard to say. For philosophy was once considered to be a guide. Now it is thought to be an investigation. In ancient times, philosophers sought a way in which individuals and societies might live life to its fullest potential. But the way has continued to broaden, due to large-brained Plato and incisive Aristotle.

These men, to some degree inadvertently, set philosophy on its present course of speculation for speculation's sake. Plato and Aristotle are greatly to be admired. But the influence of the former on Plotinus, and of the latter on the scholastics and Thomas Aquinas, led to such modern thinkers as Spinoza, Leibnitz, Kant, and the German idealists. This has left a good part of philosophy somewhat in the clouds. Still, there is much to be learned from them.

IT is most probable that Aristotle wrote the books attributed to him. They are not simply notes recorded by one of his students, as some scholars appear to think. Aristotle's works may seem dry and overly compact to the casual reader, especially when they are compared to the dialogs of Plato. But one must look closer. For Aristotle was a practical, no-nonsense kind of speculative thinker.

This can be deduced from the character of his philosophy, which is entirely this-worldly. One sees it in his scientific interest. It can be observed as well in the reported facts of his life. He would not allow Athens to make him a second martyr to philosophy after Socrates. And he tutored Alexander the Great, a man of extraordinary practical accomplishment. These facts support the character of his writings. They are a reflection of him: terse, going straight to the point without stylistic flourish, and cleared of any debris of wishful thinking.

THERE is a problem with the distinction between noumenal reality and phenomenal reality. For a distinction to exist, they must both have a structure, however that structure may differ between them. For, were it not the case that noumenal reality has a structure, how could it be conceived? And how could it exist or be said to differ from phenomenal reality?

So, if noumenal reality is understood to be the world as it is, yet unavailable to human awareness, and phenomenal reality is the world as human beings perceive it, then the advance of science should eventually take the human mind off course. For it will not reflect the noumenal reality which is the world as it is and which must therefore in some way influence the character of the world as it is perceived.

In phenomenal reality, the way the mind perceives must correspond to what is perceived. But what is perceived will, in its noumenal character, possess an underlying structure which determines the relations of the perceived structure. Yet all that can be experienced are the relations of the perceived structure.

Take an example. There is a painting by Velázquez, which is a portrait of Philip the Fourth of Spain. The painting is not large. And it is no more than a bust representation of the king. When a person stands at a distance of about twelve or more feet from the portrait, it comes alive. The flesh seems to move. And there is a sense of warmth, as though the figure in the painting were living flesh.

But let the viewer step within a few feet of the painting, and the portrait goes cold. Moreover, the viewer cannot determine by looking at the colors or brushwork what it is that makes the portrait come alive at a greater distance. So, if the viewer only saw the painting close up, she would have no idea of the underlying structural principles that were in the mind of the artist. Those are the principles which make the painting come alive at a greater distance.

Now imagine that the close up view is the phenomenal view. The twelve foot view is the noumenal view. What happens if a person is stuck in the phenomenal view and she begins by means of an acute and detailed analysis to describe the nature of what she perceives? Eventually her analysis will become so precise and complicated, she will arrive at false conclusions as to why the world is constituted the way it is.

False because the noumenal view would have supplied the underlying organizational principles that are not available to a phenomenal perspective. And there is nothing in the phenomenal view to suggest them. So the investigator must wander about in the phenomenal, constructing her science from its elements alone, as she tries to become more and more exact in her analysis of its relations.

But those relations are governed by relations she cannot see. Since she cannot see them and knows nothing of their existence, her increasingly intense analysis becomes a compounding of what she does see. Moreover, in extending her thought beyond perception, her ideas will become a collection of inferences drawn from what she does perceive. Proceeding in this manner, she will eventually arrive at a point where she is far from the noumenal truth. Thus her science will have gone astray.

THOUGH rough and complex in expression, *Thus Spoke Zarathustra* is a work of unsurpassable beauty, subtlety, even delicacy of thought. There is nothing in it of the proto-fascist, as some are inclined to believe. It is strange that this elegant, at times mystical, attack on the worldly nature of spirit and religion should not be seen as true religion and genuine spirituality.

There is no claim here that Nietzsche was a Christian or that he adhered to any other conventional religious view. But his notion, expressed in the vision of the madman in *The Gay Science*, that God is, or should be, dead is nothing more than a simple plea for honesty.

Human beings have encrusted their human views of God and spirit with so much vain, manipulative nonsense, it would seem that the only way to clean up the mess is to destroy it and start over.

INTELLECTUAL demagogues, who screen their knowledge from the people and learn nothing from them as well, do this through snobbery and a deliberate obscurity in the expression of ideas. In response, the people both ignore them and accept their own ignorance. This practice arose initially from the intimidating obscurity of science—a science which has increasingly attached itself to an expression of its principles through mathematical formulas which, in general, are not a possession of the people.

It also came from the rise of a complacent middle class preoccupied with the exclusive pursuit of wealth and comfort. Not just physical, but emotional and intellectual comfort as well. Nothing too trying, lest one's equilibrium be disturbed. This attitude has led to a loss of interest in the life of the mind on the part of most people and a resultant alienation of intellectuals from the greater portion of society.

These intellectuals, in further reaction, have learned to turn in upon themselves, creating art for art's sake and a philosophy limiting itself to a grounding and expansion of science. Thus their efforts have become increasingly unintelligible or uninteresting to everyone else. That, of course, has further alienated the practical, "working" and technical populace who, by the twentieth century, found themselves in complete social ascendance.

These workers, inventors, and technicians make practical things. And practical things make money. Moreover, in Europe these people are no longer in competition with an aristocracy of birth, which has in many cases grown financially weak and culturally effete. So the working and technical populace has dropped all interest in anything other than material pursuits.

All this has been further aggravated by the two great wars of the twentieth century, which brought about a loss of faith in human reason and in the reasonableness of the universe. In short, there is today a welfare state of the intellect. Those who supposedly dole out intellectual gifts are in contempt of those who must receive them. Those who receive them are either indifferent to, ashamed of, or confused by what they receive.

Ethical Considerations

HUMAN beings have received two gifts: courage and understanding. There is nothing else.

THE world is full of beautiful things: nature, art, fine craftsmanship, the human form. But the most beautiful thing is an open heart. This is not an easy thing to achieve. And few people attain to it. The reason is that one cannot reach such a goal starting from the normal adult condition. The disposition toward an open heart is something kept over from early childhood.

THE collapse of faith is the greatest tragedy of man. Everything good which has ever come from the human mind has been in some sense a product of faith. Faith is the means of pursuit, knowledge its conclusion. Yet the world is ever pressing in its insistence that fact is supreme. It seeks to convince people that what they conceive in imagination, unless immediately confirmed in the concrete, can never be.

SINCE facts can be called into question, sincerity is the locus for truth. For this reason, humanity's hope of salvation in truth lies in relationships, whether with a universal being, a person, or fact. But such is the nature of the world, with its ever-present encirclement of fears, that every relationship has an element of falseness in it. Thus the burning realization is often that there is no truth.

ALL religious doctrines and scientific laws are questionable in that they are always provisional. Religious doctrines become harmful to the extent that they interfere with spiritual growth. Scientific laws are negative in character to the extent that they are held to be final.

Otherwise, both are powerful tools which, like all practical human instruments, must be set aside when better ones are found.

LOVE is respect. Where there is no respect, there is no love, And nothing can substitute for respect in a relationship between people. Love professed without respect is hypocrisy. The world has been struggling with this simple and obvious fact for a long time. A kingdom of decency could be built upon it. But people repeatedly choose not to because they do not respect themselves.

IT is easier to recognize selfishness in another person than in oneself. For the judging person can always find reasons for what he does, but not for what another person does.

MUCH has been said about the selflessness of love. It would be better to speak of the sincerity of it. Where love is sincere, the right balance of self-regard and regard for others will exist. What is more important, sincerity generates an honest character. And where the loving expression of that character is unfeigned, it generates sincerity in others.

In other words, where sincerity is exhibited among people, trust begins to grow. Where trust exists, there is freedom based upon mutual respect. For where there is mutual respect, there is the ability to act without fear of censure or harm. Where there is such a balance between self-regard and regard for others, love will follow. Where love is exercised, a person can afford to be emotionally honest both toward himself and toward others. He is free to be sincere.

AN open heart is universal spirit expressed within material limitation. A closed heart, which is the normal expression of material limitation, cannot bear the exposure of a comparison to an open heart. To show such limitation up, to bring it into the light of day, is to announce the deathly progress of a living being. For a closed heart is a limited heart, which is an expression of death.

An open heart is imagination unencumbered by vanity. It does not seek another's opinion in order to form its own. It is willing to learn from others, but not to be limited by them. This is an extremely rare condition. But a heart in its openness and unlimited expression does make its appearance now and then.

THE great ethical works are not only found in philosophy. They are found in literature as well. For literature is inherently ethical. Both philosophical ethics and great literature are concerned with how the good life should be lived. The one supplies principles, the other insight into the human condition. Literature is important because an intelligent immersion in it transforms emotional intelligence in a way principles alone cannot. However, without principles, a person may approach literature as a dog approaches food: wolfing it down without tasting it.

THE purpose of formal education is to create uniformity. A self-educated person inevitably develops an insurgent character. Though he attended his share of schools, Einstein was self-educated. So was Jesus. Given his character, Caiaphas was probably not.

LIFE is an instrument put into human hands. An individual has first to evaluate, then learn how to use the instrument. To do this he must study its limitations. Then he should take note of its strengths and discover the best way to make use of them.

EDUCATION is not a matter of gaining control over facts, formulas, or whole bodies of information produced by others. That is called training. Education is the transformation of an individual through his contact with insights he has never before encountered: first those of others, then his own. This requires a wide exposure. For it develops a refined sensitivity capable of an analysis of ideas and impressions, accepting none as personally true until verified within the vision of an expanding individual mind.

Thus it does build upon what others have done. But only until that is no longer needed. For it seeks ultimately to foster a capacity for deep thought concerning relationships between disparate elements found in impressions, experience, and ideas. These are encountered—and produced as well—not by others, but by the individual who has learned to think alone.

MORAL courage is rare, much more rare than physical courage. Though human beings will upon occasion risk their lives, health, or fortune for a worthy purpose, it is rare to see anyone risk her reputation. Why is this? Why is a person's life more apt to be thrown away than her ego? The answer lies in instinct.

Human beings do have a powerful urge to protect their lives and physical wellbeing. But sometimes in the very act of doing so, they must take risks. For this reason each person has been abundantly supplied, especially in youth, with a kind of exuberance of spirit which says, "I will somehow always prevail. It is the other person who will fail." This exuberance is an instinct, a kind of joy of life that may seem to contradict but actually complements the survival instinct. The two instincts work together for human preservation and the enhancement of life.

Not so with the moral. Moral courage means that a person should follow her convictions through, even if they bring her into conflict with prevailing prejudice. But here there is only one instinct at work: the social instinct. There is nothing in the animal genome to counterbalance it. The social instinct demands that a person stick with the crowd and please it. There is no corresponding instinct for disagreeing with the crowd.

Moral conviction comes from the mind. It is intellect. It is this simple mind state which must oppose the powerful need to please the group. A person can go against one other person in the group, or even against a few, as long as she thinks the majority is behind her. She is still with the group. But to oppose the entire group on principle alone, that is a rare thing!

PLATO, Shelley, Dickens, Mozart, Galileo, Caesar, Gauss, Thucydides, Cézanne. Eschewing any standard but that of the highest mark in their individual fields of endeavor, they joined the ranks of enduring achievement. It is the only goal worth pursuing. Better to have sought that goal and missed its mark, than to have won a thousand awards in competition.

WHILE observing house sparrows at a feeder, one may notice what appears to be a tendency for the year's hatchlings to form a flock of juveniles over the course of the summer. This flock, growing ever larger throughout the summer, descends daily upon the feeder in late summer, the individual members of the flock bullying one another and any House Finches or other small and less aggressive birds and forcing them out of their way.

Human beings also do this. That is, they act like juvenile sparrows. They do it especially in the modern world, where commercial interests have created a youth subculture. When one of these modern humans reaches her teens, that individual feels a strong pull toward her peers. She may indentify with this or that subgroup, but altogether modern teenagers are separated socially from the rest of humankind. Within their subgroups, the stronger among them may bully the less aggressive or weaker members of their own and other teenage subgroups.

Upon attaining maturity, however, most young adults gradually learn to identify with and assimilate themselves into the larger body of responsible adults. That is to say, they conform to society. At least, they do so if they do not become in some way stunted in mental and emotional development, remaining maladjusted, or deviant.

But there is an important exception to this general pattern of human development, which is unlike that observed in the birds. It is made possible by the existence of human culture. This culture is a phenomenon which is greater than its creators. For they know not fully whence it comes.

The human culture creates its own anomalies. The most notable anomaly is an exception to ordinary social intelligence. That exception is the truly creative and original type of person. These individuals do also, like most of their peers, indentify with society as adults and want to contribute to its wellbeing. But they do not conform to it.

They see their membership in society in larger terms. Their sense of what constitutes society is, in fact, enlarged to such a degree that it may include both past and future, thus embracing the reach of culture rather than that of living humanity. Because of this, they can at times appear eccentric, maladjusted, or deviant to the contemporary body of society. And it is only when their contribution is eventually fully understood and assimilated that this mistaken perception of their role changes.

HUMAN beings seek happiness, find it difficult to achieve, and settle for comfort. All civilized institutions are built upon the principle of comfort. Even religion. It is for this reason that it is difficult to achieve happiness, since in doing so one is apt to run into conflict with one of the rules of comfort.

Thus nearly every person is settled into a comfort zone and secretly miserable. This is the dilemma of humankind. Should he undo the entire edifice of civilization and follow himself? If so, the risk of failure will be high. Or should he stick to prescribed modes of behavior which he knows to be false to his inner being?

With few exceptions, there can be no doubt which path the greater portion of the human race has taken. Yet there is but one life. For a person to choose to throw it away due to a threat of risk is a serious offense against himself. And when he lies in his grave, no one will care. For humanity will forget him. And universal spirit is truth: a truth not made by a committee.

FOR the most part, individual people, and the human race as a whole, learn by doing the wrong thing, not by thinking the right thing. This is the greatest single impediment to the improvement of individual character and the advancement of civilization.

PRIDE is one of the most difficult obstacles a human being faces. How to overcome it both in oneself and in others is the question. Every person knows the damage overweening pride can produce. It is ugly in its power to warp goodness. And it is operative almost everywhere and feared universally, even when it is clearly understood to be founded on weakness and a lack of self-esteem. Such is the power of divisiveness in human beings.

But the opposite of this is just as evil. If a person does not have a healthy regard for her own character, her individual merits, and the simple pleasures of her physical being, can she be said to be truly alive? Human beings care for others because they want to be cared for. They are mutually dependent in this way.

A person sees her own need in other people and theirs in her. So how can she think herself unworthy, when her self-regard is a central ingredient in thinking others worthy? The Golden Rule can be reversed: have others do unto you as you would do unto them. Show them respect, by all means, but also expect it in return.

THERE is a death which is like no other death. It is the death of a human soul. It is a common occurrence but is rarely seen. It passes the notice of most people because it most often does not coincide with the death of the body. It sometimes happens gradually. And often it is so from the beginning because it was never preceded by a birth.

This death involves the full human sensibility: imagination, reason, emotion, and will. But it is easiest to discuss it in terms of thought alone. Thought is imagination and reason. Emotion and will are the drivers of thought and are contained within it. Consequently, it should be understood that thought expresses emotion and will. It is human awareness in its fullness.

What should this awareness be like? How should people think? Confucius, Socrates, Moses, Buddha, and Jesus would supply an answer. Lao Tzu would perhaps only smile. For the answer is too simple. Human beings should be fully attuned to the business, not only of living, but of being. When a person thinks, her thoughts should be as clear and uncompromising as she can make them. When she feels, she should seek out the roots of her feeling. When insight falls upon her, she should open herself to it. When she acts, she should act out of the integrity of these sources.

Advice may come from anywhere. Social conditioning may seek to constrain her. But there is no authority beyond human thought and emotion. Should she seek the revelation of a scripture, it is because she warms to it. Should she turn directly to a god, it is because she is open to the idea of a god. Should she refuse the law, it is because she finds no reason in it. Should she love, it is because she wills it.

Whether human beings choose to accept it or not, they are at the center of their world. Each one of them is the core of meaning in her universe. How could it be otherwise? So, since each individual is the core of meaning in her universe, she should avoid materially selfish ends. For that is a limitation and denial of who she is. She should identify with all being, which, in her experience, she finds radiating outward from herself. And she should live in constant intimacy with herself in the highest integrity. There should be no self-deceptions where it is in any way possible to avoid them.

Some people never learn this and are never born. Life for such a person is a flickering flame which goes out in smoke soon enough. To burn bright, a person must both see and realize in herself the glory of being. Some people have understood this but lack the courage to believe in it and act upon it. They look to authority and hang their integrity on something beyond themselves. Either condition—that of not discovering life and that of surrendering it to something or someone else—is a living death.

EMPATHY and compassion are two elements employed in the development of an individual's ethical awareness. Compassion follows directly from empathy. For, to understand the ground of another person's experience and express commiseration toward it, a person must be able to imagine that individual's situation.

This requires both thought and experience. For thought without experience is a useless emptiness. And experience without thought is not properly human. So, as a matter of course, judgment must occur in ethical matters, including those of empathy and compassion. But the most difficult task for an empathetic person is to avoid being harsh. Any person who is in a position to judge another person should be on guard against a tendency to overcredit herself as to what she might do in a similar situation.

The humanities offer the best tools for refining moral awareness and thus gaining access to an empathetic character. History and biography are useful, if they are written with genuine insight. But it is great literature in particular which gives a reader the most penetrating and thorough illustration and thoughtful examination of emotional states. It allows the reader to encounter emotions which have not previously been known by her, enabling her to experience them in imagination, and thus giving her a means to grasp them with her intellect.

A careful reader of great literature, history, and biography sees that it is emotional discrimination, and not reason alone, which is a bedrock for human decision and action. But understanding human emotions in such a way as to profit from them requires that a reader commit herself to a profound examination of her text. For the true meaning of any written work can easily be ignored.

In short, moral understanding, which may be referred to as ethical wisdom, is a product of personal growth. To possess empathy, a person must advance in both experience and understanding. For empathy is grounded upon integrity. And integrity implies an integrated soul, embracing an interrelationship of heart and mind. Thus it requires a scrupulous honesty and an untiring effort toward achieving sympathetic insight.

It also involves intellectual principles. For moral guidelines of one sort or another must be applied to human actions. But these intellectual principles can be properly applied only after an enlargement of understanding has been brought as far as it can be by other means. For such principles must develop and attain subtlety in light of a broad experiential base which is emotional. Accordingly, it can be seen that the attainment of ethical wisdom is an ongoing process. It is never complete.

A PERSON can cite different ethical systems: virtue ethics, deontology, utilitarianism, Stoicism, etc. She may decide to follow one. So, in light of one of these systems, she can either attempt to take the "prudent" middle course of virtue ethics, recognize the binding rational principles of deontology, try to forecast the consequences of her actions as in utilitarianism, or simply regulate her own mental activity in such a way as to minimize her fears as in Stoicism.

But how often does anyone ever consistently and systematically follow only one of these courses of action in daily life? Almost never. What is generally done is that a little bit of all of them is practiced to the extent that these or those principles can be fit into the decision of the moment. And how many decisions are decisions of the moment, where there is so little time to reflect and where the most obscure knowledge of the full implications of a situation is being dealt with?

It seems that people gain most of their ethical knowledge from two things: one, the rules they are taught (or those they pick up unconsciously within the society in which they are nurtured), and two, the amount of contact they have with other human beings and the emotional experience they gather from that contact and interaction with others over the years.

THERE is a fundamental difficulty with the use of reason in ethical matters at a personal level. It is the way in which the problem thought about may shift in meaning. Let it be said that someone loves justice and would apply it wherever applicable. The problem is this: can this person keep a clearly defined, rigorously unvarying concept of justice in mind to apply to every situation? Or is it not possible that there are shifting circumstances in which she finds herself, not to mention an ever increasing tableau of her personal experience and the manner in which it changes her understanding of life and justice?

Is it not possible that these things will subtly, perhaps even unconsciously, alter the concept of justice in her mind? How then is she to govern her present and future action solely under the guidance of reason? It would be difficult for her to keep up with the minute, hardly detectable alterations of a myriad of variations of the concept of justice in her head. And that is assuming she is aware of the changes.

SINCERITY is the final definition of truth. There is nothing in the experience of nature or life which may not be placed in some doubt. But sincerity is not contingent upon experience. Rather, it reflects the character of an individual's relationship to it. Thus, when a scientific investigator uncovers new facts or laws, he must provide an assurance that what is being placed before the human mind is presented in honest simplicity. For these facts or laws will change, however subtly. And they will do so the more readily in an open environment.

SPIRIT-MINDEDNESS is difficult. For it sees with a full heart. It feels the tragedy and pain of the natural world. Nature being what it is, and human beings being a part of it, they must reconcile themselves to it. They cannot ignore it. So, when they take this spirit-minded state upon themselves, they must embrace life as it is, eyes wide open. They feel the pain. Yet they rejoice in all things.

ONE thing which is grudgingly learned over the years is that ambitions large and small possess a comparative value only in the limited, jostling materiality of the world. Outside this environment, every good purpose is absolute and of infinite value.

IT is difficult to think clearly where there is anger or offense. It is also difficult to reason out an appropriate response to a situation, if the circumstances are either not known or not clearly understood. It seems a human being is always in the dark, anticipating his own next move or an opponent's response, as does a military patrol in dim starlight and no moon.

This is a central problem in ethics. How can a situation be apprehended clearly enough to map out a response? It is not possible to read the mind and emotions of another human being. And it is here that all the secrets lay. A person can follow general principles. But these act only as rough guides.

In the final act, a decision rests upon the decider: his memories, cultural exposure, insights, principles, the stability of his emotions, the quality of his mind. When he does act, he is alone. He cannot initially see the immediate response, long term outcome, or universal estimation of what he has done.

THE writer Ernest Hemingway declared that war is life speeded up. Rather, one should say that acts of war are truer than life because they are not so thoroughly concealed beneath a layering of false civilities. In the ordinary living of life, people are apt to forget how much there is that they do not mean.

THE worship of money, science, and technology constitutes a cult of materialism. Its philosophical basis is that there is nothing beyond the evidence of the senses. Its ethical and aesthetic foundation is that appetite and a continual unfolding of subtle varieties of vanity are the meaning of life. It is an unquestionably powerful but shallow force, as social fashions often are. And it carries within it the seeds of its own destruction because it ignores the power of a creative mind to reach beyond the immediate.

THE desire for popularity, when it governs an individual life, is an expression of vanity. This drive is a waster of human lives. It is worse than war. For people can die with meaning in war. But in the grip of vanity, they pass through and go out of this world as empty vessels.

AN egoist is always looking over her shoulder to see what the other person thinks. Genuine self-confidence moves straight ahead without regard to opinion.

HUMAN egoism, in the sense of a person worrying unduly about what someone else may think of her and letting that govern her actions, is the single most destructive moral force in human existence. This form of egoism taints the very best human personalities, making any path of creative effort difficult and stony for her.

Worse yet, it vitiates in varying degrees the greater majority of minds and wills, limiting their powers to uplift the human condition or to allow others to do so. It is a sickness, which has its origin in a powerfully realized human self-awareness which is not yet strong enough to envision its own freedom.

SO many people live solely to eat, reproduce, and raise young. But they never stop to think, when they sit down to eat their beef in the evening, that that beef had the exact same view of life as they do.

SUBTLETY often accompanies malice. People tend to express their spitefulness with a smile. This would imply a strong relationship between malice and planning. Malice is spiteful behavior aforethought. A lack of malice therefore implies a lack of resentfulness burning within the secret heart of a person.

Yet it is almost impossible among adult human beings, and certainly rare, for a condition of spitefulness never to exist. When it occurs that it is never found to exist in a person, such an omission is likely to be accompanied by that person's habit of not dwelling on injuries inflicted upon herself. But this habit almost inevitably implies a drawback, namely that person's tendency to also not think of the effect of her own actions and words, good or bad, upon others.

This is interpreted as thoughtlessness, which it certainly is. But it is thoughtlessness without intent of wrongdoing. It injures others but does not mean to. Yet the very carelessness of it stands as a condemnation of the thoughtless person. So here arises a fundamental dilemma in the field of ethics: which is more important—absence of malice in the heart, or absence of the subtle thinking which usually attends malice but which also prevents injury through careless unconcern?

If the teachings of Jesus of Nazareth are to be accepted, the heart of a child is the preferred state, even with its omissions. The heart of a small child is one without forethought, often without afterthought as well, and generally without malice. For subtlety is a learned, more adult condition. Thus the fundamental question in ethics becomes: which is more important—the cause of my actions or the consequence of them? Is my character more important? Or is it my ability to do the least harm to others, regardless of my motives?

Jesus answers one way. People often answer another. This expresses the usual conflict between the naturalness of Jesus and the superficiality of present social structures and constraints. It is for this reason that it can be understood that Jesus' vision rests on something else. It transcends the material and dwells upon spirit. It looks for a universal condition of heart not yet realized, but felt, if only faintly, within every person. No Western institution has been able to consistently reflect this, not even as an idea.

THE depth and sincerity of a conversation are in inverse proportion to the number of people engaged in that conversation at one time. These are people who gather together in a single, simultaneous engagement of loosely connected tongues. Cocktail parties and many committee meetings belong to this category. They are generally more about social positioning than thinking.

A HABIT is a state of mind reinforced by repeated practice. A state of mind is a state of consciousness. And consciousness is spirit. Thus a habit is a spiritual state of mind. A mind in the grip of a bad habit is a mind possessed.

COURAGE is a product of both disposition and circumstance. Some people are constituted as more daring than others. But to have a courageous disposition in all or most circumstances, one must have the discipline of habit. As Aristotle says, "To act bravely habitually in varying circumstances is to develop a brave disposition." Sometimes discipline alone, as in military discipline, can set a person to do courageous things when he sees them as his duty and doing his duty is his daily habit.

Circumstances also give a sense of urgency or a lack of it to one's acts. In those circumstances which an individual conceives of as being of little importance, that person's response can be less than daring, especially if he is of a fundamentally retiring disposition and sees the cost of action as being too high for the prize won. But in circumstances of great importance to this same individual, all his inner resources may be called forth to meet the emergency. For this reason, it is presumption to hazard an opinion of another person's actions without knowing that person well.

HEROISM in combat is not precipitate. It can be, and often is, accompanied by hesitation, though the hesitation be but for a moment, providing a means of quick assessment. For there are no simple explanations of bravery. Bravery is not foolhardy. Rather, it combines heart with mind. In this way, it can be seen that heroism and hesitation belong together as fundamental battlefield requirements.

The former arises from a need for initiative, for decisive and aggressive action. The latter is born of the necessity that this initiative be conducted under the guidance of prudence. For, while it is initiative which carries purposiveness forward, it is prudence which increases the likelihood of its success. Thus it can be seen that courage is not bravado. It is not reckless. Rather, it is a result of a form of training which produces appropriate and measured habits on the battlefield.

These characteristics of war can stand in as a metaphor for life. There is a sense in which life itself is a battlefield. It is an arena in which forward movement is necessary. Decisive efforts are required to place new vision at the service of others. But a headlong pursuit of ambition without regard to its cost or its consequences to oneself and to others results more often in failure or ruin than success.

ANY ethical situation is an expression of trust. An unethical act is a breach of that trust. Trust is an expression of unity. Universal spirit is unity, the unity which lies behind all things. This unity which lies behind all things is one spirit out of which and within which all things material are formed. For this reason, a breach of trust is an offense against the spirit. For it is a denial of the unity.

When a person offends the spirit, that person offends the principle of unity within herself. She places an emphasis on the division inherent in material things, thus denying the unified awareness lying at the core of her being. For the division apparent in material things is an illusion. It is no more than the breaking of ice on a body of water.

BETWEEN two people there are many bonds of material necessity. Childrearing and property are two of them. But there is only one bond of spirit. That is the way one heart faces another, such as when two rooms are joined. The open door between them is neither specifically of one or the other but makes the whole a single room.

ANCIENT Israel accomplished more by not being a country than it did in all the years that it was one. For its greatness lay in its moral force. And moral understanding is never furthered by economics, politics, or the sword. These are the expressions of material limitation, not the expansiveness of spiritual insight, which the writings of ancient Israel have so abundantly provided.

THE present age does not seem to be one of the more brilliant moral epochs of humanity. Human beings live now in a time when the narrowing focus of imagination, which began in the late Renaissance, has given them great power over their physical environment. But this is a contraction of the breadth of mind.

So their appetite for abstract moral thought, particularly for deep insight concerning the central problems of humanity, has waned. Thus the long-delayed ability of people to cope effectively with major behavioral problems like overpopulation, environmental ruin, and military destructiveness.

The reason for this is that during the Renaissance, European culture gave up serious consideration of three of the four types of cause described by Aristotle. They kept only efficient cause. That being the form of cause which enters into cause-and-effect relations in the physical world, it is the one which is investigated by science. Aristotle's material cause has been subsumed under efficient cause. And so have both his formal and final cause, which consider fittingness (or value) and purposefulness respectively. These have been overlooked for four hundred years.

Such investigation as modern science offers has led to much material success. But it has disciplined the mind to look outward, away from the subjective. Thus practical scientific problems can be brilliantly solved at that focused range. But when this human vision is required to be enlarged beyond an isolated objective sphere of consideration, the mind is at a loss, even when the problems set before it are of a practical nature.

So how can present ethical problems be addressed? For example, how can the environment be preserved? Human beings, as creatures of this earth, remain an integral part of it. Thus it cannot be ignored. In addition to this, how is aggressive behavior to be curbed, given the destructive capacities with which science has endowed human beings? And what can be done about overpopulation? Finally, how can a society be built in which individual happiness and fulfillment are considered to be at least as important as the collective good, but in which, at the same time, the collective good is not overlooked?

These problems cannot be solved with science. For science is utterly blind to them. It offers special tools, but not the hands, hearts, and proper will to wield them. So there must be a return to the humanities, to a study of the human condition from a human perspective. The wellspring of moral understanding must become simultaneously internal to one person and to many.

For this reason, empirical psychology is not enough. Neither is sociology. Psychiatry is insufficiently comprehensive. And anthropology is little more than intellectual zoology, confined to one species. These objective sciences (save to some extent psychiatry) are all erected on an exclusive foundation of the senses and do not register values. They may study and classify values, their origin, development, and practice. But they do not reflect them.

So what are needed are the subjective sciences, sciences which consider the role of emotion as well as reason. They are history, philosophy, literature, art, music—that which for millennia has, or has sought to, knit the mind, emotions, and will of human beings together into a single comprehensive whole. Thus the human condition must be studied as though it were an integrated organism, sustaining its life over millennia as one mobile body. It should be understood within a full compass of mind, emotion, and will. It should be asked where it has been and where it is going.

There must be a return to a use of reason unconfined to corridors of strict material definition. An opening should be made in the range of imagination, which will be unfettered by what has been defined as an authorized objective sphere of investigation. All human beings should be taught to respect these liberated powers of reason and imagination in their social practice and in their private thought, even when they themselves lack the capacity to practice or understand them.

If this is not done, how will human beings ever come to envision such simple and obvious truths as the fact that laissez-faire capitalism, with its ethic of selfishness and greed, is a primary (but not only) cause of several of humanity's most pressing problems, such as environmental destruction and military aggression? A way must be sought to balance material progress with spiritual need.

ONE of the most problematic characteristics of the modern age is the tendency to assume any knowledge will contribute equally to the improvement of the human condition. Technical and scientific knowledge are useful. But that usefulness is primarily in the area of changing the physical environment in which human beings live. This no doubt materially improves the human condition. But it does little to affect it spiritually.

The social sciences may provide an exception to some degree. For, by advancing the knowledge of human psychology and social interaction, they increase an understanding of the human condition. Such an understanding is an important ingredient in forming ethical judgment. But it is not enough.

There must be an increase of sensibility. Sensibility should be defined as a full human capacity for awareness—self-awareness as well as social awareness. It involves intellectual and emotional development. This introduces an emphatic point: such a development must include the enlargement of moral imagination.

Art, music, literature, history, philosophy. These are the principal materials with which sensibility is to be constructed. This is so particularly in terms of ethical awareness and moral imagination. Every one of these "character building sciences" involves a subtle analysis of attitude and motive.

History, and especially philosophy, may be rational and indirect in their approach. But they are still directed toward an overall human-grounded outlook. Ethics in particular is concerned with attitude and motive because it is centered upon the will—its control, discipline, and proper employment for the benefit of all.

It is in this area that the material idea of knowledge fails. Because of a one-sided view of what constitutes useful knowledge, nations may continue to develop collectively and materially in power. But individually and spiritually they fall into decline. In the onrush of the modern, the receding ground may not be noticed.

THE five moral principles are:

To embrace life with all one's capacity.

To practice empathy with all one's reason and sympathetic imagination.

To express kindness with the consideration of a sound awareness as to how, to whom, and in what circumstances it is to be applied.

To act out of sincerity in every matter of intellect, body, and spirit.

To be thoughtful and reflective concerning one's own motives and the motives and circumstances of others.

IN consideration of the distinction between natural law and higher law, the following can be said. Natural law considers a human being as a material entity. As such, a person is understood to be liable to harm by her fellows and must herself be restrained from doing harm to them. Society as it is presently known is based on natural law.

Higher law considers a human being as a spiritual entity. It is the law of universality in perspective (everyone is my brother or sister) and is predicated upon a complete absence of fear. This is because spiritual beings, inasmuch as they are spirit, are indestructible. Hence they are not subject to fear. This is the ethical system taught by Jesus of Nazareth. It is not of this present social order.

VALID moral judgments are judgments which are of relevance to human concerns. So spiritual matters must be expressed within a context of human experience, if people are to get out of the habit of being lied to and of lying to themselves.

HUMAN beings are compelled to live by reason. If they wish to live sensibly, they cannot do otherwise. But to live by reason is to know the limits of reason. That is the paradox.

REASON is not an instrument of knowledge so much as it is an instrument of adjustment. Human beings are forever measuring the world by the yardstick of themselves and then amazedly discovering themselves in the world.

THERE is a relationship between heart and intellect. A clean heart makes a strong mind. When a heart is layered with malice and self-deception, productive critical thought must continually struggle through these barriers to clear vision. Otherwise, thought is being built upon a foundation of half truths.

This is why genius, particularly in the humanities, is always principally a matter of sincerity. Confucius, Buddha, Socrates, Jesus—these are men of deep conviction born of a desire to set the mind and emotions into balance, to restore their true function. And this aspect of who they are is what is always being misunderstood.

TO become a genuine register of an individual's character, his personal ethics must be centered in himself, not in the consequences of his actions. This was John Stuart Mill's argument, in spite of his utilitarian sympathies. It was based on the following observation. The good consequences of each person's behavior may redound to the immediate benefit of society. But if they do not reflect an elevation of character in those individuals, society will be become debased over time.

Consequences are complex in their ramifications and cannot be clearly seen at the time when a course of action is chosen. So, in addition to a cultivation of his reason, an individual must strengthen himself in emotional understanding and sympathetic imaginative response. For reason alone cannot foretell the subtle complexities toward which an action will lead.

Nor may it grasp the full measure of moral and motivational circumstances in the moment a decision is made. Emotions are elusive and at times hard to identify. For this reason, the moral domain and individual human motives are both far too subtle to be grasped by a reason stripped of emotional understanding and sympathetic imagination.

Therefore, three things should stand as the pillars of an ethically complete character. These are empathy, kindness, and sincerity. Empathy allows one person to understand another and his immediate circumstances. Kindness, as a universal principal, should always be the first expression of a moral character, subject to modification only when it is rebuffed, and then only to the degree which is necessary to a proper personal defense.

Sincerity is the bedrock of truth. So much is this so, it may be asserted that a fact can be said to be true only in the sincerity of a person's relationship to it. For it is the use of the fact which makes it relevant. Since a proper and honest use of the facts is what gives them value, facts can never be said to be isolated, morally inert entities. They must have a life in the bosom of humanity.

Sincerity is a matter of the heart. Only when an openness of emotional attitude is proffered is there sufficient personal risk in the giver to justify any risk taken by the receiver in response. Sincerity is therefore the foundation of trust, of that social bond of mutual interdependence which is itself the reason human beings come together in community. Community is so necessary to the ethical condition, it is meaningless to state without it the meaning of the word "moral."

Emotional understanding and sympathetic imagination are not simple things. Nor are they innate in human character. For this reason, education should play a role in broadening their acquisition. Since emotional understanding and sympathetic imagination have to do with human nature, though they are not intrinsic to it, it is only fitting that the humanities should play a central role in moral education. For their human connection is why they are called "humanities."

Emotional understanding and sympathetic imagination are the core of a moral awareness. The greater their development in each individual, the greater the personal and social benefit. Thus it is moral education which provides an assurance that any well intended actions should have greater certitude and reach. People will then be more likely to act as they should and to affect other people and situations with their right actions.

TRUTH is not bound up in fact. It is held within the observer of the fact. This is why facts can change or be reinterpreted. But truth remains eternal. Humanity continually reinterprets the world. So what remains is the sincerity of that interpretation. Thus the only question of relevance is, how committed is the investigator or thinker to seeing things as clearly and honestly as she can, given the present means at her disposal?

THE defining of oneself is perhaps one of the most difficult projects of life. For on the one hand it may consume all of an individual's energy in an egocentric rush toward self-proclamation. On the other, taken in a more serious frame of mind, the task may simply be overwhelming, resulting in a retreat to borrowed identity.

Part of the problem is that any definition of oneself is not only an expression of what one is inwardly. It must of necessity be an expression of the time and place in which one lives and acts. The entire struggle is toward finding and retaining the authentic inward person against the outward habits, customs, and expected demeanor of the milieu in which a person finds herself. She cannot deny the social part of herself, its acquired nuances of behavior fitting her into her world. But she must make it her own. She should transform it into an expression of her authentic inner character.

For example, a particular individual may be extraordinarily reticent and gentle. This would put her in danger of contempt or abuse, if it is not corrected somewhat, at least in outward appearance. Yet who, with an adequate sense of the good of general humanity, would counsel the adoption of a harsh and cruel character in lieu of the gentler inclination?

Such an individual as this gentle person, upon surveying the social condition and expectation of her world, should pause to reflect. For she should find a means of hardening her tone just sufficiently to project a strength of character, while maintaining a ready compassion when it is called for.

Since most human beings fear and loathe in themselves and others any appearance of weakness, such as a lack of quickness of mind, unsociability, and unattractiveness in general, it should be noted that there are many other kinds of vulnerability beyond gentleness and reticence. So the simple goal is not to have an attempt to overcome these obstacles lead into harshness of character and unreflective behavior.

For it is always precisely this sort of difficulty people are faced with—that of mixing authenticity of character with a sense of moral right and then placing it without fear into a potentially hostile social context. Doing so is an art not easily attained, which is why the best performers of this feat are invariably well known.

KNOWLEDGE requires that a thing be known. Wisdom requires that human beings know themselves in relation to that thing. This is why a great deal can be known about the sun and its affect on the earth's atmosphere in the evening. But the beauty of a sunset can only be grasped when its humanity-related meaning is understood.

The same is true of other such abstractions, such as courage and love. It is also true of their opposites, cowardice and hate. These are things which are only understand as a relationship between human beings and their experience. When these insights are integrated into a single relationship between human awareness and experience, and when this understanding has been harmoniously developed, the highest wisdom is attained.

TO say there is some sort of universal good in the universe is to assert something not known. Material things come into being. They exist. They go out of existence. That is all that can be objectively observed. However, someone can project his own feeling, his own sense of things, onto the bare, objective facts which he has empirically observed.

For instance, he might believe there is a principle of good in the universe. And he may very well be right. But that is not to say he knows it from observation. Good is a human idea. There should be an attitude of honesty about that. Then people may choose to believe what they feel impelled to believe, so long as they recognize a subjective origin for that belief. In other words, much of the problem with Natural Law Theory in ethics is that subjective values, like the good, are imposed. They are imposed upon nature. Subsequently, one presumes to infer good from nature. This is certainly a species of circular reasoning.

Values, like the idea of a universal good, are spawned and nurtured within social contexts. Thus it is in social history that their effects on human behavior, legislation, jurisprudence, etc. are observed. Noting their correlative effect in several quarters, it is decided that a law has been discovered. But the law is that of a developing idea, however variously it may have been produced. It is not of a material origin.

In short, such a complex web of socially evolved values is a world view imposed by the human mind upon physical reality. If it seems rooted in human nature, as might be deduced from its appearance in different quarters, it is nevertheless rooted in human nature only as expressed in the web of ideas which has been cast over material nature. This does not indicate that it is always present in human nature. It is in this way that such a blending of ideas and physical reality produces what is subsequently observed. And it is from this that people attempt to infer objective laws.

An alien culture might very well cast a completely different net of ideas upon the physical realm and draw a different harvest from it. In fact, has this not been done? What remains then that all people may share in common? There is a need for people to trust one another, which is expressed in every communal environment. And there are certain other essentials, like physical security and those things like property and reputation which are closely connected with it. Yet even these may be modified somewhat and have been from time to time.

THE fundamental assumption of trust, which makes any ethical community possible, is not an expression of how or why the community came together. For it does not arise from a prearranged social contract. Rather, it is an expression of what makes the community a community, regardless of its origin.

ARISTOTLE and John Stuart Mill ran into a similar dilemma. To begin with, they both defined morality in terms of a person's relationship to others. Of course, there is hardly any other way to define it. Aristotle thought specifically that the relationship between one human being and another fell to prudence, while Mill thought it was determined by results. This set their thinking in opposition.

But then Aristotle insisted that, in addition to a careful balancing of motives, the contemplative life was to be regarded over and above it as the highest form of human activity. And Mill likewise clearly considered a cultivated mind as being productive of an elevated character, which would in turn be more conducive of socially beneficial behavior.

So, different as the fundamentals of their ethical systems were—in the orientation of Aristotle toward personal prudence and of Mill toward social outcomes—it is this added consideration, concerning an elevated character arising from a thoughtful mind, which brings the two men together. But neither of them succeeded in fully reconciling the contemplative, cultivated life he advocated with the original, more obviously practical, system he had created.

THE basis of John Stuart Mill's ethics is not strictly utilitarianism. The basis is enlarged sensibility. Through the expansion of moral and conceptual imagination as a result of experience, reflection, and exposure to literature, art, philosophy, etc., the outlook and attitude of a person can become more inclusive and refined. This greater comprehensiveness and sensitivity makes for better ethical choices.

REASON dictates that women should be treated as equal to men in matters of personal dignity and intellectual capacity. Humankind's highest faculty is reason. It defines the human race. This faculty is possessed in equal measure by both sexes. So, as a part of the human race, women should be defined by the faculty which principally defines their character as a species. And that gives them equal dignity with the male sex.

Now to a human being, the human body is undoubtedly beautiful. But the human spirit (mind) is more important than the body. This is because the spiritual triumph and dignity of the human race supersedes any material, or bodily, concerns. So the conclusion is that, by all means, there should be physical activity, alimentation, sex, etc.

But there should also be a large measure of the activity of thinking, accompanied by a disproportionate reverence for higher thought, since that is what most characterizes and ennobles a human being. In other words, the pleasures of the body can be enjoyed. But this should be done without a limitation of oneself or others to them. Least of all should anyone be defined in this way.

THE vast majority of human beings are sheep. Only a small fraction of the race differentiates itself from this mass. This differentiation is accomplished, not by brilliance of intellect alone, but by a habit of reflection. The wisdom designation, twice repeated in the nomenclature of the modern subspecies—Homo sapiens sapiens (wise man)—refers to this capacity for reflection.

That is, it refers to reflection taken to its highest degree of development in considering the human condition. It is this: the capacity to think practically and self-referentially simultaneously. This has lifted humanity out of forest and savannah. But practical intellect alone is merely a tool. It elaborates and puts into use the products of reflection. In this, it originates nothing.

Science is an example of this. A few men and women have reflected deeply and given others the tools of science: original insights that may be used in a number of ways. Then follows the vast army of field and laboratory workers, who further develop and use these tools for both good and ill. The majority of them do not discover in the sense of original insight. (When they do, they are reflective.) Rather, they elaborate upon and play out the implications of those original insights. Thus their productions are not their own, except by right of labor.

IT would seem that Nietzsche, in his attempt to preserve the strength and independence of the creative individual, fails to clearly remark an important distinction in the concept of egoism. Thus he puts it all on one side. But in truth, egoism has two constituent elements. One is pride and self-confidence. The other is insecurity.

Because Nietzsche assigns insecurity to those who would oppose his supermen out of a sense of their own weakness, he attributes to the supermen only pride and self-confidence and proclaims this to be egoism. The insecurity is something else. It is an unnamable weakness of the many. Thus egoism takes on exclusively positive characteristics for Nietzsche. And it applies to the few.

But in common practice and common parlance, egoism takes on exclusively negative connotations. Because insecurity is here exhibited as the principal element in egoism, the other positive attributes are interpreted in light of it. So pride becomes false pride and self-confidence an inflated sense of one's own worth. Can Nietzsche be blamed for condemning this interpretation as false? How could he help but recognize its oppressive inclinations, especially since this is inevitably the majority view and the outlook of those of least distinction?

Egoism, in this negative sense, is the shortcut the greater portion of humanity takes in its confrontation with the conditions of life. It is the path of deceit, self-deception, and cunning. Cunning is a limited, destructive state of mind aimed at preserving the individual against threatening circumstances. Often it takes the form of an individual seeking psychological safety in social inclusion. There it becomes the type of individual who can be seen looking over his shoulder to discover what everyone else thinks before taking his own course of action.

Wisdom, on the other hand, is a path of genuine, well-grounded pride and self-confidence. It is the long, hard, lonely way, but the only path of authentic self-fulfillment. Because of the amount of insecurity that must be overcome to enter onto this path, only a few ever attempt it. Nevertheless, it is this dichotomy between cunning and wisdom which expresses the full range of ego. Both arise from the same human consciousness. They depart from one another in the matter of self-possession and personal integrity.

WISDOM cannot be produced without reference to the self. Thus a self-orientation is required, which to the unfamiliar eye looks like selfishness. And that is why there are those who will argue that selfishness lies at the root of all human acts, even altruistic acts. The problem lies in the concept of the self.

Wisdom differs from knowledge in that it focuses on relations. It is true that knowledge itself could not produce a definition without an at least implied reference to context. And while this is certainly an appeal to relation, the emphasis is upon the particular fact. In knowledge, whatever may be gathered into a fact is subordinate to the fact. Thus, if a person is defined as a rational being, it is implied that he is not a non-rational being, though the topic of non-rational beings is not broached. Here there is relation. But the relationship stops short at a definition of the fact.

Wisdom, on the other hand, though it is certainly involved in facts, is not focused upon facts, but upon the relationship between them. Therefore, if it is asserted that a sunset is beautiful, the person making this assertion is relating himself to the facts, or effects upon him, of sunlight, atmosphere, etc.

Though these facts are being related to his own person, the reference is general. For his interest is not in the facts themselves. It is in their beauty. Beauty is not a fact but a judgment. It is a judgment of his relationship to those facts, a judgment which could apply to others. They could be in a similar relationship to those facts. The same may be said of justice, love, the good, etc. All these devolve into meaning. This is not meaning as definition, but meaning as significance.

Thus wisdom, in its fullest sense, goes beyond the relationship of facts to one another. For it is not a simple relationship of one fact to another, a relationship which is devoid of any reference to the being that is contemplating the facts. Wisdom is the relationship of that being to one fact, many facts, or all facts put together.

Moreover, where it is a relationship focused on one fact or a few facts, there is always a sense of the entire community of facts. For the relationship is ultimately one which is between a person and his state of being. This is so even when such an enlarged perspective is not being addressed. It forms the general ground of the relationship.

Thus the beautiful sunset mentioned above addresses the issue of beauty in general, not only in one instance or for one person, but in every instance and for all people. For beauty cannot be understood in isolation. It is in this way that the facts have significance for an individual person. They may potentially have significance for others. Thus they have meaning.

This is the egocentric core which lies in wisdom. Human wisdom always bears a direct reference to human beings in their relationship to one fact, many facts, or all facts put together. Whatever the range of the focus, all people and all facts together are the ground of a relationship which forms the nexus of wisdom between an individual and his existence. He is humanity in a human world.

But when any fact is taken out of the integrated context of the world of facts, and thus out of its universal meaningfulness as well—when it is subjected to a limited purpose—the relationship between the person and the fact becomes one of cunning. It asks, how do I oppose or make use of this fact? This is why facts must be considered within their universal context to form a relationship with a person which is one of wisdom. The wise person asks, what is my place in the general order of things?

So understanding the reason why acting upon this latter relationship is not a selfish act is simple. If a person relates himself to all things, he cannot conceive of himself as apart from all things, all facts. Therefore, he cannot take a divisive or contrary position against them. Though his reference is to the self, he cannot express this self as ego. For the self is immersed in a universal, unified context.

OLD age and sickness are a giving back of the gifts of life, one by one. They demonstrate what has been taken for granted.

WILDERNESS is beautiful. There can be no disputing this. But the idea that nature is only beautiful if it is wilderness is ridiculous. To maintain that family farms, such as those spread out in the southeastern Pennsylvania countryside among green fields and meadows with copses of trees on rolling hills, and streams running through the ravines—to maintain that such a panorama, featuring man functioning harmoniously within nature, is not beautiful is nonsensical. It is human involvement in nature which determines nature's aesthetic, even when it comes to wilderness.

FREE will presents a paradox: choice implies freedom, but freedom does not choose. For choice involves a limitation to two alternatives, however often this condition may be repeated in a sequence of paired alternatives. That is, a choice between three or more alternatives is a choice between two, then a choice between the selected alternative and the next, and so on.

Since any act of choice involves a single pair of alternatives, and this is repeated a finite number of times, the process implies limitation. But the idea of freedom entails an absence of limitation. Hence the paradox that a person is only truly free when she is not concerned with freedom, not making choices.

FREE will can best be understood on a practical level. For, though one can neither intellectually prove nor disprove its existence, verification of it can be discovered at the seat of human emotion and of practical, everyday action. For human will is a barometer of emotional truth. It always acts according to the nature of inmost desire.

A person's will may appear at times to contradict her desire. But her acts always follow the way that is most important to her. So, looking at her motives, what does she find? She finds free will. It is free not simply because she acts according to her inmost desire, but because she believes she acts freely upon that desire. She believes this of others as well.

This is not an argument for soft determinism. There is no attempt to follow a causal chain of material facts into "an iron block, in which there can be no equivocation or shadow of turning," as the philosopher William James put it. A person's belief in her own freedom is entirely subjective. It is based on felt circumstance and does not concern itself with any objective fictions about unlimited causation manufactured in the intellect.

So to continue with an illustration of the point, imagine that such a person has an expensive mountain bike which she keeps on her front porch. One day a neighbor takes this bike, puts it on his porch, and proceeds to act as if it is his own. If the bike owner believes there is no such thing as free will, this act will not trouble her, in spite of the loss. She might grieve for the loss of the bike. But she can in no way blame the neighbor for taking it, since he does not possess a free will.

How difficult is it to entertain such a forgiving generosity of feeling? Quite difficult, unless a person has gone through extraordinary mental and emotional conditioning. That is because this person cannot let go of the idea that her neighbor is in some way responsible for his acts, especially where they affect her.

In other words, on a practical level, she believes in his free will. She believes in it because she considers him to be, in some degree, responsible for what he does. She further believes he knows he is offending her and could have chosen not to. Finally, she feels it would be shameful not to act in her own defense.

But why these attitudes? Why should anyone's behavior matter, if no one truly has the capacity to exercise a free will? There can be no blame where there is no selection of the act. And neither can any shame be assumed where there is no choice between one response and another. So the answer must be that, not only does her neighbor have a free will. So does she.

HOW is it that a person receives his fundamental moral education? He usually does so through a conditioning process involving sympathy, as opposed to empathy. Sympathy is emotional and instinctive. Drawing upon a person's natural social proclivities—that is, his need to belong—it teaches him the rules of the group. This generally begins with family influence and progresses through stages of ever enlarging circles of acquaintance throughout his life.

Empathy, on the other hand, is deliberative. It involves the intellect. Emotion will follow. But it is guided by principles. Thus, by means of an intellectual effort, emotional imagination is enlarged, extending a person's understanding to an inclusion of the tribulations of others, especially strangers.

In this way, under the active influence of the mind, a full-rounded apprehension of another person's condition is achieved. As a result, compassion, which is an expression of empathy—i.e. thoughtful sympathy—allows that condition to be seen and felt. And most importantly, it allows it to be understood.

So it becomes clear that a sympathetic attitude alone is insufficient. The problem with a strictly sympathetic attitude is twofold. First, mere sympathy does not necessarily lead a person to think matters through. So long as he has a ready set of rules to follow, or is surrounded by those with whom he identifies, he will experience little imaginative expansion of feeling, especially toward those with whom he does not share a common interest. Second, a strictly sympathetic conditioning often involves conflicting ethical impulses.

For example, religion may instruct a person in sympathy, forbearance, and humility. In contrast, popular culture—with its simplistic ideas of history and even more simplistic notions put forth in popular entertainment—may demand that a person defend his sense of honor, regardless of the triviality of the occasion.

Moreover, capitalist society is generally intolerant of any failure on the part of an individual to succeed in a competitive world. In such a society, both the laws and private rules of behavior are subtly construed to promote as acceptable a seemingly civilized means of taking advantage of the weak or the innocent.

The problem with these self-centered standards is that they are introduced within the same social environment as the sympathetic. So a direct conflict between selfishness and altruism makes them incompatible. For the human need to belong, which is variously expressed in this conflict of motives, inculcates opposing rules into an individual mind. The opposing rules put each person in conflict with both himself and others. He wants to belong to his family and his religious faith, but also to his peer groups at play and work. Yet they demand different things from him.

Moreover, he ingests the conflicting influences without trial by reflection and informed imagination. He does it in part because it is too difficult and painful to confront the complexity of these demands in a thoughtful manner. The result is that he ends up without a consistent and clearly delineated code of morals. He is left in a state of internal confusion, which he tries his best to conceal both from others and from himself.

How can this dilemma be solved? A person must begin by accepting a burden of self-discipline, which for some may be arduous and painful. First, a conscientious person should seek to recognize the conflicting messages coming from different sources. He must attempt to understand their contradictory nature. To do this, he must be honest with himself.

If he is of a reflective and sensitive character, he cannot treat the self-centered tenets of a highly competitive marketplace as though they were representative of a moral conscience. And he should certainly recognize the interest that a market-driven popular culture takes in promoting standards of the broadest, and therefore lowest, appeal in whatever it is attempting to foster upon an uncritical public.

However, should this problem be considered strictly in the light of a disinterested argument, there can be no attempt to insist on any particular standard. It may be that a rejection of self-centered behavior for the sake of material gain would seem preferable. But here the argument is taken strictly on its own merits as a means of avoiding internal conflict within a person and misunderstanding between persons. As such, it merely insists that the most fundamental demand of any civilized society should be that uniformity is maintained in whatever standard is adopted.

If the "take advantage of your neighbor within the law" outlook is adopted, and if it is practiced uniformly by all persons within the society, any individual person within that society may at least be assured that whatever deception he encounters is precisely that which he would have used himself. Thus there can be no unpleasant emotional surprises, no sense of unexpected betrayal, no letdown in expectation. Though it must be granted that this is a low expectation indeed for human relations.

So recognizing conflicting demands on individual behavior, and reforming institutions and social practices to bring those demands into a reasonable agreement with one another, is a beginning. But the most important thing which can done in seeking to better the human condition socially and emotionally is to promote a general enlargement of moral understanding and practice.

This requires an empathetic awareness which seeks to interpret, and act on, other people's problems and misfortunes in terms either of personal experience or of an imaginative grasp of experiences which have never been personal. Tempered by forbearance and gentleness—the latter of which is generally referred to as kindness—this may lead to a better world. Or at least it may lead to a less hypocritical world.

THERE are two radically different conceptions of honesty in the world, the one practiced by a large portion of the human populace, the other accepted by very few. The popular version is what might be called "cash register" honesty, since that type of honesty is based on a rote observance of rules or principles. It is often completely lacking in sincerity.

The cash register clerk provides an interesting model for such behavior. For as often as not, she unreflectively follows the rules, such as, do not shortchange your customer. Nevertheless, since her working behavior does not necessarily arise from an inner conviction, from her true self, this kind of rote observance of rules could easily allow for a good deal of subtlety and deception where conditions should permit. However, because she is likely to be under close scrutiny as a cash register clerk, she will not have much opportunity to stray.

So let a different example be taken. Let it be presumed that one person should sell another a freshly painted house that she, the seller, knows is about to fall down. The faulty condition of the structure has escaped the notice of an inspector. But it must be assumed that the seller will make no mention of it, since it would not be in her interest. The buyer will simply be expected to beware on her own account. This too would be "cash register" honesty.

Again, a trained cleric who states that she *knows* something about transcendent being or the afterlife is also practicing cash register honesty. She may wish to comfort someone in making such a statement. But her attitude is deceptive nevertheless. These are familiar enough examples. Thus it can be seen that cash register honesty is, unfortunately, the very soul of ordinary social intercourse.

But genuine honesty is quite another matter. For it is based upon reflection and has to do with a sincerity of the heart. It is not popular because such behavior requires discipline and effort and must arise from a practiced and settled character. The fact is that the word "sincerity" is such an important part of this condition, that it might easily be exchanged with the word "honesty." Thus, in stating that a person should be honest, a sincere person is what is being implied.

So, once the idea of such honesty has been brought under a general understanding that it means sincerity, it can be observed that there are, in fact, two varieties of this honesty, each of them a unique expression of sincerity. And both of them are beyond reproach insofar as a straightforwardness of attitude is concerned.

For neither of them is a product of a superficially, and often insincerely, imposed habit. Rather, one is a result of a carefully developed character. And the other arises from astringent and unavoidable circumstances. Thus, while the first condition is subjective and voluntary, the second is imposed entirely by external conditions.

The voluntary expression is an honesty of vision and purpose which is carried out to a productive and beneficial end. It is both socially and personally beneficial. It benefits others in terms of the treatment they receive and in terms of the example they observe in the actions of the sincere person. And it is good for the sincere person in its further development of her character. For the more an open sincerity is practiced, the more it becomes a settled state within her.

In fact, when this practice is carried to its most profound and universal level, it can be observed that it becomes transcendently good. For it goes beyond any immediate situation which might incidentally call it forth. This deeply focused type of sincerity is the author of genius, be it spiritual or material.

For it is the role of genius to uncover hidden truths, which reveal themselves to a profoundly searching and honest mind. Thus it benefits many beyond the original scope of activity which might have called it forth. For this reason, genius should be considered the best and rarest expression of the true form of honesty.

But let mention of the other type of genuine honesty not be omitted. For there is also a sincerity to be found in it. It is involuntary in the sense that it is not self-caused. Rather, the honesty concerned with it arises from an impersonal cause. That cause is generally war, though it may be a natural emergency. However, war is the better ongoing example. For its destructive power does not occur in a moment, but over an extended period of time.

War is a condition which, in spite of its destructive results, has the peculiar virtue of greatly simplifying circumstances. It also reduces options. This reduction in personal options is brought about by the fact that no one can be deceived about the consequences of a war. There is no reason to deceive oneself or another about its nature.

War is prosecuted in deadly earnest and can be either carried out or endured in no other manner. Thus the condition of honesty inherent in war results from the fact that war acts as a moral straightjacket. Along with its reduced circumstances and the limited alternatives they offer, it restricts emotional expectations and responses to their most elemental character. They cannot be feigned.

In combat, or when civilians are subjected to some form of terror or bombardment, no one is deceived about what the other person's motives might be. These motives are to kill, maim, terrorize, or otherwise disrupt, subjugate, or destroy the normal course of lives and events. So no one is mistaken about what should be done in self-preservation. A soldier must reciprocate. And a civilian must hide. Thus, in either case, war is always experienced in deadly earnest. And all participants understand its transparent meaning.

However, because war is an imposed condition, it does not include personal reflection and internal growth, which are the preferred state of a thoughtfully sincere person. Thus nothing enduring is gained from an experience of war, other than a saddened skepticism concerning life: a shattered innocence and a lingering fatalism about the possibilities of human nature. Moreover, it is a very costly way for human beings to find out who they truly are.

IT has often been said that humankind is *the* reasoning animal. But scientific research continues to narrow the distinction between humanity and other forms of life. Human beings were once thought to be the only toolmakers. But at this moment, there are at least three species of mammal (including Homo sapiens sapiens) and about thirty species of birds known to make tools. Moreover, birds do not appear to have a folded cortex, such as is found in mammals. So, if that distinction is considered to be an exclusive sign of intelligence, it must fall into disuse.

Can it even be said definitively that a human being is a reasoning animal? If a human being is to be individually defined, then surely he is not. For most of what people do on a daily basis is not reasoning. It merely passes for such. When an individual encounters a situation requiring decisive action or thought, his natural recourse is to mentally generate a rapid sequence of associations—a train of images—which culminates in a direction of thought or action. This, however, is immediately followed by a process of rationalization. Images are converted into concepts, reorganizing the imaginative process into a logical string of deductions. Hence the illusion that what occurred in the first instance was an act of reasoning.

Consequently, a human being cannot be defined essentially as a rational animal. On an ordinary, individual, mundane basis, he does very little logical thinking. Rather, he rationalizes a great deal and flatters himself that this is reasoning. If someone were to point to the fact that quite a few people do spend time mulling over familiar ideas in their heads, sometimes reviewing them in short logical sequences, the objection would not disturb this thesis. It could simply be pointed out that reviewing ready-made ideas does not constitute reasoning.

Claiming the attribute of reason is often a form of psychological self-aggrandizement, laziness, and personal comfort seeking, nothing more. Not to mention that most human ideas are opinions grounded in emotional wish-fulfillment and hearsay. So the dilemma remains that, individually, a human being cannot be judged to be much of a rational animal.

But what if it is assumed that he is at least potentially capable of genuine rational thought? To this it must be answered that most living forms are capable of behavior that does not distinctively define them. The fact that Socrates and Galileo reasoned a great deal is no more definitive of the whole of the species than that some dogs can walk on their hind legs.

So the present topic of interest should be the institutionalization of reason. For it is this type of specialization which is a more uniquely human trait than the universal use of reason. Like some species of Hymenoptera—in particular, those insects which are referred to as social in character—humankind does create specialized behavior among certain members of the species.

Thus, by the institutionalization of reason, what is meant is the designation of specific contexts within which reasoning not only can but is expected to occur. This would imply the use of reason as a unique discipline. It is no accident that philosophy, as a fully independent rational discipline, did not occur until the sixth century B.C.E.

Science is an excellent example of such a specialized rational context. Reasoning is not only carried on within a scientific field, but carried on in a certain manner. And when it is not conducted in that way, it is not considered a scientific activity. Economics is a field closely related in many respects to the natural sciences but differing somewhat in its intellectual operations due to the fact that it is a social science. Philosophy is a field different yet. And so are the cases of applied and pure mathematics. Etc.

Then there are the more immediately practical fields, such as law practice, manufacturing, and governmental and business activities. Here are cases where careful, but not always rationally premeditated, delineations of infrastructure are paramount. In other words, the rational structures do exist. But they come into existence by trial and error. From these an example can be taken. Let it be manufacturing.

A modern airliner is a complex and ingenious piece of work. Such a thing is possible because it originates from a precisely defined and regimented process which is external to any one person. No individual can build an airliner alone. But many people, working together along specialized and separately defined paths of activity, including some involving high levels of reasoning, others not, can collectively create the final product.

The paths of reason, such as aeronautical design or electrical engineering, are not principally governed by habit, emotion, or instinct. But in addition to these, there are electricians and metalworkers who operate within specific corridors of expertise. Corridors which depend more on memorization and repetition than reason.

But even these specialized tasks require some use of reason. The demands of the task to be performed are learned in a professionalized formative process, perhaps a trade school or an apprenticeship. Here the novices learn what is to be done in a variety of closely related situations. Thus the professional development in these trades somewhat resembles that of soldiers training for battlefield service. Minimal thinking is required. Rather, memorization and practice are strongly emphasized. For the final activity will not be carried out in a place of contemplation.

Then there are those who bring about the integration of these tasks: managers, supervisors, assembly line facilitators, accountants, etc. Yet not one of all these individuals—neither those on the paths of reason, those plying the trades, nor the managerial and accounting specialists—can perform the roles of all the others.

In spite of this division of knowledge, the airliner gets built somehow and actually flies, the flying being done by another mind trained in another way. Flying is also not primarily a thinking discipline. It is a highly sophisticated trade. Though it does require extensive mental preparation. And in certain situations, it may require good mental and emotional habits resulting in quick, and sometimes even creative, responses.

What is being pointed to is the fact that reason has been institutionalized, segmented, and put to specific uses in ways—some complex, others less so—which are alien in context and procedure to one another. So much is this the case, that there is no overarching, controlling rational source from which all the others are derived. This amazing feat has been made possible because reason has been set upon certain deliberative paths from which there can be little or no deviation. It has been institutionalized.

An aeronautical engineer goes to work and enters upon the business of thinking about aeronautical issues. An electrical engineer does the same in his specialized sphere of expertise. There may be some communication between them. But only in generalized terms. Each must rely on the arcane knowledge of the other, without knowing much about what it is or how its processes are arrived at.

However, when the aeronautical engineer takes a coffee break, he returns to his intuitive, sub-rational habits. He does so at home as well. For in most cases, it is not likely that he performs small talk, reads a newspaper, or converses with his wife in a tone of intellectual discourse. He is thus once again the animal humankind and not much the reasoning human.

So things being what they are, how can it be said that humankind, defined individually, but as a type of the species, is a reasoning creature? For reason is only being used intermittently in special circumstances. And there are quite different forms of reason when it is in use. Other than as an undeveloped potential of behavior, these forms of reason do not come into existence by any means but training and special circumstance.

A potential property is not enough to define something. It must be inherently characteristic. To say a human being is capable of reasoning is not to say he characteristically does so. Moreover, the metal worker, welder, or assembly line worker reasons little on the whole. Certainly not enough to excite the epithet "wise," which is implied by the label affixed to the subspecies to which human beings belong: Homo sapiens sapiens.

So it can hardly be the case that any of these people is a predominantly rational animal, an animal which could not be otherwise. Nor is it a matter of some people choosing not to be. For the great majority reasons very little, if at all. And it is a minority which chooses to practice reason, and usually then only intermittently and in specialized ways.

But defined institutionally, human beings can be considered rational. For it is this institutionalization of reason, where in some cases thinking is required to be logical, that has spread the human species over the face of the globe. And many of the problems faced by humankind, such as climate alteration or the destruction of the earth's biodiversity, are problems precisely because no one has figured out how to apply new institutional procedures adequate to a solution of them. Solutions will be found because they must. But any search for the right intellectual mode of organization is always time consuming and often itself not a strictly logical process. There is a good deal of random trial and error.

There is one last note to be considered. Human beings should not think of themselves as automatons needing to be controlled by a regimentation of the thought process. A free play of imagination, both conscious and unconscious, fulfills a vital role. The greatest innovations come from dreams, hunches, and occasional flashes of insight. These are individual acts of imagination.

So there should always be room for a person to move freely within the larger social body. But to be effective, his insights must be fitted to a logical mode. For logic is the invented language of the group. It is a social language. Thus it is within institutionalized paths of reason that rationality is harnessed.

To take an example from among the seemingly least rational activities of man, consider the painter. If he is original, he may have to go outside the art community and its rational assumptions to suffer critical opposition. In fact, if he did not go outside the respected canons in some degree, he could not be original.

But no matter how original, he must eventually be accepted by the art community. The canons of that community, which are the invented rational structure he wants to be accepted within, may have to change to accommodate him. But as rules which are generally—i.e. communally—accepted, they must remain as canons. And what are they but a regimen for defining procedure and taste?

This thesis can be extended by means of analogy to the sciences, philosophy, mores, and so forth. Though in the sciences, going outside the accepted structure poses a more immediate disturbance of order and progress. The point is that a civilization subsists through the rational structures which define it. But it grows and changes through imaginative innovation. In short, humankind is collectively rational in its institutional form. But human beings cannot be individually confined to the rational.

Thus the species is not inherently rational. It deviates from reason far more than it follows it, because it is natural for it to do so. However, human beings are social in character. Thus an individual person, living in his individual way, unheeding of any institutional demands, is an anomaly. Yet a person who never deviates, though more common, is equally unacceptable. For he lacks a center of truth in himself. And truth cannot come from the group.

This is why the faculty of reason is innate only in potential. Its completed structure is found in the communal mind, not the solitary individual. Though the relations of logical terms are imaginatively associative, reason's development into a logical form, and that form into a practice, is invented. Moreover, its habitual employment is socially induced, specialized in one department of thought or another, but intermittent in common practice.

ADVOCATES of the humanities have lost their way in allowing themselves to be intimidated by science and technology. What is meant by this statement? It is that advocates of the humanities (literature, history, and philosophy) have lost sight of the grounding of these fields in fundamental human thought and emotion. That thought and emotion, though immediate and familiar in experience, is more mysterious in its origin and character than the deepest probings of experiment and hypothesis.

Many people are able to enjoy Sophocles' play *Antigone* after two and a half millennia of its existence. But it is not because of the circumstances in which it was originally written that the majority of these people do so. Nor do they admire it because they have knowledge of the Attic tongue, its beauties and complexities. Neither do most of these people have more than a scant acquaintance with the elements of ancient Greek culture.

What they do recognize in *Antigone* is its grounding in a fundamental emotional situation: Antigone's struggle between her own personal values and those of the state. This is a struggle people can easily understand. That is why the play appeals to them in a powerful way. The same thing can be said for reading the ancient historians Tacitus or Thucydides. The facts of history alone do not compel anyone to read them. But Tacitus does not only provide history. He submits himself to the reader as a typical upper-class Roman of his time. His attitudes now belong to the world.

Thucydides provides more than a historical narrative as well. He explores events taking place in ancient Greece through a voice which understands fundamental, universal motivations, good and bad. In fact, his sense of good and evil cuts through to the bedrock of human experience. It transcends cultural specifics to ground itself in fundamental human emotions, emotions founded upon the maintenance or betrayal of trust. People in any epoch can readily recognize these situations.

Again, does anyone read philosophy and ponder its eternal questions about what is known, and how it is that what is known can be known, simply because in the West there is a cultural fixation concerning such questions? If so, then why does the Biblical book of *Job*—a philosophical poem—raise impenetrable questions only to refute them as being beyond human reach?

Why do the *Upanishads* and the *Bhagavad-Gita* of Hinduism—also philosophical works—attempt to answer such questions by pointing to an illusory grasp of sensory reality and then taking the reader beyond that into the ineffable unity which they believe transcends the physical world?

To understand the limits of what is known is a fundamental human need. Such an understanding would explain what human beings can expect and not expect in dealing with the circumstances of life. People are anxious about these circumstances, no matter what lengths they may go to to avoid acknowledging their anxiety.

Not least, as already mentioned, there are the mundane realities of trust and betrayal, which are an elemental ground of human ethics and social organization. Moreover, there is the role of individual conscience in sifting through the labyrinthine coils and conflicts of personal fulfillment and social obligation. Can it be denied that such concerns are always present in life—in varying degrees, a weight and burden to all? These issues are fundamental. They appear in every age and human condition. They compose the ground of the humanities.

So why the intimidation by science and technology? Science and technology produce *things*. They manipulate the physical immediacy of the world to the perpetual wonderment and dismay of its material-hungry denizens. But they do not answer the eternal questions which continue to haunt heart and mind, to make them uneasy and restless.

Questions such as: Where have we come from? What are we? Where are we going? The French painter Paul Gauguin posed these questions when he made them the motif of one of his paintings. They are embedded in the fundamental insecurity of the human condition. And no amount of technical wizardry or empirical explanation can satisfy them. For science asks only the questions it can answer, avoiding those it cannot. Which, of course, leaves people with the hidden agitations of an abiding insecurity.

Aside from religion, which frequently encourages no thinking at all, only the humanities can fulfill these deeper needs: not, to be sure, by supplying answers, but by reiterating the problem. While there may be few satisfactory answers to these questions, there is a satisfaction in establishing a wholesome confrontation with the facts of existence.

These are facts which tell human beings they cannot know everything, that their progress in understanding their condition is an advancement down an infinitely long tube enclosed within an infinitely large box. All that is outside the tube remains unavailable to their probing curiosity. And the end of the tube is never reached. Nevertheless, it is lovely to stand before the void and acknowledge the possession of a courage to wonder!

Now let it be asked what the advantage of the humanities could be from a social point of view? Certainly, what can be gained in this sphere is more modest than philosophical probing. But it is no less important. A civilization is an edifice built by man, riddled with faults. If it is to be kept a vital and living thing, the flaws are perpetually in need of confrontation and correction. To ignore them is to bring about a prolonged, but certain, social death. Civilizations do not fail because people run out of answers. They fail because people run out of questions.

A civilization is, of course, above all a context for human relations. These relations ought to be founded on an understanding of the elemental emotions which are securely grounded in human nature. If they were, as the English poet William Wordsworth noted, people could hardly go astray. But they do go astray. Human history is one long saga of men and women struggling in darkness against their own unrecognized, self-inflicted ignorance.

As the French philosopher Jean Jacques Rousseau observed, civilization corrupts. Through its complex layering of values and needs based on vanity and a false sense of what human beings truly are, it leads people further and further from the heart of themselves. They learn not to know themselves but only to be concerned with what is expected of them. And much of that is in direct contradiction to what would do them the most good. They become lost, frustrated, privately frightened, desperate, and vicious.

So what is it that has been lost? What has been lost is a knowledge of the human condition, its purest emotions, its most essential intellectual and spiritual needs. Henry David Thoreau tried to remind his countrymen of these things. But America, along with the rest of the Western World, was on a speeding train which was moving too fast for an enjoyment of the landscape. The train continues to accelerate. And the question becomes, does this train have any brakes? Does it have a destination—a destination grounded in human realities?

Rousseau noted that civilized peoples had lost their innocence. He might have said, their goodness. But goodness is a complex matter because good and evil are concepts worked out in a specific social environment, an ethical milieu. Human beings do not come into the world with an innate knowledge of good and evil.

What they possess are essential emotions and nascent ideas, emotions and ideas which, at their beginning, are a product of a common human nature. How these emotions and ideas are twisted, bent, combed out into an ethical perspective is a matter of history, sometimes insight, and often deliberate blindness.

Once again the humanities make their appearance. When they function as they should and are not themselves warped out of meaning by the prejudices of a moment, they pursue a cleansing role. They rub the human psyche down in oils of a calm assurance and anoint that assurance with reminders of simple truths. Those truths are the elemental emotional, intellectual, and spiritual foundation of the human condition.

Index

Made in the USA
Middletown, DE
22 June 2023

33228907R00166